FINDING ANSWERS

FINDING ANSWERS:

The Essential Guide to
Gathering Information
in Canada

Dean Tudor

M&S

Canadian Cataloguing in Publication Data

Tudor, Dean, 1943-
Finding answers: the essential guide to
gathering information in Canada

Includes bibliographical references and index.
ISBN 0-7710-8637-7

1. Information retrieval. 2. Library science – Research – Canada.
3. Information science – Research – Canada. I. Title.

Z669.7.T84 1993   028.7′0971   C92-094717-4

Typesetting by M&S
Printed and bound in Canada

McClelland & Stewart Inc.
The Canadian Publishers
481 University Avenue
Toronto, Ontario
M5G 2E9

CONTENTS

To all of my students: former, current, and future

INTRODUCTION

Give a man a fish and he eats for a day; teach a man to fish and he eats for life. – Chinese proverb

He who knows where knowledge dwells has it within his reach.
– James Luce Kingsley

Finding Answers introduces the elements and principles of information resources, information-gathering techniques, the organization of information, and retrieval patterns of different types of resources, such as articles, documents, and online computer databases. Selected major sources of bibliographical, biographical, statistical, business, and governmental information available in both print and non-print formats are examined. These are presented in a uniform manner so that students, for example, can use this guide "in the field." In addition, this book examines the roles of libraries, computer databases, associations and institutions, governments, and experts as resource persons, thus enabling researchers to decide on the kinds of materials necessary to answer questions. Such decision-making is absolutely crucial to research: the act of reviewing available information and then formulating queries as a means to further gather and organize information. With a sound base of knowledge about information resources, researchers striving for accuracy will be able to develop the strong research techniques called for in documentation work.

This book is directed to a varied readership, but its expected audience is those at a beginning research level. Those who will find useful information and techniques here include librarians, market researchers, college students in different programs (but especially library studies and communication-journalism studies), journalists and writers, professional researchers, business people with a need for business-related information, and anyone else with a recurring need for information. Experienced researchers already know the contents of this book, but some might want to wander through the index (serendipitous browsing) or the chapters (analogue behaviour) as a sort of *aide-memoire*. One *can* teach an old dog new tricks; I am learning from my own students all the time.

The basic way to use this book is to skim through it. Master the structure of information: find out how systems are supposed to work and how they actually do work, and note any differences. Find out how to work around the system by privately obtaining information through a network of contacts.

There are several different approaches to writing about information resources. I have used all of them in various chapters, so researchers will find lots of material in this book about:

- resource tools – what the different kinds of reference books are and how to use them and the library catalogue, as well as online computer facilities;
- search strategies – how to determine information needs, locating and using resources, availability of documents and experts, and tips and advice on both a subject-oriented and a need-to-know basis;
- discipline knowledge – the kinds of resources available in the key areas of business and finance, politics and government, law and courts, society and individuals, science and technology, and culture and the arts;
- types of information needed – parameters for establishing routines to research current events, people, places, statistics, consumer data, and a company or a government agency.

Of course, not all of this material is needed all the time or even at the same time. After skimming this book, read it slowly and absorb it a little at a time to avoid information overload. Then, when the need to know strikes, return to the book. Look at the parameters in

Chapter 5 and subjects in Chapters 6 through 11. Check out the index. Without this slow and need-to-know approach, the entire book can become a blur and have no meaning.

Unfortunately, the book cannot cover every single instance of research need or present all the various unique methods of doing research that are applicable to one narrow field. Specific topics for in-depth research demand specific sources and varying search techniques; these should be brought out in small group discussions, if this book is to be used in the classroom. This kind of information is also available in many different subject guides. Researchers do not need to know every little trick or resource; they only need to know where particular information is stored and how to access it. Obviously, the first places to check are good tools for introductory background and subject guidance.

The ability to do research is transferable from one subject to another; only the specific topics change. Each researcher needs to develop the following expertise: (1) mastering general search techniques and research methods, augmented by strategies that are unique to one subject field; (2) knowing the major organizations, associations, government departments, and contact networks in that field; (3) knowing the specialized publishers, trade journals, and newsletters in the subject; (4) knowing the particular information centres and special collections of materials available in that field.

The "pre-writing" stage of research enables writers to visualize the structure and form of their final pieces – by knowing where all the major sources of information lie, by determining the information's credibility, and by deciding how to use the information of varying quality that has been uncovered.

What Is in This Book?

Each chapter begins by listing the key points to be discussed. Chapter 2 deals with the nature of information: accuracy, errors, verification, critical evaluation, research matrix. Chapter 3 covers the triad of information: warehouse, documents, experts. Chapter 4 discusses the linkage of information: bibliographic trail, vocabulary control, BRITE, research log, paper trail, search strategies. Chapter 5 covers the key parameters of all search strategies: background, definitions, addresses, names, places, current events, reviews, multidisciplinary subjects, statistics, and polls. Chapters 6 through 11 look at key topics of search strategies: business, government, courts, society, science, culture. Chapter 12, the conclusion, discusses the researcher mode: shortcuts, failures, successes. Of the two bibliographies in the appendices, the first deals with additional sources for reading about research techniques, the second is a basic listing, arranged by category, of printed or computerized resource tools.

What Is Not in This Book?

This book does not contain sample pages from printed tools, with an indication of how to use them. Sample pages are actually a disservice to the beginning researcher: too many times these stand in place of the actual tool for instructional purposes and encourage the researcher to leap right into the source. I have seen too many texts padded with samples and I get a severe case of MEGO ("My Eyes Glaze Over"). There are *no* shortcuts to learning about research. The baptism by fire includes actually reading the fine print of, say, the preface to an index to determine what is in it, how it was put together, and how to use it properly to obtain the required information. Nothing else will do. Some tools, such as the *New York Times Index,* even excel in presenting their how-to-use-this-book information. Many tools offer preliminary sections with sample passages and charts, plus an explanation of the symbols and abbreviations. Actually, by not reading the preface to a research tool, the beginning researcher misses out on quite a few descriptions of indexing shorthand that aid in finding the very data needed, both quickly and accurately (see Chapter 2 for a story about the misuse of *Who's Who in America*).

This book does not contain all of the normal bibliographic data for the major resource tools. Resources are cited mainly by title only. Over the years, editions change, as do publishers. Place, publisher, dates, pagination, and frequency after each and every source used would only slow down the reading of the text (again, MEGO). Does anybody really care who publishes the *Encyclopaedia Britannica,* or when the *Guinness Book of Records* was first published? Any library will either have the tool on site or have the bibliographic data otherwise available. Beginning researchers need the experience of pulling out bibliographic data from the title page of the latest edition of the source.

This book is not meant for those of the general public who have infrequent information needs. Researchers – whether professional or freelance – have a distinct edge over the general public when it comes to ferreting out information. In addition to knowing all about information as a system and about the specific workings of subject areas, they have contacts and inside sources who can privately obtain documents, facts, or statistics. An ordinary person does not have this support network. Members of the general public cannot walk into a traffic court looking for a probated will (for one thing, that's the wrong courthouse), or request a death certificate, or get a company's balance sheet relatively quickly. Researchers can plead deadlines to be met, or can freely consult with media advisers working in corporations and governments, or can get a toehold with public relations personnel. Anyone seeking information on an occasional basis simply does not have such ease of access. This book, then, cannot solve specific information requests needed on an irregular basis by anyone who is not planning to spend some time on research. It will not answer specific, trivia-type questions.

In fact, this book will not provide definite answers of any kind. Rather, it suggests places to go to find answers. Inevitably, that means, too, that some of the more highly developed resource centres, government agencies, and experts are based in Ontario. That's a fact of life in English-speaking Canada, and that's why most examples are drawn from this part of the country, on the understanding that something quite similar should be available to a researcher in Quebec, Alberta, Nova Scotia, or the Yukon. If nothing similar has developed in those jurisdictions, then that is a signal that perhaps such resource tools might be needed there, or that the phone/fax machine must be used to obtain data from outside the region. This book, then, will not provide researchers with specific lists of, say, courthouses by province, or vital statistics offices, or branches of Revenue Canada. These can all be found by phoning information or the appropriate government agency.

Some parts of the present work may be outdated when researchers begin using it. This seems to be inevitable, for new books are
being published all the time, governments (and their policies)
change, and businesses collapse (or, in better times, new businesses
start up). For example, not every province will allow people to trace
licence plate numbers; this service was recently closed off in British
Columbia. The strategies described here should remain the same,
no matter what happens in the near future, but the actual specifics
might not since these are based on an end-of-1992 cutoff date.

But this book *does* provide a framework for indicating where information lies, how to use that information, and what strategies should
be generated to reach the information. It attempts to create an infor-
mation-literate person (one who is able to recognize when information is needed and has the ability to locate, evaluate, and use it effectively) by linking theory and practice, by making the connections.
Reading this book now, and referring to it again for specific
need-to-know information, will save researchers much time and
effort when they start "finding answers."

PART 1

THE THEORY

2

THE NATURE OF
INFORMATION

Research is to find out what there is to know about a subject by reading previously published material, interviewing people, and digging up statistics or other facts. It is material found out about a subject, either in note form or on tape. – Words for Sale, Periodical Writers Association of Canada

Let's put it this way about research and that kind of thing. You have to touch that material at some point, even if someone else collects it for you. Even if someone else goes and gets a book, you have to read the book, you have to touch the material, you have to understand what's in the research so that you can collect it, interpret it, analyse it and then present it in a way that has some meaning. – Lloyd Robertson, 1976, then CBC newsreader.

This chapter deals with the nature of information. It presents material on: how to verify information accurately; how to use the research matrix; how to evaluate sources with some measure of critical thinking and problem-solving skill.

In an ideal world, we would all know everything. But we are far from perfect, so we do not know everything. We do, however, know some things, and some of us know more than others. Indeed, quite a few of us even know how to find things. The key to understanding knowledge is knowing how to find knowledge. And for that key we need to know the nature of information.

Information lies all about us. While the words "data" and

"information" are used almost interchangeably throughout this book, "data" can actually be thought of as a predecessor term. A *datum* is a unit, something not organized. It merely exists. At a step up, *information* is a collection of data that has been classified and organized. At this level we also have *misinformation, assertions, disinformation, omissions, opinions,* and even *errors.* At the next level, *knowledge* is processed information, information that has been evaluated and considered. *Wisdom* is what we do with this acquired knowledge. Recognizing the facts, learning the facts, and recalling the facts – all of these fit into the understanding that comes with wisdom and the skills of research.

But regardless of the level at which we know information, it really means nothing until it is needed. At this point someone writes a report or an article based on the gathered material, taking that found information and giving it form and, one would hope, making it interesting. Without that, information just exists and quietly waits for a need. This makes it difficult to describe the information system because there is no context on which to hang it – unless the learning motivation is strong, as in a textbook for a course. In that case, the need for information is the need for a passing grade.

The types of information that exist about a subject will affect the research technique or research method. At its basic level, all of established knowledge can be found in books and reference resources. Current events and opinions can be found through newspapers and magazines, while current research and research-in-progress can be found through scholarly journals. Along the way, researchers will pick up distinctions between primary and secondary sources, as well as uncover names of experts and authorities. To pry loose all of this information, researchers must analyse and evaluate written materials (reports, documents), observe the data around them, and begin asking questions of people through the interview process.

This planned inquiry encounters three difficulties. First, there is the question of *accessibility.* Is the information readily available or not? Are the experts willing to talk? Are the right questions being asked? Can relevant data be recognized? Are some documents missing? Are some documents available only through private sources? What information is available will determine the focus in any research.

The second difficulty is the *time* factor. How much time is available to locate experts and arrange interviews, to visit sites of unique documents, to deal with obscure matters, to wait for the mail or for callbacks, or for in-depth analysis of data? When the information is available will also determine the search strategy to be employed, for alternative, quick sources must be used if the time frame is short.

The third difficulty is *cost*. How will computer time be paid for, or the expenses of long-distance telephone calls and personal on-site visits? How much the information will cost can determine the grade or quality of the research obtained.

Five major technological innovations (photocopiers, microfiches, personal computers, cellular phones, fax machines) have placed a massive amount of information at the fingertips of researchers and have greatly reduced the time and cost of actual research while increasing the quantity and quality. The information has always been there; it was simply not as easily accessible before these innovations. Researchers should be able to take widely scattered documents and sources and bring them together to give a clear, accurate, concise description of the way a system works or doesn't work. Such organization takes initial time, but it is well worth the investment and effort.

Thus, time, money, and availability are all interwoven. Some information might be available if the researcher could wait for it, or if she or he could pay, for example, for a computer search. These limitations are unfortunate, but they are inevitable. And this is why, when one searches for information, one must have an alternative search pattern in mind. An alternative search strategy will be of value in many ways. When time, money, or availability is a definite problem, then an alternate strategy is useful for determining new, additional information sources. An alternate strategy will also produce a list of more sources useful in verifying the main documents or original resources. And an alternate strategy will produce sources that can serve as a cross-check on interviewed experts. Since an astute researcher will cross-check and verify anyway, then the production of new information sources for problem areas is a bonus.

Research principles are straightforward, and they have been commented on in every book on research methods. Here is a brief summary:

1. Draw a clear statement of the problem; the researcher knows what kinds of data he/she is looking for.
2. Begin by backgrounding the problem through research; formulate precise queries.
3. Design a strategy for collecting data; this will take many forms, but the strategy is basically to list the sources most likely to yield information within set time limits to maximize the results of a search.
4. Collect the data by observing, interviewing people, reviewing references, looking at documents, and checking indexes and computer databases.
5. Organize the data by coding them; begin to eliminate items irrelevant to the problem.
6. Analyse the data; review the organized files for confirmations, contradictions, discrepancies, chronologies, relationships, and reliability of sources and documents.
7. Begin an objective evaluation by drawing conclusions.
8. Write the paper, report, study, or article.

The search techniques for finding, abstracting, classifying, and evaluating data will vary according to the circumstances of each research problem and the approach brought to the problem by the individual researcher. The research principles are the same, but the actual implementation will be idiosyncratic.

Accuracy and Errors

"Accuracy always" is the motto of both thorough journalists and researchers. Journalists are committed to giving balanced viewpoints of current issues, but too often there are impediments such as these Four Horsemen of the Apocalypse (journalism division): *contradiction, inaccessibility, jargon,* and *misinformation.*

Researchers need to minimize their own mistakes, to be careful at all times. Their eyes and ears can deceive them; they can misinterpret what an event means or misjudge its importance. They can misspell names, transpose figures, confuse the names of participants, identify people in a photograph from right to left instead of left to right. Researchers learn to double-check everything at each level of activity: when they research information, when they organize it, and after they have evaluated it. No statements should be accepted at face value; a good healthy dose of cynicism is needed, for people will often lie or distort the truth as an expediency. As Ernest Hemingway wrote, "The most essential gift for a good writer is a built-in shock-proof shit-detector."

Both the *authority* and the *reputation* of information derived from a source (whether a book, a public record, or a person) demand attention. This is especially true with the use of statistics or attributed facts. To be of value, information ideally should be authoritative, comprehensive, bias-free, and current. Anything else simply won't do, and researchers must check to see that the information source is indeed extremely reputable and that the information comes from the widest possible selection of sources and is as up-to-date as today. Non-authoritative types of information fall short, for they can be full of contradiction and misinformation, leading to the perpetuation of errors, the loss of credibility (and even libel suits), and the enormous expense of backtracking and redoing.

Inaccuracies begin to creep in when the researcher accepts what is read or spoken, and fails to find further explanations. Unfamiliar sources and incomplete interviews are responsible for the bulk of recorded errors, and these are compounded when there is little time to verify the data. Because of this, the researcher might cover only one side of an issue. Researchers need to remember that not all facts are equal. Some are more important than others, and all must be carefully weighed before presentation. A series of minor facts may give a slanted impression. Researchers need to ask themselves if important experts give out only important facts.

In journalism, the chief complaint that poll respondents have against newspapers and magazines is not bias, distortion, suppression, sensationalism, or invasion of privacy. The major criticism is *inaccuracy*. Indeed, some magazines employ fact checkers to look into a writer's research and verify each fact. They check statistics, legal documents, and historical records by telephone and by making trips to libraries.

Newspapers, because of their deadlines and the volume of news, cannot do this. They rely more on the writers and editors. Here are some depressing facts from a 1983 American survey: of 591 spot (i.e., current) news stories, only 319 (54 per cent) contained no errors. The inaccurate stories contained an average of 1.67 errors; these errors were divided into subjective (errors of omission, improper focus on the personality and not on the issue, under- or over-emphasis introduced by editing, illogical conclusions, headline distortion) and objective (wrong numbers, misspelled names, wrong ages, times, dates, and locations).

Typical errors are also jargon-related, coming from both writers and researchers too cocky to use a dictionary. Some examples: Is *quid pro quo* an Italian seafood dish? Is *peccadillo* an armour-plated mammal? Was *falsetto* a Shakespearean character or a Verdi opera? Is *photosynthesis* made by Kodak or Xerox?

Misinformation, even when corrected, becomes part of the permanent record, enshrined in files from which it can be retrieved by naive researchers who don't check it out (perhaps "chuck it out" is a better term!). Very seldom will researchers come across totally clean data from the past, especially in secondary sources or in the popular press. The printed word carries a special authority and a misstatement, once published, can become "fact" with its inaccuracy perpetuated. For instance, somewhere in the morgue of the Montreal *Gazette* there is the sentence, "It was as if someone had discovered that Michaelangelo didn't paint the Mona Lisa." American General William Westmoreland launched a libel suit against CBS; he dropped his suit after he admitted that he didn't check his facts first. A *Time* magazine writer testified in court that his own reading "between the lines" was the basis for a report that Israeli defence minister Ariel Sharon discussed revenge with Lebanese Christian leaders; Sharon sued and won. An American "liberal" writer accused two "conservatives" (Robert D. Novak and Norman Podhoretz) of being "war wimps" who avoided military service, despite his checking their entries in *Who's Who in America*. He did not realize that the abbreviation "A.U.S." (explained in the prefatory matter to *Who's Who in America*) stood for "Army of the United States," and thus he had to apologize to them.

The sad thing is that in each case above, the printed or equivalent version still stands on the record, for future generations to misuse. Researchers need to be aware that "clean" information is rare. What are some of the causes of errors and inaccuracies? Here are some typical excuses:

1. Not enough time – to background; to gather information; to resolve contradictions; to write reports; to scoop the competition.
2. Not enough space – to include everything; to include enough; too much edited out of the articles; wording changed too much; inaccurate paraphrasing.
3. Misunderstanding between people – sources, contacts, writers, researchers, editors, readers – resulting in incorrect, unclear, or misinterpreted data.
4. Carelessness, lack of interest, lack of direction or focus, cynical speculation.
5. Misunderstandings about topic and complexity of subject matter, leading to slanting (such as using "breakthrough" to describe a new medical development and thereby encouraging false hope) and inappropriate paraphrasing of jargon.
6. Message discrimination – some researchers will only "see" what they want to see.

Journalists take information and make it interesting. In the journalistic process information must be made readable, that is, it must become a "story" that will grab people's attention and make them want to read it. Journalists are trying to make complicated material simple enough to understand and interesting enough to attract attention. In doing so, they will use a variety of sources and paraphrase complex ideas. Without verification or checking, this type of writing is prone to inaccuracy. Here are some of the main elements in factual inaccuracy:

(1) *Guessing.* Reporters ought not to write stories that they do not understand, for their audience won't understand either. In doing so, they have done worse than fail to inform: they have *mis*informed. If researchers are not certain about something, they either check it out or leave it out. They should use only facts of which they know the origin.

(2) *Statistics.* All numbers need to be double-checked and attributed to a source. Statistics should not be manipulated but should instead be used in a comparative sense so that the figures are

meaningful. Many sets of statistics require interpretation and deciphering by the use of visual aids such as graphs and charts. Many errors, however, can occur in the creation of these visuals.

(3) *Names.* These should be checked with the original source and cross-checked in a reliable directory. Researchers should learn to ignore public-relations handouts unless they are verified. Addresses, ages, titles, and other identifying information should all be checked.

(4) *Dates and places.* Calendars and up-to-date maps should be checked, twice if possible.

(5) *Quotations.* These must always be attributed, to document the story. Complete documentation is necessary because all quotations are taken from a larger context and the quote, thus, is incomplete or may furnish an incomplete answer (this clarifies responsibility for the ultimate authority of the answer).

(6) *Personal experience.* Did you try it out yourself, or are you taking someone else's word? If the latter, did the source provide you with all the crucial details? How do you know nothing was left out?

(7) *Omissions.* Basic facts may be ignored, more sources may be needed, or different parameters may need to be searched. The constraint of time should not be an excuse for shoddy or incomplete research.

(8) *Not enough time.* Haste makes waste, yet somehow there is always enough time to do it over again. Obviously, then, it's best to take the time to do it right from the beginning.

(9) *Hoaxes.* Some people like to feed false information to the media for the simple joy of fooling them and their audiences. Facts need to be verified and explained. In looking for the explanation, the researcher may happen upon the truth.

(10) *Technical errors.* Jargon problems occur in the areas of science, finance, law, and medicine. Extra research is needed, and facts must be cross-checked with additional sources.

The best prevention against inaccuracy is careful research and checking, verification, proper attribution, a careful re-reading, and re-checking afterwards.

Verification

Verification of the facts is absolutely necessary because when people (and this includes researchers) read a fact, they do one of four things: (1) they *accept* it because it appeared in a source that they trust; (2) they *reject* it because it does not square with what they think likely happened; (3) they *suspend judgement* until more information appears; (4) they *ignore* the difficulty altogether.

This *message discrimination* is pervasive and must be recognized by the researcher. It helps to be a sceptic who can doubt the facts until they can be verified. Examples range from getting a person's first name correct, to establishing someone's age, to proving that a document is both genuine (not forged) and authoritative. This discrimination relies on attention to detail, on common-sense reasoning, and on a feel for institutional and human behaviour. Along the way, verifiers (or fact checkers) absorb huge quantities of miscellaneous information.

Researchers are like pack rats – they take ideas, facts, and opinions, and in their place they leave behind an organized study of complex ideas. They collect and file and shift an incredible collection of evidence, all of which has been verified so that no biases are revealed and a proper understanding of context has been maintained. Facts are established and corroborated by source credibility, attributable quotations, cross-checking of identification, reconciliation of contradictions, clarification, and collation (comparing sources). Scepticism throughout the process is a valuable attribute.

The same information can lie in different places, whether in several government agencies or levels of government, or in different people's minds. This is useful to recall if one is engaged in verification or if doors are closed and alternate sources are needed. Every memo, report, or document has been created by someone for someone else, and thus at least two copies probably exist in two different files. Even everyday encyclopedias can be used to cross-check each other for inaccuracies and contradictions. A beginning researcher could look for answers to just about anything in five or so encyclopedias. No two encyclopedias will be alike: some articles contradict each other, others furnish additional data, some do not even mention the subject matter, still others can provide access to the answer only through a machine-readable search, which will call up every article that contains the specific search term. Verification skills are, of course, transferable, whether the researcher is working with elementary tools such as encyclopedias or specialized sources within a narrow range of sub-disciplines. In information work, the key to unlocking many details lies in "asking the right question," and this is true for the verification side as well.

Critical Evaluation and the Research Matrix

The mere existence of information does not mean that it is contextually truthful, valid, or even useful. All information must be evaluated critically. One key to good research lies in the researcher's grasp of the interplay between "general categories" and "specific examples." This is, to be sure, stating the obvious: the relationship between deductive thought (from the general to the specific) and inductive thought (from the specific to the general). This will also be part of vocabulary control (see Chapter 4) and search strategies (see Chapter 5).

With deduction, a researcher starts with a general idea of how things are supposed to work and then applies this to the specific current case; with induction, a researcher generalizes after she or he has examined specific cases and identifies their combined general effect. In essence, a deductive mode of reasoning gives support for a system while an inductive mode of reasoning creates a system from the situations. Critical thinking, evaluation, and the reasoning process balance the general and the specific, the abstract and the concrete. The researcher who knows where he is on the sliding scale of general, specific, abstract, and concrete will be in a better position to understand how the evaluative process works in the context of moving about the critical thinking matrix, also known as the *research matrix*. This is a spectrum of information flow, and the researcher must be cognizant of where she or he is on the spectrum at any moment; her or his position will vary from subject to subject, resource to resource, contact to contact, and even researcher to researcher, depending on one's previous knowledge of the subject area and of research techniques in general.

An evaluation of information is an attempt to draw objective conclusions from all the information gathered, analysed, and synthesized. One straightforward method of evaluating is simply to make a list of the conclusions or implications derived from analysis and synthesis. Another way is to look at the information related to each specific aspect of the researched topic, dividing material into objective matters and subjective matters, and applying tests of evidence.

According to all the texts on research methods and rhetoric, there are twelve standard tests of evidence, which I have modified slightly to take into account the mode of research. These are:

1. *Recency.* Do the data appear to be the most current on the subject or the most appropriate for an historical time period?
2. *Relevancy.* Is there a direct correlation to the subject? Is the tone of the source popular, scholarly, or technical?
3. *Authority.* What is the reputation of the data? What is the reliability of the source (history, context, viewpoint)?
4. *Completeness.* At what point has the researcher gathered sufficient data to produce a relatively unslanted report? Can the subject be understood by the researcher and the intended audience?
5. *Accuracy.* Does the source furnish background data and/or in-depth data? Are complex issues oversimplified? Are terms adequately defined?
6. *Clarity.* Can bias be recognized? Are there any logical fallacies? Are all assumptions (hidden or otherwise) identified?
7. *Verifiability.* Can subjective materials be verified? If not, why not?
8. *Statistical validity.* Can the conclusive data be supported by standard statistical testing? Was statistical inference needed? Are there clear explanations for using "averages" or "percentages"?
9. *Internal consistency.* Do the data contain internal contradictions?
10. *External consistency.* Do the data reflect any contradictions among the source documents?

11. *Context.* Do the data reflect some sort of common sense or experience of the world within the context of information demand? Can fact be distinguished from opinion? Are sources taken out of context? Can the document be placed within the era and circumstances that produced it?

12. *Comparative quality.* Are some data clearly inferior to other data? Which are the "best" data in context of the above eleven tests (i.e., the most recent, the most relevant, the most authoritative, the most complete, the most accurate, and so forth).

Some of the more straightforward objective matters that can be evaluated include the spelling of proper names and titles, and the basic factual information of correct locations, dates, quotations, and historical references. Some of the less objective situations that need clear thought and more tests of evidence concern adequate and correct descriptions (e.g., did an event happen as described? who described it? how reputable was the describer?) and ranking and comparative information (e.g., is it a valid comparison? are all needed data collected for ranking and statistical testing?).

But the fuzziest area concerns the subjective analysis of information derived from human sources, with their penchant for misunderstanding through miscommunication and faulty memory. Some of the questions to be asked concerning subjective information include:

- What is the actual source of the information (e.g., informed opinion)?
- What are the connotations applied to words, phrases, jargon?
- What is likely to happen in the future?
- Is there a logical flow to the mode of reasoning, or do the facts lead to wrong conclusions because of misinterpreted data?
- Is the analogy used an apt one?
- Are two facts or more juxtaposed for prominence or by accident?
- What about balance, emphasis, exaggeration, vagueness, ambiguity, tone?
- What about speculation, or proper use of examples?

Answers to serious questions of subjective matters can come only to a researcher who has had the experience of doing research. Experience simply means lots of reading to find out what exists, lots of interviewing to help fill in the gaps in the written record, lots of observing to gather information about how things look, feel, sound, and smell, and plenty of reasoning, which demands time to sit down and think and recognize the importance – or unimportance – of what one has. Such experience about subjective matters will also tell the researcher that more of a certain type of data is required, or will at least point in the direction of where recent or relevant or reputable data of a higher grade might be found. In conjunction with both deductive and inductive forms of reasoning, the researcher can slide around the research matrix and begin to fill in any holes in the collection of information. This process of evaluation, together with knowledge of the nature of information, the triad of information (see Chapter 3), the vocabulary control needed for information (see Chapter 4), and search strategies for specific subjects (see Chapters 6-11), is at the heart of any in-depth research. Researchers must know where they are on the research matrix at any one time (see also Chapter 4, especially about research logs), for this will allow them to move around at will.

After checking facts and looking at documents such as licences, transcripts, certificates, or maps, after trying to get the highest grade of data possible and evaluating the worth of such basic information, the researcher still must deal with the "report" (a primary study or a secondary piece) done by another writer. This report can take many forms, such as a free-standing publication, a magazine or newspaper article, or a technical study. How does one gauge its overall reliability? Studies have shown that in all of the social sciences, for example, reports contain more errors and erroneous conclusions than a researcher might believe. Intense analysis of facts and figures has shown carelessness and misinterpretations; much published research is not completely trustworthy, and thus the popularization of social research in magazines and the press is even less so. Here are some questions that researchers should be asking themselves, not about the facts in any report, but about how the facts fit conclusions and how the tone of the report leads to these conclusions.

(1) How does one know what one knows about the report? Does

one rely on common sense, or seek advice from opinion leaders, or produce one's own research (which might be counterproductive)?

(2) What kind of information needs to be known about the report? Examples are types of controls used, amount of possible error, to whom the report applies, the methodology used, the currency/obsolescence of the data, and other tests of evidence.

(3) What was the purpose of the report? Why were the data collected (official communication, research study for a marketing company, recordkeeping, propaganda, publicity)?

(4) Who was responsible for collecting the data? What built-in biases have been developed from its sponsorship? Is there a hidden agenda? What is the intended audience for this report?

(5) How consistent are the data obtained from one source with data available from other sources? How were the "bias" and "noise" (mechanical errors) minimized?

The careful researcher will be suspicious if there are few answers to these questions; scepticism is useful as a beginning point to evaluate reports. But the only way to have confidence in results is if those conclusions have been replicated elsewhere. Finding similar data in other sources is extremely useful for cross-checking, verifying, and strategizing in case of document non-availability. This searching for alternate sources should always be done, for it will result in automatic and quick confirmations. Indeed, multiple sources will show that there is yet another question to be addressed, which is:

(6) What has been left out of the report? The original writers simply cannot see everything even if they want to – there are always limited vision, limited recall, some distortion, some interpretation based on editing or bias, and some measure of expectations. Even the act of establishing an hypothesis sets up the reader to know that, in all likelihood, the hypothesis will be proved – why else was the study written? – and the reader is less likely to suspect or to question the results than perhaps he/she should. What has been omitted from a report may not have been useful to the writer but it might have been extremely useful to the researcher. In such cases the writer needs to be contacted for a follow-up interview. Were only the best results used? What kinds of assumptions, interpretations, and inferences were considered and/or discarded? Was any information buried? And if so, how (smokescreens, effect of language, operational and circular definitions)?

The framework for the report needs to be examined, for whatever was left out may have been left out only because the writer considered it not to be important or relevant to the conclusions. Some ways of stating an hypothesis can restrict the scope of a study, and the report on that topic may not be quite what the researcher is looking for. The report writer may have chosen not to do research on the aspect of a topic that is most important to the researcher. What has been researched is not necessarily what is important – that's for the current researcher to dig out and assess. One must constantly ask if the results apply to the case at hand, evaluating these results and making decisions largely from one's own knowledge of the immediate situation and needs. The researcher will be limited because he almost always knows less than he would like to know about the report, especially about any missing information and the general trustworthiness.

In a similar sense, the tests of evidence and what has been left out of a report apply to human source credibility. Journalism, for example, relies heavily on the expert – for data, for confirmations, for explanations, for opinions, for attributable quotations. And experts, in the same manner as the trustworthiness of reports, need to be evaluated. Here, cynicism reaches its full strength: people do lie. There are total lies, half-truths, coverups, policy lies, personal lies, black lies, and white lies. There are "dirty trick" lies. Some people often do not believe they are lying, for the lie has become the truth in their own minds.

Experts are continually deciding whether certain information should be revealed, which details should be highlighted or discarded, and when the data should be offered. Every decision is an act of manipulation, and while this may be a huge ethical problem in the minds of a few, it is something that is acknowledged and lived with by journalists. Because information is quite often traded back and forth between expert and journalist, there is a feeling of mutual back-scratching and promotion. Often, experts become journalists and vice versa (or they even co-exist: some journalists work both sides of the street). As they evaluate experts, journalists realize that experts have different motives.

(1) A *well-rehearsed* expert who promotes a line of propaganda may be involved in public relations, the aim of which is to supply information on behalf of special interests, such as an organization, a

political party, or an individual. Researchers need to screen out what is valid from what is distorted or inflated. Public relations sources are used only for certain parts of research work, such as background or ease of access to other experts; they supply reports (which in turn must be tested), texts, statistics, illustrative materials, references. They willingly give their time to answer questions because that is what they are paid to do. It has been said that public relations personnel are employed to get a firm's name into the media and to lobby, and to get a firm's name out of the media and to lobby – it all depends on whether promotional value or damage control is being stressed.

(2) A *self-interested* expert protects his or her ego and identity. He or she will be misleading and self-serving, with inaccurate observations and selective perceptions based on selective recall and distorted reactions. Such experts are the ones who inflate themselves in the "who's who" published entries (these data are only spotchecked by the editors) or in organizational curriculum vita sheets (which are never checked). They may attempt to cast aspersions on policies or embarrass opponents.

(3) A *well-used* expert is one who agrees to talk with just about any journalist or researcher. This does not necessarily make such an expert better; it just makes her or him more visible and available. But if an expert is frequently used, this usually attests to reliability, or at least to a certain glibness. These experts know what researchers are looking for and cater to it.

(4) The *inside* expert can provide background on what is taking place or information that can only be privately obtained. He or she confirms or denies rumours or suspicions, but the person's name is never mentioned in the context of hidden agendas. Ultimately, this expert, who wants to influence events and policies, can have several motives, all dealing with power. These are the "contacts" that lead journalists to business or political stories; it takes years to develop a network of such sources. A Harvard survey of former U.S. government officials found that over 40 per cent were sources at one time or another.

There are other types of sources, although these better fit a journalism-as-reporting model than a journalism-as-research model. Such sources, who are screaming for the kind of publicity that television and the daily press give in times of crisis and controversy, are not to be trusted: the risks are too great for the non-media researcher. These sources include the following.

- The *leaker* has something to gain by giving a reporter private information or gossip – media play or future credit when the favour can be returned.
- The *vendetta-ist* attempts to damage reputations by spreading information about improprieties, business corruption, alcoholism, mismanagement, and womanizing.
- The *whistle-blower* is usually a middle manager or civil servant who wishes to expose wrongdoing by blowing the whistle.
- The *planter* passes on authorized data about new policy or appointments as trial balloons. If the public is appalled, then the material is denied by the organization. Sometimes plants are used to counter rumours or correct false information ("set the record straight").

In all of these cases there may be a series of "brown envelopes" containing documents. Sometimes these documents have been "fixed" so that they look truthful; other times the material has been classified by government and its possession is illegal. Certain government agencies even have unique paper at photocopiers so that if officials retrieve copies of a purloined document then they can pinpoint the machine and thereby reduce the number of suspects.

All of these kinds of sources operate in both government and business, that is, in the public sector and in the private sector. They occur at universities, at foundations and charities, within organized crime, within spy circuses, within law enforcement agencies – everywhere. Most researchers learn to "consider the source": to make a judgement about the bias, or point of view, that motivates a person to want publicity. Motives must be examined or else the researcher will be trapped. Scepticism prevents embarrassment. In accepting information from any source or expert, *caveat emptor*: who wins? who loses? and why?

While these sources may not be trusted in the short run, they can be used as confirmation that research is headed in the right direction. Sources like these can be used as starting points for research, but they must be triple-checked with supporting evidence and documentary facts. The absence of an absolute denial means that the researcher is on the right track. Foot-in-the-door leverage is possible, in which one source can be played off against another. Armed with partial information, a researcher can ferret out more from a second source, a third source, and then go back to the first source for additional confirmation or new data. This is called "whipsawing," and it is not unlike the research matrix. The more information that is uncovered, particularly the more versions of the same information, then the more sound and accurate will be any evaluative conclusions.

It is sad to say that in today's society, there is the inevitability of hidden agendas, the need to know, and the dance of government-press-business. As in spy circuses, there are overt and covert activities, with much of the covert exposures relying on contacts and inside experts. Even in a simple research situation, such as obtaining a certificate (of death, marriage, or birth), it helps to know the clerk at the Vital Statistics Office who just might bend the policy and produce the needed document either as a certified document, as a photocopy, or merely as a glimpse for fifteen seconds, simply because the researcher is a "friend." Where the law is not explicit and subject to interpretation, information and documents could be forthcoming – if the researcher knows the right person to approach. A skilled private investigator with a network of contacts and sources, plus insiders from the legal system, can quickly amass mounds of biographical details about a person or a business, far more than the paper-only experienced researcher can. In this sense, contacts count for more than ability because the material was privately obtained.

There is a clear distinction here between the up-front overt activities and the backroom covert activities of sources. Up-front material from a source or expert is ultimately publicity-seeking, with disclosed information helpful to operations and/or image, and occasionally there might be tones of censorship if the information is a privileged "advance" look. The backroom material from a source or expert is full of secrets that may have been leaked or of confidential documents unofficially released. On any kind of a beat – politics, business, police and crime, sports, fashion, food – where reporters and specialized researchers are close to the subject matter, the leaks of covert material are like money: the data are circulated, spent, banked, invested for short- and long-term gain, and used to pay off debts. The manipulation of such data may be perceived as unethical or simply "not nice," but it is inevitable and it is part of the trade of journalism and of research. Protection for the researcher, though, lies in a proper evaluation and understanding of the data at hand. Applying the tests of evidence will help the researcher sift through the information harvested and separate the wheat from the chaff. As Sir Arthur Conan Doyle said through Sherlock Holmes, "Once you have eliminated the impossible, then whatever remains – no matter how improbable – must be the truth."

Summary

Exploring the nature of information, this chapter stresses the importance of accessibility, time, and costs in determining the quality of data. Alternative search strategies are needed so that additional material can be found and originally located material can be verified. Research methods are noted, as well as the research matrix. The types and causes of inaccuracies are explained, as well as the resolution of errors based on contradiction, inaccessibility, jargon, and misinformation. Researchers need to become accurate, and their verification methods include the use of message discrimination to filter out irrelevant data. Sources should be evaluated with some measure of critical thinking and problem-solving (inductive and deductive reasoning), using the standard tests of evidence. In addition, both informed opinion and flawed reports need further analysis. The credibility of experts and contacts needs to be examined in light of hidden agendas, leaks, and plants.

3

THE TRIAD OF INFORMATION

I work. I eat. I sleep. I stay in touch with family and friends. These four things take me full time. There's a world of news, art, science and music going on every day that I miss. A whole universe of ideas and information goes right by me because it takes me full time just to get through the four main things I have to do. I'm a four-channel receiver in a 198-channel world. – Cathy Guisewite ("Cathy" comic strip, *Globe and Mail,* 1983)

A scoop isn't a matter of luck; you work, you dig, you make calls, you grab the discrepancy, the loose thread, and you pull. And you have to have been paying attention in the first place. – I.F. Stone

This chapter covers the triad of information resources. It describes the "system" of information, presenting material on: the warehouse source databases of libraries and computers with their lists; the document sources of the public and private sectors, as well as legislation allowing access to information; the expert sources of networked contacts.

Information normally has no value whatsoever to people who don't know that they need it. Information assumes value only when someone needs it. And value can be a factor of packaging – it is only when information is made interesting that people are actually attracted to it. For instance, writers give information a focus by creating stories from data. This packaging promotes recognition of the information needs and creates an audience for its use.

There are three large packages of information distribution systems. Some researchers might categorize them into primary, secondary, and tertiary sources, but this only recognizes the world of print. Others may think of this system in terms of information controllers (bibliographies, indexes, databases). My preference is for a clear distinction among the forms of mass dissemination, unique documents, and people.

(1) *Warehouse sources.* These are databases in libraries comprised of published, non-confidential, stored data in books and periodicals, usually accessed by lists in the form of catalogues, indexes, and bibliographies. The warehouse also has computerized online databases that allow researchers to tie into any number of external services, for example, to find a recent Supreme Court decision, to look at the financial records of Algoma Steel, to check on the progress of a bill in the House of Commons, or to read the latest Statistics Canada news brief – all from a keyboard.

(2) *Limited-quantity documents.* These are generated by both not-for-profit institutions (e.g., government agencies, the courts, citizen groups, associations, law enforcement agencies, research centres, and governments) and for-profit institutions, such as commercial laboratories, trade associations, and corporations.

(3) *People.* Experts, as we have seen, can be sources and contacts. They include public relations officers, politicians and bureaucrats, researchers, librarians, academics, and consultants.

The Warehouse Sources: Libraries

Both libraries and online databases store information. Such storage of information implies both a structure and a series of products in abundant supply. (The antecedent to the library is the *arkheion,* the Sumerian building where religious and government records were stored.) Interposed between the library user and the information resources are the library staff, whose main function is to interpret and guide researchers through the collections, like a user-friendly computer software program.

Unfortunately, many people view libraries as merely a collection of books, magazines, and encyclopedias, with only books being allowed to circulate. But the researcher knows better: a library is a mix of stored information and retrieval services organized for relatively easy use, cared for by a professionally trained staff, and available for all.

Most perceptions about the library are those of the *public* library, with its novels, magazines, records, children's books, and students. Vaguely, many people remember a kind of *school* library where delinquent pupils spent detention or read a newspaper while ostensibly doing homework. Some adults have seen an *academic* library at a college where, it seemed, all the needed books were either on the reserve shelf, missing, or vandalized. A very few people work for a firm or a government agency with a *special* library, yet they never use it much because it doesn't have novels or it remains the near-exclusive territory of the administration heads and economic planning departments.

And all of this is sad, because there is much more beyond this facade. The researcher can turn this to an advantage because every library has some hidden unexplored resources, and every library is underutilized.

Researchers can get better-quality data faster, and verified, through libraries than through almost any other route. Nearly every expert has been asked for data that were recorded more accurately and more completely in monographs, periodical articles, and reference books than that expert could possibly recall. No expert can remember everything, not even from the very materials that he or she has written.

Library collections contain materials from among the following formats:

- books
- periodicals (magazines, journals, newspapers)
- vertical files (with pamphlets, brochures, news releases, leaflets)
- clipping files
- photo and picture files (postcards)
- telephone directories
- technical reports
- university course calendars
- mail-order catalogues

- high school yearbooks
- manuscripts, rare books, archival materials
- dissertations and master's theses
- newsletters and looseleaf services
- government documents
- microforms (microfilm, microfiche, microtape)
- audio: cassette tapes, phonodiscs, compact discs
- video: films, videocassettes, filmstrips, slides, transparencies
- audiovisual playback equipment
- art reproductions, prints
- computer software
- online computer databases
- electronic newspapers
- organized research files on trendy topics
- many different levels of lists (people, places, addresses, bibliographies, indexes)

which are used by the researcher:

- to gather background data
- to check dates and spellings
- to resolve contradictions in background information
- to identify experts
- to check previously published materials for the scope, bias, angle, or focus of the subject matter
- to avoid duplication of coverage
- to select and identify visual material

through basic searches of:

- controlled vocabulary (subject headings)
- keyword or free text (computers)
- citations (indexes, bibliographies, abstracts, annotations)
- browsing (systematic or serendipitous)
- asking knowledgeable library staff.

It is not this book's intention to explain how libraries are administered or set up. That can be found in Jean Gates's *Guide to the Use of Libraries and Information Sources* (McGraw-Hill, regularly revised) and other similar books. Researchers don't need to know how things

work in a library, but they do need to know how to take advantage of
what works and how to acquire the procedures for getting data.

All libraries have similar characteristics. Every library has a *classification* scheme, such as the Dewey Decimal, the Library of Congress, or some other specialized – often localized – system. Classification promotes effective physical location of the material, and most
times the material is thereby arranged for browsing (that is, each
book is placed next to a book on a similar related subject). Researchers accept classification systems; the arcane nature of these systems
is no different from anyone's methods for arranging books on home
shelves, except that using standard classification schemes makes
libraries look remarkably similar, and one can use any library in
North America knowing approximately where the bulk of the books
one needs are shelved. Obviously, not all materials are filed together,
especially since classification schemes deal only with books and not
government reports, newspapers, magazines, assorted microforms,
and other non-print materials.

Every library has a *catalogue,* ranging from a collection of 3" x 5"
cards to microfiche to computer printouts to online systems. The
catalogue is an inventory of what the library owns, with a description
of each item's contents. This catalogue has three major kinds of
entry points: author, title, and subject matter. By searching under
the name of the author or the title of a book, one will find out whether
the library owns that book and where on the shelves it will be.
Searching under the term given for a subject or topic provides a list of
all the books the library owns on that subject. This subject access
shows how subjects are related to each other; cross-references in the
catalogue will guide the search.

But it is not always that simple: things do go wrong, and one has
to keep a sharp eye on the individual letters and words being filed in
the catalogue. For one thing, there are several different ways of
alphabetizing (the two leading forms are "letter-by-letter" and
"word-by-word"); for another, computer sorting can be cranky and
constantly needs to be proofread. Entry points can be misspelled by
the inputter; researchers themselves could have transcribed an
author's name wrong or keyboarded it improperly. Subject terminology is extremely variable (see Chapter 4) and capricious when
one attempts to apply it to all of the print and non-print forms of
information resources. And just because a particular library does not

own a needed book does not mean that book does not exist. One can try another library or have the first library get the book through interlibrary loan (see below, on networks). In other words, no library catalogue is fully correct (even the Library of Congress estimates that its own catalogue is about 4 per cent misfiled), nor is it fully comprehensive.

Every library has *reference services,* headed by a staff that will answer questions and furnish information. They will help in finding information and give answers to questions asked in person, in writing, or by telephone/fax. They will do some or all of:

- compile lists (indexes, abstracts, bibliographies, annotations);
- indicate what's available at other libraries;
- perform online computer searches at no cost beyond vendors' fees;
- get material from other libraries through the interlibrary loan process;
- send/receive fax of library materials;
- provide photocopy services;
- do translation work;
- provide after-hours telephone reference service;
- give information about and help in using community services;
- give tours and talks on library usage and research;
- interpret the card catalogue and classification scheme;
- provide an entrée to other libraries through a variety of networks.

Reference services also include the reference book collection. These are the "fast fact" books (see Chapter 5) – the encyclopedias, dictionaries, directories, atlases, almanacs, indexes, and bibliographies – that answer basic needs quickly by helping the researcher to find:

- a definition of a word, object, or concept;
- biographical identification of a person, famous or obscure;
- directory information on a given company, government, or association;
- magazine articles on a specific topic;
- a source for a quotation;

- reviews of a film, a book, a disc, a wine;
- a statistic;
- a bibliographic citation to a book or journal;
- a recent textbook on a subject;
- some subject headings or a thesaurus to search for more data;
- a description of a place;
- an address;
- a specific fact and to verify it;
- background summary information or overviews.

If researchers have any trouble getting such data, then reference librarians can help them get the fullest value from these sources. They can be especially proficient in digging out and explaining arcane terminology and in producing lists of places that will furnish both experts and additional data.

Many libraries have also been charged with keeping back files of reports, internal publications, and working papers from the recent past, depending on the space available. In this sense, the library acts like an *arkheion*. A school library may keep school yearbooks; a public library may seek out vertical file material about local and regional history (tied in with the newspaper clipping files, city hall council minutes, and other items); a special library may control the records management of its firm; and an academic library may have an archive collection of specialized material, as well as rare books and manuscripts for research purposes. The procedure, then, is to find out why one would use a particular library, where these libraries exist, what they contain that might be of value, when and how to get into these libraries, and whom to ask in a library when one runs into difficulties.

As noted above, there are four main types of libraries. The public library is funded mostly from municipal taxes, with a combination of grants-in-aid and unconditional grants from federal and provincial levels of government; its mandate is to provide educative, informative, and recreational material to the general public, with equal access to all. Equal access, though, does not mean equal service or equal circulation, and in many places one needs to be an adult tax-paying resident before one can take books home or even get services.

Nevertheless, polite requests from strangers will result in most staff bending over backwards to accommodate their information needs. Public libraries are noted for:

- generalized collections;
- eclectic vertical file collections;
- regional and local archives;
- knowledge of the community;
- access into a larger series of networks (including setting up appointments, giving letters of introduction).

In general, public libraries have the same Dewey Decimal classification scheme and cataloguing system, as well as a "service" orientation. Even the smallest library branch prides itself on having access to lists of bibliographies, indexes, and addresses. If it doesn't have it, it knows where to get it. Every municipality has a public library, and their specialties are noted in regularly revised directories such as *Canadian Library Yearbook* (Micromedia), *American Library Directory* (R.R. Bowker), and *Directory of Special Libraries and Information Centres* (Gale). This last directory is useful for locating highly specialized collections within the larger public library.

The school library is funded by the school board; its mandate is to supplement the system's curriculum. Chronically understaffed, the school library has not much value for the researcher, except for collections of school history and yearbooks, access to education libraries, audio-visual materials, and simplicity of use.

The academic library ranges from the community college to the post-doctoral level in collection depth and in funding by the provincial governments; its mandate is to provide educative and research materials to its faculty and students. Anyone can walk in and use such a library, although some places will require identification. One must belong to the academic community to sign out books. This means that the Reference Department and the Special Collections areas are open for most researchers to work in. For sheer impressiveness in information resources (if bigger is better), the academic library wins. It has everything a public library has, plus the research materials needed to support its curriculum. For example, a university library with a Ph.D. program in urban planning would be a good place to begin an urban studies research project. Likewise, an

M.B.A. program would suggest business resources strength, while an LL.B. program would mean strong legal resources.

The academic library, though, has minimal staff. Students and faculty (and outside users) are expected to know how the library works and what is there. This is all part of the research process taught at universities. Staff members are expected to help out but not to write papers for students. Thus, they can point the way by suggesting research strategies. This is good for the researcher because it helps focus thoughts and suggests alternate paths of discovery. Academic libraries are noted for: their subject collection depth; their archive collections in many fields; their satellite libraries with many specialties; their historical depth; their immense collection of lists for addresses and names of experts.

Beginning researchers should start their projects in the Reference Department of a large academic library – there is enough strong material on any topic to get started and to get bearings. More information about the subject coverage in academic libraries is available in the three sources mentioned above, as well as in: *Encyclopedia of Information Systems and Services* (Gale); *Subject Collections: a guide to special book collections in North America* (R.R. Bowker); and *Guide to Published Library Catalogs* (Scarecrow).

The special library is the information centre attached to a profit-seeking company or a non-profit agency or organization; it quite often does not even look like a library. It is special because it provides "specialized" forms of information, usually restricted to a narrow subject coverage in terms of the goals of its parent organization, and it is run for that organization's employees. Normally, it is closed to outsiders, but a phone call or letter of introduction is usually sufficient to gain entrance. Every institute or group has an information centre of sorts, whether it is a hospital, professional society, government department, or university; in addition, every major business has a centre, usually linked to a public relations, communications, or market research branch. All information centres have common setups and responsibilities. After one has learned to use such an information centre, then one can use them all, especially with a letter of introduction.

Special libraries look after information that is needed by a group to make decisions.

- They are staffed by experts.
- They provide depth of analysis and control over their subjects.
- They feature online computer searches.
- They have selective dissemination of information programs that automatically generate pre-selected topics to their clients.
- They have listings of experts, both within and without the company.
- They collect internal studies and unpublished reports, many of which are unique and not necessarily confidential.
- They evaluate information, prepare papers, write reports.
- They collect and disseminate data by publishing.
- They provide an entry to networks of like libraries.
- They have less traffic to deal with and offer peace and quiet at most times.

Personally, after I get my bearings and develop a rough strategy at an academic library, I usually head for a relevant special library. I call in advance, after finding out the name of the person in charge, and on arrival I produce all kinds of identification and letters of introduction, if needed. I don't have to do this if I've used the library in the past. I begin work in a corner after taking a quick tour or overview of the facilities, and I am quiet, bothering no one. The staff respects me because I seem to know what I am doing. I try to stay on good terms.

So, where does one find these special libraries? Numerous regularly revised directories are available, from the local or regional level up through the international. The approach is by subject matter. Besides *Canadian Library Yearbook*, *American Library Directory*, and *Directory of Special Libraries and Information Centers*, the following directories can be helpful:

- *Aslib Directory* (covers about 7,000 centres in the United Kingdom and Ireland);
- *Encyclopedia of Associations* (Gale; covers about 20,000 U.S. and international associations, and all of them have information centres);
- *Directory of Associations in Canada* (Micromedia; covers about 9,000 Canadian groups with centres);

– *Encyclopedia of Information Systems and Services* (Gale; covers 3,500 sources from the U.S. and seventy other countries).

For a regional directory, one could consider the *Directory of Special Libraries in the Toronto Area,* listing over 900 Toronto-based centres with an appropriate subject index. Another local tool is *Newspaper Libraries in the United States and Canada,* a directory that also lists the specialized collections at newspapers; this is good for gathering regional information. For research centres, which contain an amazing wealth of information, there are three regularly revised directories from Gale Research Publications: *International Research Centers Directory* (covers about 2,500 international, university-related, independent, and government research organizations of the world, arranged by country); *Research Centers Directory* (covers 14,000 in North America, cross-referenced under 2,400 subject categories); and *Government Research Centers Directory* (covers 2,500 government-funded facilities). In addition, Gale has *Research Services Directory,* a listing of for-profit facilities such as testing laboratories. Much foreign data can be gleaned from *European Sources of Scientific and Technical Information* and the *World of Learning* (Europa). From these can be learned that the Canadian Music Centre has as its goal "to promote, disseminate, and make available the music of Canadian composers," while the Community Information Centre of Metropolitan Toronto seeks to link "people with human services ... provides individuals, organizations, and governments with information on resources available." The Arthur and Elizabeth Schlesinger Library on the History of Women in America (housed at Radcliffe College within Harvard University) has over 45,000 books and related vertical files, while the Arnold Schoenberg Institute at the University of Southern California has a small collection of materials – scores, manuscripts, recordings, archives – devoted to his music.

All this said, there are two major problems with libraries. One is the public perception. Librarians have been remiss in allowing their image to become degraded over the past century. While the profession thinks a lot about its skills and service orientation, it has done a miserable job in public relations. People may view the library as a "good thing" but may also see it as an archaic institution. Very few know what it can do beyond being a book service. Few people actually know how to find information. Students are frustrated because scores of them clamour for the same book at the last minute, and then they wonder why that book is not on the shelf. Most libraries are inadequately staffed, poorly funded, and structurally forbidding. Libraries lack the pizzazz of computer-based information retrieval.

A second problem has been that the library is concerned traditionally with only larger units of bibliographic information, such as books and magazine articles. It operates with superficial indexing of a wide spectrum of subjects. Most books get two subject headings for the catalogue, yet hundreds of headings are indicated in a book's own index. However, as the information hierarchy narrows from broad subjects to highly specialized topics at special libraries, the intensity of subject analysis does increase. Here, there is often a minute breakdown of subject matter into smaller units. For example, newspaper libraries have large files of very brief units – clippings and photographs. Law libraries have files on specific cases. The total size of a library is less important than the strength of its collection in the subject area in which one is researching. A government environmental library will have more relevant material than a large academic library with a general collection. One solution is to subscribe to online computer search services, with their retrieval by keyboard and free text. Still, libraries are a good beginning point for any kind of research, so long as one realizes their limitations.

The Warehouse Sources: Online Computer Databases

Computer use has been touted as the key to success in every field imaginable. This viewpoint has been created by the software industry in conjunction with business solely to create markets for their products. Computers are merely an aid for information retrieval, and they are useful only under certain conditions.

First, the computer is *fast*. It can save research time, for what formerly took ten hours will now take ten minutes or even less. Saving time means saving money, and this allows researchers to handle multiple assignments. For businesses and the media, the competitive edge and the scoop are important. Being first is all that matters for profit-making firms. Slow, methodical library searches are being replaced by quick, efficient computer searches.

Second, the computer is *comprehensive.* It can search a wide range of subjects at once, and it can search through a large number of files at once. It can search for every single letter or number within a database, if it is told to, for what it is really doing is comparing and sorting discrete series of electric charges at extremely high speeds. It can combine concepts that are difficult to index in print versions and can retrieve occurrences of these combined concepts – e.g., it can retrieve any reference where "organized crime" and "waste management" are in proximity.

Third, the computer is *up to date,* perhaps as recent as seconds ago in the case of stock exchange reports, though fifteen minutes is the norm. Certainly, the computerized version of magazine indexes is weeks ahead of the printed format.

Fourth, the computer is *reliable,* especially since the database is usually the same one sent to the typesetting-composition room for printing and publishing. In other words, it has the same reliability as the print version. In addition, corrections are easily made and added to the original document. This is impossible to do to the printed version unless it is reprinted.

Fifth, the computer has *unique material.* Many databases are unavailable in print form (statistical tables). Some computerized versions of print indexes have been "enhanced" by the inclusion of items not found in the printed version, thus forcing researchers who use the print copy to also check the computer version if they wish to be thorough. Also, for a multidisciplinary cross-approach, a computer database cannot be beaten.

Sixth, the computer can *manipulate* data for the creation of unique files. It can sort, order, and rank material into new configurations because the computer searches on every word. It pulls out and compares facts so that it can alphabetize on any number of principles, provided, of course, that the material is in the database to start with. For example, a search of a reference database of "who's who" factual biographies of Canadian prime ministers would soon yield information about who was the oldest Prime Minister when elected (or when defeated or when retired), who was the youngest, who was the tallest, who was the shortest. The best application of manipulation is to numbers in tabular form.

Seventh, the computer is *accessible* for searching twenty-four hours a day. A few systems shut down overnight or on the weekends, or for a few hours for "maintenance." But most files are available on different systems and in different time zones. Provided that one has a password or personal identification number (like a bank convenience card), one can access several online search systems all day long. The only thing that comes close to this are one's own home resources. All libraries, except for media libraries, normally close overnight and on the weekend, so it is here that computers can win the hearts of researchers.

And eighth, the computer can produce information in a new display, known as the *mosaic theory*. It works this way: although small items of non-classified data may be harmless when viewed in isolation, computerized databases (by shooting a keyword arrow through the whole system) have the potential to allow experts to pull together the widely scattered pieces into one big jigsaw puzzle that in total could reveal classified or sensitive information. Assembling all the pieces of data from several wide and disparate sources and documents, a researcher can produce a "mosaic" that was previously hidden. A good example of this concerned the revelation of the secret cargo of the American space shuttle Discovery – a satellite surveillance system. This information, despite the government's attempts to hide it, was ferreted out and published in half a dozen newspapers before the January, 1985, liftoff. The same thing happened before the September, 1985, liftoff of the Atlantis shuttle. By using databases that concentrate on trade journals, technical reports, newsletters, papers from foreign governments, conference proceedings, and other "grey" literature that previously was virtually non-retrievable by manual practices, researchers can summon up all kinds of information and base their conclusions on a series of disclosed fragments. By piecing together individual facts that somehow relate to a topic, researchers can get a much better whole picture. This is a simple inductive technique. And once a researcher has a conclusion (or an "answer") he or she can start a fishing expedition by browsing for confirmation. Once answers are known, discrete facts can become startling. Suspicions can be quantified by getting a wealth of statistics to justify viewpoints.

Inevitably, there are drawbacks to computerized searching. One is the unreasonably high price of $5 to $50 a minute forced on researchers by the profit motive of business. After all, searching is a legitimate business expense and thus tax-deductible. Database producers and the distribution networks are extremely wealthy. They have discovered that good information can be sold over and over. Some of the prices can be rationalized by the extreme currency of the data; also, CD-ROMs (Compact Discs – Read Only Memory) are available, and these allow for unlimited use after purchase or lease, in the same way that a set of encyclopedias can be used over and over again without paying on a per-use basis. It is best, though, to remember that not everything is mounted on a computer. Manual searches of the printed material are still needed for information published before 1975 or so. Also, it is expensive and time-consuming for researchers to become computer-literate in searching.

A second drawback is that precision is needed for retrieval. Researchers must be able to spell the right word correctly. While people recognize homonyms, computers don't. And a misspelled word is lost forever inside a computer. Subject headings, descriptors, keywords, and free texts must have a proper input, both by the creator of the database and by the user. Search terms must be carefully thought out and a specific search strategy devised. The extremely limited capability of browsing by computer does not allow for recognized mistakes. People can cast an eye over a print copy and get an overview, but computers cannot recognize errors: garbage in, garbage out. There is a vast difference between the hierarchical-relational structured print searches by subject headings and the free-text structured computer searches. The latter is more precise and not forgiving of mistakes. Thus, searches need to be specific, for limited denotations or stock concepts. It is really a different manner of searching, for all computerized databases have "commands" and features that vary from manual searches. These features simplify searches, but at the same time they are a function of the free-text mode of searching. Some examples of searching that may seem strange to a print searcher include:

- wild-card commands;
- suffix expansion;
- proximity searching;
- bulletin boards;
- global databases.

The computer is intellectually inflexible – it searches *only* those terms you tell it to, and it cannot distinguish relevant from irrelevant word contexts. Each of the vendors, the distributors of the databases, has different search protocols, and each must be learned separately by a searcher. It takes a lot of time and experience to learn which databases offer the best sources for a query, and the best sources can change every time the searcher has a new question, even on the same project. Many researchers can simply leave it up to a database search librarian at a larger public or academic library; the cost is normally free for the library staff's time, with payment to be made to the vendor for the use of the service. I let librarians do all of my searching because they know how to reach databases all over the world that contain a variety of information, from trade statistics to patents to child abuse to environmental studies. They have the hardware, the software, the modems, the networks, and the printout paper. And when the material comes in (whether it is full text or just citations) I am already inside the library ready to begin my search to confirm the text or find the article/book. I read the database-generated printout to narrow my search and focus on my needs, often discarding many references that do not apply. If the material I want is not in the library, then I try to get it on interlibrary loan.

A third drawback is more an attitude problem of false hopes. Computers have been touted as solving problems. But they don't. The computer will find information, just as a print search will. It does it better in most cases, but it does not produce "answers." One still has to read, dig, evaluate, and come to conclusions. Computerized databases are not the solution to finding answers. Too many bells and whistles on computerized devices, in addition to false and misleading statements by some vendors, create a flashy, sometimes impotent product that promises everything but might actually deliver little. The computerized warehouse is just a faster and more expensive version of a library warehouse. Once the search is complete, in most cases the researcher is given a list of citations – and he or she is back to the point of the manual search, still in quest of an elusive document. This quest might take longer than the actual search for references. A list of fifty citations can be printed online in a matter of minutes, but actual delivery of the full texts may require days. Full-text databases do not exist for everything yet, and all of those that do exist are very expensive. A fax machine will help, provided that one can locate the original material. But even this costs some money. The best document delivery would be through artificial intelligence: ask a question and get an answer. As it stands right now, however, you ask a question and get a list of documents that might contain the answer, or an article that must still be read and evaluated.

Most specific databases will be covered in Chapters 5 and 6, which deal with parameters and subject matter. With a handful of exceptions, computer databases are created by companies that make use of the information themselves. In many cases, these databases are simply instructions to the computerized typesetting process that produces the printed, paper copy, much like a newspaper or a magazine. To generate extra revenue, the companies offer the databases to anybody who is willing to pay the price. This is usually done through a vendor, who also collects a wholesale charge. The fee structure is staggering: there can be charges for simply signing on, for using the database, for using the system, for long distance telephone usage, for every reference found (with additional charges for every reference printed up), royalties to the original database, plus local charges of telephone usage, computer time, modems, paper, searcher's time, and so forth.

There are thousands of databases: some are confidential, some are restricted to national citizens, some are directly available for public use. Most of the 10,000 or so world-wide are accessible through the English language, the lingua franca of database territory, although many contents are in French, German, and transliterated Chinese (the commands and procedures are in English). Three major directories, regularly revised, monitor database progress: *Data Base Directory* (Knowledge Industry Publications) describes about 5,000 databases available directly in North America, while the *Encyclopedia of Information Systems and Services* (Gale Research) lists about 10,000 databases, networks, and systems around the world in its three volumes. *The Espial Canadian Database Directory* covers almost 400 databases with Canadian content in all subject fields.

There are different categories of databases.

(1) Online and CD-ROM *bibliographic* databases list books and/or periodical articles by library or by subject, sometimes with annotations and abstracts. For books there are the American *OCLC* and

MARC (from the Library of Congress) and the Canadian *UTLAS*. The *NLCATBN* database includes, among its 600,000 records, Canadian material catalogued by the National Library and a variety of microforms from the pre-1900 period; 50,000 items are added yearly. The National Library's *ROMULUS* CD-ROM locates serials in Canadian libraries (200,000 records). For journal articles and reports, there are *CA* (Chemical Abstracts), *GEO-REF, ERIC* (for education), *COMPENDEX* (for engineering), and *MEDLINE*. For magazines and newspapers there are the *National Newspaper Index*, the *Magazine Index, Newsearch* (200 magazines and newspapers), the *Canadian Magazine Index*, the *Canadian Periodical Index*, and the various Wilson indexes such as the *Reader's Guide to Periodical Literature*. There are also specific subject bibliographic databases, such as *Quakeline*, developed by the Information Service of the National Center for Earthquake Engineering Research (in Buffalo, New York). It contains over 15,000 records, from 1987 to the present, drawn from books, journal articles, conference papers, and technical reports. Database topics include earthquake engineering, geology, seismology, seismic design, hazards, mitigation, emergency response, and preparedness. As is often the case with these special-purpose databases, *Quakeline* contains information that is not indexed elsewhere and it can be used, without real overlap, in conjunction with other databases. Normally, for all bibliographic databases, the search mode is by keyword or descriptor, not by free text.

(2) Online and CD-ROM *full-text* databases present both the bibliographic data and the entire article. Normally, the search mode is free text. Some examples from Canada include *InfoGlobe, Infomart* (Southam), *Newstex* (CP), and *Québec-Actualité*. From the United States there are Dow-Jones News, *VU/TEXT, NEXIS, Datatimes, USA Today, New York Times, Los Angeles Times, Washington Post*, and many other newspapers and magazines. The value of full-text retrieval is that one does not have to search for the article: one already has it. The computer fee is higher, but there is no need for the additional step of trying to find the article.

(3) Online and CD-ROM *numeric* databases present tables and statistics or other sets of figures that can be manipulated as needed. Some examples include the economic time series of *CANSIM* (Statistics Canada), various public opinion poll data banks such as the

Institute for Behavioural Research collections of Gallup polls, spreadsheets of econometric models, census tapes or CD-ROMs, government nine-track tapes of aggregated personal information, and the collection of numeric data banks held by Reuters Canada Holdings (formerly I.P. Sharp Associates). An experienced researcher who has constructed databases and spreadsheets can do some number crunching, producing new facts by meshing one database with another. This will show relationships, links, and trends.

(4) Online *vendor* systems can mount any or all of the databases already mentioned, plus others. These systems make it easier to sign on and off, and there are similar commands within each system. Some examples: for Canada, there are *QL Systems* and the federal government's *CISTI* (with *CAN/OLE*); for the rest of the world (with Canadian content) there are *DIALOG, BRS,* and *NEXIS*. For researchers not living near larger libraries, the National Library of Canada has offered, since 1972, computer searching on topics in the social sciences and humanities. Fees are modest, but they are in addition to what is charged by the commercial vendors. Over fifteen major automated systems are covered, providing access to about 2,000 databases; although these systems specialize in Canadian topics, they are not limited to such topics.

Here are some relevant examples of actual usage of computer databases, accessing information that is hard to find otherwise.

- Five minutes after learning the name of a would-be assassin of Pope John Paul II, a researcher at CBS News searched *NEXIS* and found thirteen stories about the suspect, some of which recounted a previous arrest and a death threat.
- A researcher in Toronto identified and located several obscure brokerage houses.
- Eight useful citations were found when a reporter sought articles and information related to an income tax evasion hearing for a doctor thought to be both a charlatan and connected to a religious cult.
- To stay abreast of her beat, a medical reporter regularly searches the online databases for professional articles by Ontario researchers to see what they've published.
- A researcher needed current data on AIDS and successfully searched *MEDLINE*.

- An investigative reporter found a wealth of information through a database search on a company suspected of dumping hazardous waste.

Other questions that have been answered include:

- methods of measuring the levels of ozone in the environment;
- Canadian pension funds: size, growth, management, and average return on investment;
- discrimination and disparity in the treatment of defendants in Philadelphia criminal courts;
- inequities in property tax assessments;
- analysis of U.S. child death certificates showing that countless child abuse deaths went undetected because of poorly trained coroners and botched investigations;
- eyeglass frames: channels of distribution, retailing, and marketing in Canada;
- effect of high and low teacher/pupil ratios on learning in elementary schools;
- racial discrimination by Atlanta's home-mortgage lenders;
- analysis of U.S. occupational safety and health records showing that workers nation-wide were dying on the job and employers were going unpunished.

The Document Sources: Public and Private Sector

Top American investigative reporter I.F. Stone's sources of information were not so much people as they were documents. He specialized in finding contradictions and inconsistencies in the official printed records of American government. He used these documents to attack McCarthyism, racism, the nuclear arms race, the Vietnam conflict, and countless other events.

Documents are instruments that furnish evidence or proof of something; they are also referred to as "records" or "certificates." They can be:

- official forms such as licences, certificates, permits, applications;

- letterhead correspondence and internal memos;
- diverse reports, technical studies, and analyses;
- polls, surveys, and statistics;
- financial data (revenues, expenses, accounts, audits, wages, taxes, profits, budgets);
- legislative materials (tabled documents, statutes, regulations, hearings, verbatim accounts, Question Period responses);
- company filings required by regulatory agencies.

Documents are useful because they are written, tangible evidence containing details no one person could possibly remember. Some, such as reports, cover a scope of activities and information from varying sources so extensive that it would be prohibitive in cost for a researcher to duplicate. Others contain verbatim accounts made in front of witnesses. And still other documents are regularly issued, allowing for historical comparisons.

Documents, while they might be truthful, are not always neutral. Text, commentary, and opinion are bound to have built-in biases and slanted data. Documents can try to persuade, to build a consensus, to seek approval for changes. They contradict each other, as I.F. Stone noted, when they emphasize or de-emphasize contentious points. Data selection is used to prove a point or to muster support. A healthy scepticism is needed when assessing textual documents: what has been left out can be as valuable as its contents. Whether the institution is a business, association, or government, everybody wants to look efficient and productive, to look good.

Institutions and organizations, as well as their staffs, are responsible for copious amounts of data and information needed for the proper running of society. Most such records are for internal use or for transmission to another institution for *its* internal usage. Some of these are on the public record (such as ownership of a publicly traded company); some of it is widely disseminated (such as an annual report); some of it is aggregated (such as tax returns). But most of it is treated as confidential; for example, it is considered an invasion of corporate privacy to dig into such things as an inventory of goods ordered, received, and sold or a record of how many employees worked for how many hours for what wages.

However, data *about* those goods (excise taxes, duties, provincial sales taxes, goods and services taxes) are kept and sent off to the appropriate revenue collector. These data are compiled and become a measure of the business conditions in the region. Even so, these data are usually rendered as totals of taxes collected, arranged by month collected, by type of product, by area within the region, and so forth. It is next to impossible to get sales tax records for a private company unless such data are needed for disputes – and then it becomes public record in most legal cases. The major reason for this is the marketplace – a company does not want to give away its competitive edge! Yet it wouldn't mind finding information about *its* competitors. This is the major usage of business databases and of legislation that provides access to information: one company trying to find information about another.

To continue with the prior example of employees: records of staff, such as pay rates and work hours, do become part of the public record if there are disputes (such as whether a worker got paid for his hours worked or whether payroll taxes were properly transmitted) or if the company has a labour dispute and wages and hours are splashed all over the local papers. Newspapers contain so much scattered information about institutions that computer searching is really mandatory: simply use the name of the company, the government agency, or the industry to retrieve stories. A few short paragraphs on a labour dispute in different stories over several days buried within the newspaper have the same weight (to a computer) as a major airplane crash or a declaration of war on the front page. The stories might reveal pay rates, taxes, profits, and the names of people associated with the disputes. Even a minimal amount of data generated by a small company can assume awesome proportions in the context of needed information. And even more data and documentation could be privately obtained.

In the public sector, a much more complex production of information is needed to determine public policy. For example, a government agency may decide to shut down residential care facilities (group homes) for young offenders and to send these residents back to either their local communities or correctional centres for further care. A substantial amount of data is needed for a proper evaluation of these cutbacks, and while undoubtedly some information already exists, much more will be needed. Thus, the agency study will produce new and different data that will be used to defend the change. Internal impact studies are done with different scenarios (no cutbacks, deep cutbacks, transfers, eliminations), but at some point the public must be informed. Either a report is released, along with its appendages of figures and raw data, or external comment is called for from other players in that service sector (community groups, agencies, individuals). If the policy change is too sensitive, the agency will consult with the government in power to check on the political expediency of the move (i.e., re-election prospects). If the policy change appears to be routine, then the agency might just go ahead without consulting with the government. An example of this would be the decision to raise the number of beds in the average group home by one. And if the policy change lies midway between sensitive and routine, then public consultations and hearings may be called for.

The *vox populi* should be taken into consideration one way or another, and at any point along the way "leaks" or "plants" from government agencies may appear in the media, thus generating even more information. Justifying any change is exceedingly difficult because legislators, the media, and citizens must be persuaded that change is a good thing. Background data are needed, and words must be chosen with care. If citizens are to form enlightened opinions, they need access to a wide range of sources of data. Questions and objections/support must be considered. If the closing of the group homes is adopted, then there must be a plan for doing so, and more reports and data must be transmitted to the appropriate bodies. Several levels of government may also be involved, as well as several different agencies or boards and several different regions.

Before the issue is resolved, an enormous quantity of data is needed and must be evaluated by policy-makers. For the group home example, the following steps may be part of the process.

(1) The cabinet (based on its own studies) decides that social agencies need to make cutbacks (documents are generated to and by the priorities and policy committees, and to and by individual ministers, as well as the government leader's office).

(2) The line departments and agencies make a response: senior officials target various existing programs; evaluation and planning branches assemble "special study" teams who work on cost-benefit

analyses with different scenarios. (On many policy issues, environment assessment panels are formed.) All of this generates documents that discuss policy and alternative proposals that might suggest government preferences.

(3) Central agencies become involved (the Premier's office and the Management Board for political implications; the Finance Department for expenditure implications; the cabinet minister responsible for social development).

(4) Advisory councils will be consulted, such as a social planning council or a university affairs group at a provincial level.

(5) Different levels of government will be brought in, if needed (regions and municipalities need to discuss the closing of the homes; their organizational setup parallels numbers 1 through 4 above).

(6) The legislature and political parties need to be involved if there is to be new legislation or if the issue is politically sensitive. Documents are generated through Question Period, legislature committees, political party research units, party caucus, and legislative libraries with prepared background data. If there is policy change, then the government may table a Green Paper containing legislative proposals for discussion or a White Paper that actually outlines government policy in a particular area and the direction of future actions, including legislation.

(7) Policy institutes and "think tanks" may respond. Documents could be issued by groups such as the C.D. Howe Research Institute, Conference Board of Canada, Institute for Research on Public Policy, Canadian Institute for Economic Policy, Fraser Institute, Centre for Policy Alternatives, National Foundation for Public Policy Development, Canadian Council on Social Development, Canadian Tax Foundation, Canada West Foundation, and others working on a provincial and regional basis.

(8) Lobbyists may be involved (they need to file documents and to present their briefs openly).

(9) If the issue is hot enough, a royal commission may be appointed to defuse the matter. In Ontario, this is an investigatory body appointed by order-in-council under the Public Inquiries Act to inquire into a specific public concern. The Act, administered by the Attorney-General, governs the methods and procedures used by the commission, e.g., subpoena powers and hearings. The royal commission investigates sudden or catastrophic events, examines

the conduct of public service employees, or assists the government in determining policy; the investigation could go on for years and cost millions of dollars. Many research studies are generated by these commissions.

(10) Larger issues will generate academic research grants for testing hypotheses, polls and surveys to gauge public opinion, and involvement of the media for special coverage.

Not all steps will apply, and at any point along the way the agency or the party in power could change its mind. To make a decision and implement it, the agency needs information. Further, it needs data to justify its actions to the people and to seek a consensus. For this, it requires good public relations and a supportive press.

Thus, at each step staggering amounts of data are produced, and at each step some – if not most – of the information could be made available to anyone who needs it or who can privately obtain it. For any one issue there might be hundreds of people involved in gathering and disseminating data from and to a wide range of sources. Multiple copies of reports and studies exist, and if one department doesn't have a set available for researchers, then maybe another one does. Understanding the process allows researchers to make good educated guesses in the paper trail of documents. Many of these documents are available for the asking when one can figure out whom to ask. But the researcher must know what records exist, which are likely to have the information, and where to find them. Most government agencies make public records available for inspection and (sometimes) photocopying. But a researcher needs to know which agency has what and if it means anything.

For this, researchers need to know the structure of governments, how they are administratively set up. This includes the national government of Canada with its three branches and agencies, boards, and commissions; the similarly structured provincial governments, duplicated ten times, as well as the territorial governments; the regional and city councils; the embassies, consulates, and chambers of commerce of foreign countries in Canada; and the vast number of international agencies such as the United Nations and its sections, the Organization for Economic Co-operation and Development, and the General Agreement on Tariffs and Trade.

A good guide for Ontario is the *KWIC Index to the Government of Ontario*; other jurisdictions have their own organization manuals (such as the *Guide to Federal Programmes and Services* for Canada) or directories and phone books. Legislation itself may include lots of documents, and for these the researcher needs to check the appropriate statute and any ensuing regulations. These can be found through the various statute citators, such as the *Ontario Statute Citator* and the *Canada Statute Citator,* to make sure that all of the regulations have been covered, or through the government gazettes, such as the *Canada Gazette* and the *Ontario Gazette,* for announcements or for the actual regulation that has been indexed. Open records laws (discussed in greater detail later in this chapter) can also be employed; they have opened up many records that were previously kept closed but they have also closed some records (in the interests of privacy), thus creating other problems for the researcher. In addition, researchers might have to wait for some time for a satisfactory response from the Act's administrators. But each Act has a register of files, so that at least one knows what records are kept where.

It takes money and time to ferret out what is within the government, obtain a copy, and analyse it. Data in one record are often revealing when meshed with information from another document. For example, a developer's connection with local politicians, on the one hand, and organized crime, on the other, can be traced through numerous sets of documents – election campaign records, corporation reports, zoning variances, court testimony, licensing commission reports. In fact, it may be possible to show that the developer is actually a conduit through which the politicians and criminals can be linked.

The major types of public and non-public records and documents include:

- vital statistics (births, deaths, marriages, divorces, name changes, census data demographics);
- trade statistics (manufactures, imports, exports, sales);
- police and law enforcement records (police blotters, informations [data supplied on forms when someone is charged], criminal records, complaints, investigation files, parole and probation records, RCMP and CSIS files);
- tax records (property taxes, corporation taxes, tax payment records, tax liens, income tax returns, regulatory filings, tax court cases);

- budgets and audits (payrolls, purchase vouchers, travel expense vouchers, auditor reports, personnel reviews, budget worksheets for agencies);
- directories (government phone books, government listings, organization charts);
- corporation records (incorporation papers, nominal and beneficial ownership, business name records, stockbroker registrations, business directories, regulatory bodies' actions and records);
- licensing records (business, professional, automobiles, and drivers with relevant names and addresses, franchising data, qualifications, and so forth);
- property records (land titles and transfers, mortgages, property assessments, deeds, taxes, zoning variances, building permits, building and housing inspection reports of electrical, heating, plumbing work, construction permits, planning reports, and maps);
- contracts awarded for materials and services (tenders, contracts, bid specifications, purchase orders);
- health records (local, provincial, national; medical records, admission records, hospitalization payouts);
- laws, by-laws, and regulations (judicial interpretations, case law and opinions);
- court records – criminal court files and transcripts, charges and indictments, prosecutors' case records, arrest records, coroners' records, young offenders' records; civil lawsuit files (e.g., breach of contract and libel and the resultant discoveries, transcripts of testimony, exhibits, depositions, pleadings), probate court records on estates and executor appointments; divorce court pleadings, transcripts, financial statements; bankruptcy files; insurance claims; administrative tribunal files; and the various appeals of judgements, sentences, and awards;
- records of regulatory agencies, boards, and commissions (ABCs): reports, hearing transcripts, files, licences;
- government programs and Crown corporation records (e.g., CBC, Canada Post, Agriculture Canada, Ontario GO Transit);
- lobbyist registration reports;

- legislative indexes and committee hearing transcripts (witness indexes for those who have appeared on the record as supporters or opponents to an issue, lobbyists, and arguments for proposed changes in the law);
- speeches (on-the-record addresses to legislatures, such as Hansard, public pronouncements, publicity news conferences);
- minutes and agendas (meetings, hearings, transcripts of legislative committees, civic councils, attendance reports on elected officials);
- registrations of charities and foundations (forms, filings);
- grant applications to government bodies and responses;
- financial disclosure statements (personal finances of elected and appointed officials with an indication of potential conflicts of interest; on-the-record blind trust statements);
- enumeration and voting lists;
- military discharges, veterans' records;
- election campaign spending records;
- labour union reports filed with the government (collective bargaining contracts, grievance reports);
- archives and records (historical);
- welfare case records;
- letterhead correspondence and internal memoranda.

Researchers need to note that not everything listed above is completely private. Some records are available only at the whim of the bureaucrat; this should not be so, but it is (this will be looked at later). Other records have legislative seals, yet are susceptible to leaks or plants. There is a fine line between the right to know and the right to privacy, just as there is an apparently similar line dividing overt and covert sources of information. Non-public records ostensibly include law enforcement intelligence files, criminal records, parole records, income tax returns, young offenders' records, welfare case records, and medical records. This is all in the name of privacy, since these files deal with individuals and not governments. Occasionally some files will come to light, through leaks, plants, introduction as evidence in court cases, or just plain carelessness. There is no inherent right to these records, and many are floating around but are not publishable. These records may be useful as springboards or confirmations to get sources to go on the record. But researchers need to tread carefully here.

Private-sector documents are similar to those of the public sector. There are two main kinds – those needed to run a business and those needed for compliance in law by submitting to a regulatory agency.

With records in regard to the operation of a business, there is no inherent right of access because they are all private. These include:

- credit bureau reports;
- telephone call records;
- bank records;
- insurance investigation records;
- private investigators' files;
- employment records;
- union records;
- real estate development plans;
- financial records;
- internal memos.

Nevertheless, industrial spies uncover these data by bribing officials or clerks or by engaging in nefarious activities. Researchers might be able to get at bits and pieces of this information, but it can be slow and laborious, not to say questionable. Lawsuits, contempt of court, threats, and the like will follow if private records become publicly available. Certainly, though, as with the public-sector records, documents can be used as levers or springboards to get sources to go on the record and be quoted.

The second category of material – legal compliance – reveals a wealth of detail from sources that will be explored in Chapter 6. The requirement that publicly traded businesses must file reports to regulatory agencies and that even private companies must seek licences and file private reports means that a great deal of information about a company is available on the public record *through the government*. Indeed, most online computer databases that deal with business are derived from government reports. And the highest use of these online services is by one business trying to get a line on what another competitive business is doing, to get that edge for increased profits. Also, the highest usage of the access to information legislation involves businesses trying to find out what competitors are doing. Most information available from the government about a business has been mentioned above: statistics, tax, corporation, licensing, and property records, contracts, civil lawsuits and criminal charges, administrative tribunal files, ABC records, lobby registration reports, charity registrations, labour union reports. The best data come from those regulatory agencies that require information at regular intervals – this will allow researchers to plot changes in names and finances.

The private sector also includes a large number of groups that exhibit public-sector characteristics – that is, groups that have banded together for some common goal, usually on a non-profit basis. These are loosely called "associations." Some types include:

1. Universities and learned societies, devoted to research and investigation.
2. Professional, union, and trade associations such as the Law Society of Upper Canada and the Canadian Manufacturers' Association, or local chambers of commerce.
3. Non-taxable institutions dealing with welfare, culture, and education such as charities, performing arts societies, foundations, and religious institutions.
4. Social organizations such as hobby and leisure groups.
5. Political groups: political parties, lobbyists, citizen action groups, public affairs interest groups.

All of them have vested interests, and they would care enough to collect information on the themes that interest them. For example, if statistics on insurance companies were needed, then one would get in touch with the Insurance Institute of Canada; if biographic details about a University of Windsor graduate are needed, then one would get in touch with its alumni association. If business data about a city are needed, then one would contact the Chamber of Commerce. Associations exist for every conceivable subject area, and they would be happy to share their information. But researchers need to remember that associations are chauvinistic to their cause; they are one-sided. They have their own agendas, and they try to play down any negative sides to an issue. Researchers need to be aware of the biases here and try to verify their data. The easiest way to do this would be to check with an opposing association and then with a research centre.

Associations are used to handing out information; if some of them appear to be too glib, then that is because they are in the communications business. Associations do most of their work with their members (handling industry complaints and exchanging information), with legislators (lobbying for favourable legislation), and with the media (trying to promote a positive image about the industry or special interest). Sometimes they can be useful as a counterbalance to government information sources. Often, their knowledge of how government works and whom to see is better than the government's itself.

But associations have a long memory, and they'll never speak again to any researcher who has burned them. Every association is powerful, and information is released cautiously with an eye toward protecting its members' vested interests.

Normally, associations can be found through directories, beginning with *Directory of Information Sources in Canada* (Micromedia's directory of about 1,500 Canadian information sources), or the regularly revised *Directory of Directories* (Gale Research; an annotated guide to business and industrial directories, professional and scientific rosters, and other lists of all kinds). The latter contains listings of about 10,000 North American directories arranged in major subject classifications such as public affairs, science, and business, with an index of about 2,600 specific subject headings. Full bibliographic data for each directory are provided. This tool is used when an address is needed or if a directory's existence needs to be known. Both *Directory of Information Sources in Canada* and *Directory of Directories* are kept up-to-date by the *Public Affairs Information Service Bulletin*: new directories are recorded under the heading "Directories," and new editions of older directories are also noted. Other useful master directories are the regularly revised *Current British Directories* and *Current European Directories,* covering the United Kingdom and Europe, respectively.

For direct access to the association names themselves, take a look at the regularly revised *Encyclopedia of Associations* (Gale Research, covering 20,000 U.S. and international associations in twenty broad subject areas), *Directory of Associations in Canada* (Micromedia, covering 9,000 Canadian groups with over 800 subject categories), *Sources* (which has paid-for listings), *Directory of Labour Organizations in Canada, Connexions Directory of Canadian Organizations for Social Justice, Corpus Almanac and Canadian Sourcebook, Canadian*

Almanac and Directory, Yearbook of International Organizations, Directory of European Associations, Directory of British Associations, various encyclopedias and yearbooks (since these contain listings), as well as the phone book (most associations seem to start with the name of the industry, or the name of the region, or the word "Association" – just look it up under any of these three names).

For data on learned societies and university research centres, researchers check out the regularly revised Gale Research editions of *International Research Centers Directory* (2,500 international university-related, independent, and government research organizations of the world, arranged by country), *Research Centers Directory* (14,000 North American university-related and independent centres, with 2,400 subject categories), and *Government Research Centers Directory* (2,500 government-funded facilities). The latest editions of the following volumes can also be useful:

- *World of Learning*
- *International Handbook of Universities*
- *American Universities and Colleges*
- *Directory of Canadian Universities*
- *Scientific and Technical Societies in Canada*
- *Scientific and Learned Societies of Great Britain*
- *Scientific, Technical and Related Societies of the United States*
- *World Guide to Scientific Associations and Learned Societies.*

Just about all directories concern themselves with national associations. It is difficult to track down local citizen groups; these underfunded public interest groups change all the time, and they have limited resources. If they have a phone, then they will be listed. If they don't, then maybe a similar group can help, or intrepid researchers can try at the local public or newspaper libraries. Many of the directories cited here are also available as online computer databases, which considerably speeds ups searching time. Information, from both print and computer versions, includes a wealth of names, addresses, branch locations, phone numbers, history of the group with founding date, staff rosters, what companies are represented, objectives of the association, what publications are produced, affiliated organizations, name changes over the years, annual meeting sites, and information centre location. Association listings are extremely useful for: (a) getting names of expert people to contact about a particular subject; (b) getting into an information centre, which will have lots of data, especially statistics; (c) getting the association literature (publicity releases, newsletters, magazines, books).

Foundations and religious institutions are also very useful. Some foundations support charity causes and groups of people; others subsidize activities, such as the arts, that are not supported in the marketplace. They report to an appropriate government level on their financial affairs and expenditures. Religious institutions intersect with governments at all levels, and they maintain records of vital statistics as well as organizational structures (membership, clergy selection, youth clubs, missionary work). They exhibit the characteristics of any association, with information centres, experts, and particular positions on social issues. However, the potential for scams in religion and foundations is so strong – because of the favours of the tax-exempt status – that governments keep a tight rein on their activities. As non-profit groups they can be used as tax shelters by individuals or corporations. Government files bulge with data about charities, and since they are public groups, such information is freely accessible. To find information on these groups, researchers use the various directories listed in the previous section dealing with associations, as well as the following directories:

– *Connexions Directory of Canadian Organizations for Social Justice*
– *Canadian Peace Directory*
– *International Foundation Directory*
– *Foundation Directory* (American scope)
– *Canadian Directory to Foundations and Granting Agencies*
– *Canadian Donor's Guide to Fundraising Organizations in Canada.*

In 1989 Canada's Lobbyists Registration Act came into effect. Under this Act, people who are in contact with government as part of their job registered as either Tier I lobbyists (trying to influence national legislation, regulations, programs, grants, and contracts) or Tier II lobbyists (trying to alter the course of government affairs). Most of these lobbyists work for associations and foundations. Information has to be updated and submitted annually. As of December, 1991, there were 773 active lobbyists. The City of Toronto also has lobby registration (since 1990), as does the United States national government (since 1946). The value to researchers here is twofold: they learn the names of key groups who are interested in a specific subject and the names of experts who can assist them in the pursuit of their inquiries.

The Document Sources: Open Records Laws

If this book is to be a guide to sources of information, then it must cover how to access government information files. But the issues of what government information should be private and what should be public are beyond its scope. Researchers already have reasonable access to documents, more so when these are published and made available in multiple copies. But what about those files that have been denied by a bureaucrat who is unable or unwilling to cite a specific regulation that forbids dissemination? One technique of access is through the various open records laws in Canada, some of the provinces, and the United States. While government shares some of its information with the public, there are exceptions, such as military secrets, business competition, covert operations in the name of national security, law enforcement, and information given to the government in confidence.

The first country with an open record law was Sweden, over 200 years ago. The United States Congress passed the Administrative Procedures Act in 1946; it had a clause stating that records were open to the public unless they were deemed confidential for good cause at the discretion of the public servants. This established a principle of openness. That clause and other legalities were consolidated in the 1966 Freedom of Information Act. This Act also had provisions that any citizen of any country could use it, and thus Canadians use the American law to access information about Canadian branch plants (there are more stringent filing regulations for American businesses; hence, more data, such as upper management salaries, can be made public concerning those Canadian businesses with American corporate headquarters), or about the Free Trade Agreement or anything else that impinges on Canada. An estimated 80 per cent of the requests made under the U.S. Freedom of Information Act have been made by companies seeking information about the trade secrets of their competitors; the balance is mainly from journalists, students, and researchers. Compiled figures from the U.S. House Government Operations Subcommittee on Government Information show that more than a quarter of a million requests are submitted annually, and about 90 per cent of properly submitted requests were granted in full. The highest success rate was reported by the Department of Health Services (98 per cent) while the lowest was the State Department, with 29 per cent.

At the national level in Canada, the Access to Information Act was proclaimed in 1983, as was the Privacy Act. Generally, the former is for allowing public access to non-personal records only, within certain strictures; the latter is for protection of privacy of government-held information of a personal nature (but this is not an inherent *right* of privacy). Government secrecy seems to be inherited from the British system of democracy; the prevailing philosophy throughout the Commonwealth is that all government files are closed and classified unless they are specifically designated as being open. In the United States the 1946 Act was the reverse: all files are open unless specifically closed. In Canadian law there are many file closures, beginning with the Official Secrets Act (oaths of secrecy, court bans on publication of evidence, the illegality of actually "receiving" confidential documents), the Criminal Code (s.314 on tampering with the mail, s.173 on trespassing at night, s.465 on wiretap evidence), the National Defence Act (s.157 closes court martials), the Anti-Dumping Act (tribunal hearings may be closed), the Income Tax Act (a taxpayer as plaintiff may request privacy), the Statistics Act (privacy of census materials), the Young Offenders Act (banning publication of identity), and the Combines Investigation Act (misleading advertising tribunals can be held in private).

Eight provinces have passed legislation enabling access: Nova Scotia in 1977, New Brunswick in 1978, Newfoundland in 1981, Quebec in 1982, Ontario in 1987, and Manitoba and Saskatchewan in 1991. British Columbia's will be law in the fall of 1993. P.E.I. is still talking about it, while Alberta remains opposed to any access. Both the Ontario and Quebec laws give the information commissioner the power to *order* the government to disclose documents (the national commissioner must go to court for such an order), and both provinces have also included municipalities and special purpose boards as subject to disclosure. Ontario passed a separate act for this, effective in 1991.

A major difficulty still remains: while legislation specifies what is protected as private and what can be disclosed as public, much information falls ambiguously between the two designations. The question here is one of conflicting values: where is the line dividing the public's right to know from the individual's right to privacy? The Canadian Charter of Rights and Freedoms guarantees an outright freedom of the press to publish anything (section 2(b)) while it also guarantees, in section 1, the freedom to do virtually anything in Canada "subject only to such reasonable limits prescribed by law as can be demonstrably justified in a free and democratic society." Thus, there can be a range of expression available that might just be determined by how broadly disseminated the "free expression" becomes. For example, is there any difference between disclosing information before a national television audience of four million and printing it in a weekly newspaper read by 500? How widely disseminated is this public knowledge? This could affect the availability of documents through intent to use. It is one thing to "look at" a divorce file on the public record; it is another thing to publish it in a local paper read by 500; and it is yet a third thing to splash it all over national television. Where is the line to be drawn?

The *use* of the information could be a factor in deciding whether the researcher will have access to public documents or not. It should be noted that this situation can exist even in the commercial marketplace. American labour unions were denied direct access to a computer database about business companies, even though anybody who paid for computer time could access it. The unions, after lodging a complaint that did not work, simply accessed the online service through libraries. A result here is that more requests for information through the freedom-of-information system are being handled by information brokers who do not disclose the names of their clients and certainly not the ultimate use being made of the information. Thus, a business wanting information about a competitor could hide its name by using an intermediary. Also, the Canadian federal Access to Information Act can be accessed only by Canadian nationals, so that a foreigner or offshore client needs the services of an intermediary. Both Canada and the European Community have a continuing concern about trans-border data flow and knowing who the ultimate users are.

The Canadian national government possesses the largest volume of information in the country, collected through the regulation of taxation, immigration, law enforcement, environment, business, and so forth, stored in well over 1,500 databases. The Access to Information Act provides a right of access, but within limits. I will not explore the many facets of the Canadian law: such examination can be found in the succinct pamphlet *Access to Information* (Canadian Daily Newspaper Association) or in Heather Mitchell and Murray Rankin's *Using the Access to Information Act* (Self-Counsel Press). Both have summaries of usage and tips, as well as cautions, strategies, and samples of forms. In bare outline, the Canadian law provides for access to files listed within *InfoSource (Sources of Federal Government Information)*, which breaks down classes of records kept by national departments and agencies. Over 100 chapters on the national departments and agencies covered by both the Access to Information Act and the Privacy Act describe their background, responsibilities, legislation, organization, and information holdings, along with names and numbers of public inquiries units, departmental libraries, and other national offices. This is available both as a book and as a computer database. The requester fills out an official form or letter of request for a particular file or files. The book and the forms are found at all major libraries.

The requester is seeking access to existing records and files containing such material as correspondence, memoranda, books, plans, maps, drawings, diagrams, graphics, photographs, films, microforms, phonodiscs, audiotapes, videotapes, computer records, and the like. Public servants will not prepare answers to questions. Once the official form or letter of request has been submitted, the government program has thirty calendar days to process it (77 per cent of requests are handled thus) or to state why the requester cannot have it – unlike the United States, where the wait is a mere ten days and the success rate is about 90 per cent. Of course, one can appeal, but the Information Commissioner can only recommend that a government program release a file. If it is then refused, either the appealer or the Commissioner can take the case to federal court within forty-five days.

The Canadian Act is so fraught with delays, costs, denials, and weaknesses that most researchers and journalists use it only as a last resort. All formal and informal channels are used first, followed by approaches to information officers within each government program. Time, though, is on the side of the government. Unless they are prepared to wait for about six months, researchers should not use the Access to Information Act (ATIA). There are many exemptions to providing the files, based on the necessity to keep information hidden (law enforcement, information obtained in confidence, personal information, trade secrets, statutory prohibitions). The Act has had limited success mainly because there are about 490 exemptions. Programs can base their refusal on these exemptions, which are derived from what is known as the "Mack truck" clause (named thus because the clause is so broad that one can drive a Mack truck through it), and the government can deny access to all sorts of documents and files under this clause (section 69(1), which refers to confidences of the cabinet) by simply calling these items "cabinet papers."

Most citizens remain unaware of the Act. The public needs to be educated about it, but unlike the American or Ontario legislation, there is no provision in the ATIA for public education. The government has also achieved a state of paranoia by feeling that it cannot win: release of a controversial record may cause embarrassment while denial of a file implies sinister motives on its part. Government figures show that there were 2,978 requests under the ATIA in its first eighteen months of operation, far short of the 70,000 originally anticipated. Indeed, there are so few requests that it is possible for all the deputy ministers themselves to look at each request and see if it is for any sensitive documents (or if it is part of a trend) and then, if so, to recommend a denial or to alert the minister as to the nature of the request. Bureaucrats are far more experienced in using the law to stonewall than citizens are in using it to obtain information.

Nevertheless, information can be ferreted out, as in these examples:

- the costs of Prime Minister Trudeau's swimming pool;
- public opinion polls on Senate reforms;
- a report on a prison riot at Archambault;
- a military report showing that a dead army cadet was not wearing safety equipment;
- lists of Conservative Party lawyers appointed to handle federal government legal business in Ontario and Alberta;
- minutes of the Atomic Energy Board meetings showing its

staff and Ontario Hydro battling, for the past decade, over the safety of the latter's nuclear reactors;
- conflicting reports on lead additives in gasoline, released by two different departments;
- embarrassing expense account vouchers (transportation, hotel, food, bar bills).

In addition, the ATIA has been used to find data about its underusage by the public!

The ATIA and other such legislation are basically slow to respond, capricious in their demands, and outright frustrating to use, but there are times when they can be used efficiently.

(1) Fishing or browsing expeditions: reports and files can provide leads to additional or new information, as well as reveal discrepancies. Fishing can produce interesting juxtapositions, as in the mosaic theory (see the previous section about computers). Browsing can turn up all sorts of unexpected information.

(2) Declassifying information: under the stress of a request for files, the government has actually changed its mind in a variety of cases. Previously classified information was subsequently released, sometimes casually, sometimes after a court battle, sometimes with fanfare.

(3) Documentation of rumours: files contain statements, facts, and figures that are not indexed because only the larger unit – the file itself – is subject retrievable by indexation. Embedded information (which the government program itself might not even remember is there) can confirm or deny suspicions, gossip, rumours, and allegations based on tips, enough so that these sources can be quoted.

The Expert Sources

The other major source in the triad of information is the expert, generally defined as a specialist having knowledge derived from experience or training. Experts come in all different shapes and sizes, and they operate under different kinds of rules when the media dance with the institution.

The researcher's choice of expert will be influenced by what he or she learns in an overview of a subject area. Much valuable information consists of data obtained only through experience: impressions and experiential conclusions are often the only information available. There are bound to be situations in which expert opinion is the only source, such as the speculative "what if" type of inquiries. Such information needs to be sifted carefully, balanced with other experts, or acknowledged as biased. In every case, opinion must be separated from fact. A good question to ask experts (particularly if one expert is being balanced off another) is: how do you know this is true? "Expert opinion" can give credibility to any report or newspaper account, explaining behaviour patterns of people and institutions. But it is important to note that not all experts are equal. Some are more authoritative than others and their "facts/opinions" have a greater cachet. Researchers need to remember that not all statements are of equal weight, that some have more credibility than others. The "who" of information sourcing can determine the validity of the facts (see Chapter 2 on evaluation of experts).

An expert can be one of three types. First, a *source* is someone who tells you something you need to know, giving you information. A source is not necessarily an expert, although a source can be authoritative simply by working for an agency that has the data you need. You go to sources for information, but occasionally a source will come to you with a leak or a plant. Second, a *contact* is someone known to you, someone you have dealt with before, maybe as a source of information, and with whom you have developed some kind of rapport. You go to a contact for information, for tips, for documents, and to confirm other sources. Finally, an *authority* is consulted when you are stumped or when you need guidance. An authority can provide specific data that have not yet been published, or are not indexed anywhere, and can evaluate documents and published materials for you. An authority can give you names of other authorities as experts, although these latter authorities may be cut from the same cloth. With a good rapport, authorities can become contacts and part of a researcher's network.

Where does one find experts? Let's begin with the obvious. You already know somebody: family doctor, lawyer, accountant, teacher, minister, siblings, students, relatives, neighbours. Everybody is an expert at something. It's safe to assume, too, that you know somebody who knows an expert in a field. Go through your friend, after first getting a reference. Experts, of course, can be used to find experts. Always try to come away from an interview with a name or a recommendation to somebody else, a new place to go, an association, and continue with the search for experts by going all the way back to the library and the computer.

You can search through biographical directories that have occupational or subject indexes, such as *Biography Index*. These will locate names attached to professions. Let's say you want to locate information about trombones. Simply look under "trombones," or if there are no entries there, try related terms such as "brass instruments" or a broader term such as "musicians." This will produce names of people who are associated with trombones. The online versions of many of these biographical directories, such as the *Who's Who* series, have the added capacity of locating names of people in *your* town; this is a parameter not found in the printed version. Also, you can look through databases under the name of the occupation, with the sub-category directories, and this will lead you to references containing people's names in one particular occupation or field of endeavour.

Book authors are automatic experts, and they can be found by looking up subject headings in library catalogues or *Subject Guide to Books in Print*. The computer version of the latter also includes listings of new books expected to be published in the upcoming six-month period. Living authors can always be contacted through their publishers. In addition, you can search for magazine and newspaper *writers* by checking *Magazine Index, Canadian Periodical Index, Canadian Magazine Index, Canadian News Index, Reader's Guide to Periodical Literature,* and *Newspaper Index* (all of these in online, CD-ROM, or printed formats) under the subject headings. The more times a name appears, the more likely it is that the writer will be an expert. Writers on a beat can be found through *Bowden's Media Directory* or *Matthews Media Directory* for Canada; the *Working Press of the Nation* covers the United States.

Even more authoritative experts can be found by searching under subject headings in specialized indexes. These authors are usually *scholars* and they publish in respected academic journals or the trade press. For example, for authors of material about trombones, you could try the *Music Index*; for the business side of music, try *Business Periodicals Index*. Depending on the scope of your subject, you could look at *Social Sciences Index, Humanities Index, Applied Science and Technology Index,* and a wide selection of others (see Chapter 6). When you look up their writings, be sure to give proper attribution to any of their quotations that you use. Citation indexes such as *Science Citation Index* or *Social Sciences and Humanities Citation Index* indicate which experts have been cited or quoted the most, which ones are at the top of the heap. And those people themselves who do the quoting form part of the information network for the field.

Specific tools of *names* are geared to finding experts, such as:

- *National Directory of Addresses and Telephone Numbers* (American)
- *Sources; the directory of contacts for editors, reporters and researchers* (Canadian)
- *Directory of Federally Supported Research in Universities* (Canadian)
- *Canadian Register of Research and Researchers in the Social Sciences*
- *Connexions Directory of Canadian Organizations for Social Justice*
- *Directory of Information Sources in Canada* (contains 1,500 handbooks, lists, market surveys, membership rolls, with a cross-referenced subject index)
- *Directory of Experts, Authorities, and Spokespersons* (American)
- *Directory of Special Libraries and Information Centres*
- *Consultants and Consulting Organizations Directory* (lists 10,000).

Look for groups to which experts are likely to belong, such as *associations, research organizations, labour unions.* These groups should be able to furnish names. Search the subject indexes of:

- *Encyclopedia of Associations* (for North America)
- *Directory of Associations in Canada*
- *Directory of Labour Organizations in Canada*
- *Guide to Federal Programs and Services* (Canada)
- *KWIC Index to the Government of Ontario*
- *Corpus Administrative Index* (Canada and the provinces).

Check the subject indexes, too, of the various information/research centre directories covered in the previous section.

Universities, of course, can be useful in locating experts. Many have academic programs devoted to specialized subject matter. They have directories that identify expertise, operate a speaker's bureau for presentations, and co-ordinate alumni association rosters of famous graduates who may be experts. A simple phone call, or a quick check of the university calendar, will establish what and who are available. You should be able to use universities for a local angle, too. In this regard, sometimes you need only use the local board of education for a knowledgeable high school teacher.

Try also the *government* at all three levels, plus the boards and commissions. There are telephone directories and organization manuals available such as the *Corpus Administrative Index* for Canada and the provinces, the *Guide to Federal Programs and Services* for Canada, and the *KWIC Index to the Government of Ontario* (see Chapter 7 for more details). For Canadian government sources, try *Reference Canada,* available nation-wide through various 800 numbers – one per province or territory. For an American source, try the National Referral Center of the Library of Congress in Washington, D.C. These will give you the names/departments to try within the government, as well as non-governmental sources. Political parties, especially the opposition, are also great sources here.

Another large database of names consists of the directories of *research centres and government agencies* mentioned earlier, such as the *Research Centers Directory.* These will have staff "researchers" who often don't publish, academics doing work on contract, as well as a variety of unpublished materials. Some examples include museums, data analysis centres, research institutes, laboratories, and opinion leaders and think tanks such as the Conference Board of Canada, the C.D. Howe Institute, and the Fraser Institute.

Depending on your subject matter, experts can also be located through registration lists of *lobbyists.* Professional lobbyists are paid by clients to contact or arrange meetings with both politicians and bureaucrats to influence legislation; they may be lawyers, government relations consultants, public relations people, or employees of the client. The computerized Lobbyist Registration Act Registry is available online through the Department of Consumer and Corporate Affairs in Ottawa, with data about the clients, the handled subject matter, and the lobbyist; 773 had registered by December, 1991. This is an extremely rich source of experts on matters pertaining to government, politics, and business. Other names can be found through the *Government Relations Handbook* (Southam Business Communications), which gives names of federal government contacts, federal laws, federal departments and agencies, associations, government relations consultants, and some case studies.

Free *hotlines* have grown extremely useful in the past few years. Not only can you get answers (but these are usually self-serving, and must still be checked) but you can also get the names of experts. Some government examples: Heatline advisory service from Energy, Mines and Resources Canada at 1-800-267-9563; Investment Canada at 1-800-267-0490; Statscan 1-800-263-1136; Bureau of Labour Information from Labour Canada at 1-800-567-6866; Charities Division of Revenue Canada at 1-800-267-1871; Canadian Centre for Occupational Health and Safety at 1-800-263-8270; CORCAN Service (Correctional Services Canada) at 1-800-267-0354. Private hotlines are run by various writer groups. Requests are answered either while you wait on the phone or within ten minutes, usually by return fax. Some of these include Medialink (1-800-387-4643), which will put researchers in contact with any of 350 businesses who pay for the service; Sourceline (1-613-564-3891, not a toll-free number), which is operated by the Canadian Association of Journalists to put researchers in touch with reporters with specializations who in turn can provide source names and contacts; and SIS (Science Information Source; 1-416-425-5613, not a toll-free number), operated by the Canadian Science Writers Association as a 2,000-name contact list for science specialists, mainly academics. Bell Canada has a directory of 800 numbers in Canada, but not all the 800 numbers from the United States are accessible in Canada.

Public relations firms will also supply experts, but you must be cautious here since most will tout the business line or the subject topic they are associated with. Still, public relations people are useful in supplying industry spokespersons and people representing their clients. It is up to the researcher to separate the truth from the hype in reports, texts of speeches, statistics, illustrations, bibliographies, and names of so-called "experts." Public relations firms and communication sections of corporations can be found in *Sources; the directory of contacts for editors, reporters and researchers,* for Canada, and

O'Dwyer's Directory of Public Relations Executives, for the United States and parts of Canada. But beware of the spin doctor!

Every industry has *watchers* – these are market analysts. They number about 1,500 in Canada, and they analyse specific sectors of the marketplace to provide expert market advice to their investor clients. They work for banks and brokerage firms, among others.

The *witnesses and survivors* of an event, often tragic, but sometimes happy, are "experts" on the event. You can find their names and descriptions through newspaper accounts of the event or through oral history programs. The latter can be accessed through the *Directory of Special Libraries and Information Centres,* through the Oral History Association (U.S.), or through the Canadian Oral History Association; they are excellent sources for descriptions in their own words.

For *experts no longer living,* consult their diaries, correspondence, autobiographies, or other writings. You can no longer communicate with them, but they can still have some meaning to you.

Finally, cultivate the *master investigators.* (1) Reference librarians are knowledgeable about printed resources and computer databases; they can suggest leads, focus points, subject approaches, and broad strategies. (2) University scholars are knowledgeable about every important printed resource and computer database within their specialty. Their techniques emphasize thoroughness through the scientific research method, producing new data or bringing forth the previously buried accounts of events, dredged up from archives and libraries. (3) Investigative journalists are tenacious and quick, with an ability to interview and write about experts. They know how to find sources, how to ask the right questions, how to interpret responses. (4) Private investigators and police detectives are knowledgeable about human behaviour patterns. They are quite often able to get inside sources such as classified documents, credit records, municipal archives, confidential indexes, and credit ratings. (5) Professional researchers are knowledgeable about where the sources of data lie; indeed, they combine all of the above characteristics and use all of these people as experts. They know the fastest and simplest way to get needed information: they have access to in-house files and databases created by information providers and information vendors, to local and global networks, and to research banks. Collectively, they can provide background data, survey research, corporate and government reports, industry profiles, online computer database searches, demographic data, and international research. In addition, a good information broker (as they prefer to be called) can find confidential competitive information, access closed information centres, make inquiries on the client's behalf without anyone else knowing, and handle rush jobs or projects on an instant's notice. Of course, unlike the other experts, brokers charge a fee for all of their services, for this is their occupation.

How does one get experts to help? There are so many different approaches here – so much that falls within the realm of psychology, so much that depends on the subject matter, the topic, the interviewer, and the interviewee – that several books would need to be written. Researchers can get swift help from John Brady's *The Craft of Interviewing* (Vintage Books) and Paul McLaughlin's *How to Interview* (Self-Counsel Press).

But here are some immediate, useful strategies of a beginning nature. First, you should make it easy for experts to reply. This means try the telephone and take collect callbacks, use return postage on correspondence, and be polite. Second, you should win respect by knowing what you want before you approach the expert. You have to verify and cross-check the data at some point anyway; do it in advance as part of the preparation work. Third, you should cultivate contacts who would be willing to supply information when needed and who do not feel as if they are merely being used. This can lead to a long-standing relationship that can establish credibility both for you and for the nascent expert. Fourth, you always need to handle experts with kid gloves, for at any moment they might turn on you or do whatever suits them. They can be tough and play hardball, telling you things that are *on the record* (you can quote and identify the expert) or *offering background information* (you can use the data but attribution must be vague) or *deep background* (you can use the data but there must be no attribution), or they may choose to talk only *off the record* (you cannot use the data, and thus the source certainly cannot be revealed).

You either accept the rules or you don't play – unless, of course, you are mightier than they are, as in the case of a nationally syndicated journalist.

Summary

As the world becomes more complex and as researchers tackle increasingly difficult projects, knowing what questions to ask often becomes crucial. Understanding how information is structured and where it is facilitates the asking of questions that will get answers. The most common problem among beginning researchers is just being able to get a "handle" on the data: where to start from among the welter of sources. The best advice is to find out how the system works, and here, how the "information" system works. This chapter explores the three sources of the information system: the warehouse, the document, and the expert.

The warehouse source database of libraries necessitates a discussion on their classification schemes, their catalogues, their reference services, and their types of outlets (public, academic, school, and special libraries). The section on the warehouse source database of computers includes a discussion on their value: they are fast, comprehensive, up-to-date, reliable; they contain unique material and can manipulate data; they are accessible. As well, the mosaic theory is brought out. Costs are explored and weighed against the time saved in unique searches.

The document sources of both the private and the public sector are: official forms and certificates, correspondence, technical studies, polls and surveys, financial data such as budgets, legislative materials (laws, hearings, debates), the regulation of business, law enforcement, and court records. Privately obtained materials are mentioned, in light of institutes and associations within the profit and non-profit sectors. Lobbyists are also considered. Freedom of information legislation is described, along with its pitfalls.

A distinction is made among experts as to sources, contacts, and authorities, with some strategies on how to find experts and how to get them to help researchers.

4

THE LINKAGE
OF INFORMATION

It is fun to learn how to dig out information. This knowledge is a confidence builder. It arms you with a methodology that enables you to understand the daily activities that you must explain to readers, viewers or listeners. – John Ullman, assistant managing editor, *Minneapolis Star and Tribune*

No piece of information is superior to any other. Power lies in having them all on file and then finding the connections. There are always connections; you have only to want to find them. – Umberto Eco, *Foucault's Pendulum,* 1989

This chapter discusses the linkage of information. It presents material on:

- the information controllers with their bibliographic trails;
- vocabulary control and thesaurus structures;
- BRITE strategy as a process;
- the research log for project management;
- the paper trail of documents;
- generic search strategies.

Information Controllers

In the last chapter, libraries were noted as specializing in lists; to a great extent, these lists are the *information controllers.* Lists can be directories of addresses (hence, a regularized control over who is listed and who is not, over a certain time period), directories of books (control over the subject knowledge of the world through bibliographies), directories of magazine and journal articles (control through indexes), even directories of words in a computerized database (each word in a computer file is given an "address," and it is this address that is searched, not the actual word itself). Special types of information controllers are union lists, bibliographies, indexes, abstracts, lists, and directories. They all have a role to play in working out a bibliographic trail.

Union lists are compilations of publications with a note about which libraries physically possess them, what time period the subscription was for, and whether microforms are available. A researcher uses a union list to see if a visit to a particular library will be profitable. The researcher can find, for example, three locations for a particular master's thesis – will the library lend it or will the researcher have to visit the place? What charges are incurred? These finding devices are exceedingly useful, especially since many of them are now computerized and therefore up-to-date. Some of the more common ones found in libraries include the *Union List of Manuscripts in Canadian Repositories* (which pulls together all the physical locations for the writings of specific persons), *Directory of Canadian Archives* (use the subject index), *Canadian Theses* (for locations of master's papers), *Union List of Serials in Libraries of the United States and Canada* and *New Serial Titles* (which together will give physical locations for both older and newer magazines and journals), *Union List of Canadian Newspapers*, *Union List of Scientific Serials in Canadian Libraries*, and *Guide to Periodicals and Newspapers in the Public Libraries of Metro Toronto* (which is not a guide but rather a listing showing which of the many library branches have particular copies); similar lists may be found for other cities. Most academic libraries have a list of their own magazines and journals, indicating where on campus one could find the issue, how far back the subscription runs, whether there are microforms, and the like.

Bibliographies are listings of books and other materials that have some relationship to each other. These lists include the name of the author, the title, the publisher, the date, the pagination, and sometimes other descriptive matter. Some bibliographies evaluate their materials: these are known as critical bibliographies or annotated bibliographies. They are valuable because someone has read the materials and has made an assessment of their worth. Other bibliographies (without a written evaluation) may be called "selective bibliographies"; here, the compiler has just given a blanket blessing to the worthiness of all the materials cited, with the added implication that books not mentioned are not important enough. Some of the more valuable bibliography tools are discussed below.

Bibliographic Index indexes bibliographies by subject matter. It picks up smaller listings found in book chapters and in journal articles. Its specialized nature makes it a top source to consult for a few basic articles in a tiny area or to suggest other sources to consult.

Books in Print is a bibliographic listing of all trade books available for sale in the United States by commercial and academic publishers. For Canada, there is *Canadian Books in Print,* and for the United Kingdom there is *British Books in Print. Subject Guide to Books in Print* re-sorts the data by broad subject headings, so it will be possible to see at once who has written recent books on French wines. The value here is twofold – one, to consult the new books, and two, to consult with the authors who may be approached through the publisher. A similar bibliography is the *Cumulative Book Index,* which goes back to 1898. While this tool has listings for every English-language book published in the world regardless of country of origin, the listing appears just once in the annual volumes. To use this tool effectively, researchers must know the book's publication date: English-language authors of French wine books will be listed on a year-by-year basis. But at least researchers won't need to know the nationality of the author. The *Books in Print* series are all available as computer databases and CD-ROMs, with the former being updated weekly. This series even has a *Forthcoming Books in Print* – a six-month look ahead at what is new. Under the right circumstances advance proofs can be obtained from the publishers, as well as interviews with the author.

Large libraries often have catalogues of their holdings. *Canadiana* is the published catalogue of the National Library of Canada, *British National Bibliography* is for the British Library in London, and the *National Union Catalog* covers the Library of Congress in Washington, D.C. These jumbo tools list all the materials acquired by these national libraries. *A London Bibliography of the Social Sciences* is the library catalogue of the London School of Economics. Many other catalogues are published, and these may be found through the *Guide to Published Library Catalogs*. *Subject Collections; a guide to special book collections* and *Subject Collections in European Libraries* are useful tools for showing what types of books exist in highly specialized libraries in both North America and Europe.

A "serial" is a publication issued serially for an indefinite period. If it is issued at a regular frequency, such as weekly or monthly, it can be called a "periodical." Types of periodicals include (and here the terminology is very loose) newspapers, newsletters, magazines (popular, trade, or house organs), and journals (scholarly, technical, or professional). Other types of serials include annual reports, meeting proceedings or transactions, and yearbooks or annuals. Serials are both current and timely, serving to update existing book information. They often deal with minor or obscure items, and they present opposing views on these same items. Articles tend to be short, specific, and to the point: the better ones are abstracted (see below). Serials also contain quickly changing data of immediate short-term interest such as opinions and statistics. The advertisements, illustrations, and reports of research-in-progress are rarely indexed, and indeed many are not yet available even on full-text databases; thus they are extremely difficult to access. To find out what serials exist in any subject area in Canada, look at *Canadian Advertising Rates and Data*, which lists by format and broad subject just about all periodicals in Canada that accept advertising. For additional titles and for the non-profit sector, look at the *Canadian Serials Directory* and the *Gale Directory of Publications and Broadcast Media* (the latter is arranged geographically and covers North America), or *Ulrich's International Periodicals Directory*, which is arranged by subject and is also available online. For Great Britain there is *Willing's Press Guide*.

Indexes point out where data can be found. The most common index is that at the end of a book: an alphabetically arranged list of subjects and names, with subheadings, cross-references, and page indications. Periodical indexes are quite similar, except more bibliographic data are given in the text of the index. Since the periodical literature in a subject discipline may be very large (for example, in the field of psychology there are well over 1,000 journals published in many languages), then the only real way to gain access to all these articles – and hence to the data they contain – is by means of the index. Some indexes are multi-disciplinary, such as the *Canadian Periodical Index,* which indexes 200 or so Canadian periodicals covering a wide range of articles; others are highly specific, such as the *Funk and Scott Index of Corporations and Industries.* Some cover certain types of literature, such as the *Short Story Index*; others are specific to a particular periodical, such as the *London Times Official Index.* Some indexes cover books, theses, and technical reports; others cover only journal papers. In using indexes, researchers must remember to use the most specific one possible, for in this way they will capture more bibliographic references in the shortest possible time.

For example, if a subject is popular in scope (or if it is Canadian, whether popular or scholarly) then researchers will use the *Canadian Magazine Index, Canadian Periodical Index,* and *Reader's Guide to Periodical Literature.* For academic and scholarly materials, they will try the *Humanities Index, Social Sciences Index,* or *General Science Index.* For research-oriented materials, they will use abstracting services (see below), while for technical and business orientations, they will use online databases.

Indexes can be land mines, for they are full of abbreviations and many of these are not transferable from one index to another, or even to their own online database format. While all indexes work the same way and look the same, many have hidden, arcane ways of treating entries. Always read the preface to the index to see how it is set up and what the abbreviations mean. Because of required exactitude in online services, this understanding of the set up of an index in a computer database is mandatory. Once researchers know how an index works, then using it is relatively easy. Briefly, then, researchers:

- select the subject headings, being as specific as possible;
- work with a backsearch (searching backwards from the most recent), keeping an eye out for review articles that summarize previous findings;
- revise the subject headings, noting any suggestions given such as cross-references;
- keep a logbook, with a record of subject headings and indexes searched, along with notes about all relevant bibliographic references that lead to more sources of information;
- use an abstracting service wherever possible since the

abstract may contain the exact information needed and will invariably determine whether or not the original article needs to be read; also, while the original article may be in a foreign language with which researchers may not be conversant, there is a good chance that the abstract will be in English.

Abstracts, then, are indicative summations of the source being cited. They contain the same bibliographic data as an index, plus a brief summary of the article. All abstracts are highly specific, such as *Sociological Abstracts* or *International Political Science Abstracts.* Researchers use them the same way they use an index, at least to find articles, remembering that the abstract just might contain the exact information needed, such as a research method employed, or a date, or a statistic, or a conclusion suitable for quoting. Abstracts cover periodical articles, publications of learned societies, reviews, and anthologies. An index that looks like an abstract, and the format used by the *New York Times Index,* is the *fact index* – a mixture of headlines and summaries in one or two sentences. Again, while using the *New York Times Index,* researchers can find a fact or a statistic or a conclusion – without having to turn to the newspaper and read the entire article.

Bibliographic Trail

To become familiar with the organization of a discipline and to control the information in a readable form, there are a number of books that researchers can read; these will allow researchers to place the discipline in perspective (see Chapter 5 for the titles of some of these). Obvious candidates include special-term dictionaries and specialized encyclopedias that will furnish specific background data, definitions, and additional readings, such as the *Encyclopedia of Bioethics*; guides to the literature, which outline and survey the available sources of information as well as discuss search strategies and specialized research methods unique to just that subject field, such as Bart's *Student Sociologist's Handbook*; annual reviews of progress, such as the *Canadian Annual Review of Politics and Public Affairs*; and textbooks and histories of a particular field, which define the parameters, briefly discuss all of the subtopics, with a perspective, give substantive background information, and, of course, provide the main facts and names in the development of the subject field. These and other books can be found simply enough through the library's *list* – or catalogue – of books that it owns or through other tools it has access to. The easiest way to find these books is by searching the "subdivisions" of the subject headings. These are all well standardized by the listings in the National Library of Canada or the Library of Congress. "Form" subdivisions list types of information tools that exhibit similar characteristics. Under the form subdivisions are lists of particular resource tools to handle specific parameters of one topic. These subdivisions are usually indicated by a dash between the subject and the form, although on the printed page of an index they might be centred or they might use a different typeface such as italic. Under the heading "oil," for example, one would find such typical form subheadings as:

- abstracts
- bibliography
- biography
- case studies
- catalogs
- collections
- congresses
- dictionaries
- digests
- directories
- encyclopedias
- exhibitions
- handbooks, manuals
- history
- indexes
- outlines, syllabi
- pictorial works
- public opinion
- societies
- statistics

- study and teaching
- tables
- yearbooks.

All of these should be followed through for the bibliographic trail:
the sequence of bibliographic references that occurs when one item
is linked to another.

The bibliographic trail can suggest to researchers ways to get at
facts, figures, and names that are unknown. Even though researchers don't know the answer or even a source for the answer, they do
know several ways of finding out, albeit through trial and error.
Beginning researchers need to think about looking around from the
point of view of what they already know. Through various links
between the forms of information controllers they can begin a con-
necting link. For example, if they need to find the names of subject
specialists in oil, then a quick check through the bibliographic trail
will produce in minutes any or all of the following.

Subject Guide to Books in Print will establish current book authors
in oil and related topics. They can be approached through their publishers, whose addresses are at the back of this resource tool. *Forthcoming Subject Guide to Books in Print* (merged with the *Subject Guide
to Books in Print* in the online version) will establish book authors
who will be publishing within the next six months. Again, approach
them through their publishers, and even try to obtain advance proof
copies or galleys of their books. *Bibliographic Index* will establish who
has written important articles recently on oil and who has created a
bibliography for additional reading. Authors can be approached
through the magazine or book publisher, whose address will be in
Bibliography Index. *Biography Index* is an index to biographic articles
and books. While the main index is arranged by surname, there is an
"Index to Occupations." Check under "oil" and related terms for
names of authors, experts, and oilmen who can be approached.

In addition, newspaper and magazine indexes can be used to find
names of reporters on the oil beat (environment, business, science),
and citation indexes can also be checked (*Science Citation Index* and
Social Sciences and Humanities Citation Index are two examples).
Essentially, a citation index is an index to the footnotes (i.e., the citations) in the articles published in scholarly journals. Researchers

then know the networks that comprise the scholars' "invisible college." If researchers have found a useful article on oil by Morgan, for example, and Morgan refers to a work by Hayward that might be interesting, then the researchers would like to see what else Hayward has written on oil. This is following through on the footnotes, endnotes, or bibliographic references. By using the citation indexes, researchers can also determine which authors have cited Hayward's work and then can move to those authors' own works, which might contain more information on oil, and perhaps even better or more relevant information. Researchers could even check exclusively on those authors who have cited both Morgan and Hayward in one article – and this would be extremely valuable if there was controversy in the field fuelled by both authors.

If researchers have a shortage of names or are otherwise unhappy with who they have, then they can pursue various avenues. (1) Redo the search. Remember that many of the names have already been found by trial and error. By cross-checking sources and strategies, researchers may find new names from the context and the use. (2) Begin contacting people right away to generate new names. (3) Watch for the embedded name. Begin reading the books and articles to see what names turn up. This is especially useful for newspaper and magazine articles in which reporters reveal the names of their attributable contacts and sources. These, of course, can be pursued. (4) Shoot the existing names through any accessible online databases and see what other names may be generated in that context.

Vocabulary Control

While the bibliographic trail can clearly show linkage of information, the controlled vocabulary or thesaurus lets the researcher peek inside diverse books, articles, or clippings – while still maintaining a linkage of related ideas.

Many different terms can be used to express the same idea. Thesauri are built around this principle, both print examples like Roget's and any online version in a word-processing package or in a searchable index database. The principles of vocabulary control are really very simple. All subjects (normally called "subject headings" in a library and "thesaurus" in a computer program) are hierarchically arranged: every subject is related to every other subject, no matter how tenuously. And the same is true of classification schemes, whether it is a scheme for flora or fauna, such as the Linnaeus classification, or for a collection of books. Every subject heading has a BT (broader term for a more general subject), an NT (narrower term for a more specific subject), an RT (related term for a cross-referenced subject), and a UT or UF ("use term" or "use for" from a subject heading not used in this listing). For example, the subject heading "Pets" has a BT: Animals, an RT: Animals, Domesticated, a listing of NT: Cat, Canary, Gerbil, and a UF: Household Animals (this term not used). In chart form, it would look like this:

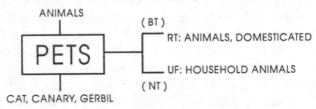

In the listing with references, there would appear statements such as "Pets, see also Animals, Domesticated" and "Household Animals, see Pets" or "Household Animals, use Pets." Other UT or UF examples would be "Cabs, use Taxis" or "Departments, use Agencies." If the NT: Cat was to be used as the base term, then the hierarchical display could be BT: Pets, RT: Dog (because "cats and dogs" are often linked and researchers can find additional, related data under the other term, in this case "dog"; an RT for Dog would, of course, be Cat), NT: the name of a breed or several breeds, and UT: Feline (a term not used in this list of headings). The major purpose of all this is *unity*: libraries like all necessary and relevant data to be brought together or cross-referenced to one place. All the material about pets in general should be tied in together, as should all the material about cats. But some sources deal with cats as pets, so there needs to be a link. As well, other sources deal with "American Exotic Shorthair" and "Himalayan" and "Siamese" as particular breeds of cats, and these need to be linked to both cats and pets.

Where it all gets complicated is with the use of different indexes in searching. Each index has its own needs and target audience. A cat index will not have general terms such as "Cats" or "Household Animals" or "Pets" except in the context of specific issues. Each index uses its own headings and there is no guarantee that the same heading will be employed throughout different indexing systems. This is precisely why many researchers prefer to use full-text databases: these usually have no controlled vocabulary. Here, the search is directed by the simple use of a word or phrase in context, mainly in today's meaning. But while these databases are easier to search, they cost more because more time is used in reading or printing out the articles. They also do not show relationships to other subjects, produce more garbage articles to wade through (and to pay for), and are good only for the previous ten years or so, since before 1980 there were hardly any full-text, free-text databases. Researchers looking for pre-1980 data will still need to know about vocabulary control.

Here are examples of different indexes and their entries on the theme of "controlling health-care costs."

1. Library of Congress subject headings, used by many libraries, including the National Library of Canada, for their book collection, and by many indexing firms (all subject to local modifications). Terms may include: Medical Care – Cost Control; Hospitals – Rates; Insurance, Health.

2. H.W. Wilson indexes try to standardize their headings based on Library of Congress headings. For popular accounts, researchers look at *Reader's Guide to Periodical Literature*; for business and financial data, they would look at *Business Periodicals Index.* A similar index, not from Wilson, is the *Canadian Periodical Index,* covering Canadian magazines. Terms in all of them are the same as in the Library of Congress subject headings.

3. *New York Times Index, Canadian News Index,* and other newspaper indexes use broader terms for their subject approaches: Medicine and Health; Medical Economics.

4. *Index Medicus,* an index specific to the medical field, jumps directly to the issue. Terms may include: Cost Control; Health Services – Economics.

5. Canadian and British indexes may add additional headings,

such as: Socialized Medicine; State Health Services; Health – Medical Costs; Medicare, while American sources will add Medicaid and Health Services Administration.

Semantic relationships between words need to be explored and fully understood if any sort of use of BT, RT, NT, and UT is to be made. Information not found under one heading might be located under another. It is yet another manifestation of the bibliographic trail.

One example is *synonyms* – and this is where the thesaurus excels. Almost every word has another, related term that should be searched, particularly in a full-text database (e.g., kill/slay/murder). Words also have *antonyms*, and information can be buried under opposite terms (e.g., hard/soft). A hierarchical arrangement such as "subject headings" means that the broader-term/narrower-term relationship should also be searched. This is the inclusion relationship (e.g., green/colour). In heavily jargoned fields, terms will occasionally be replaced (e.g., caccitis/typhlitis). Sometimes there are temporal historical changes (e.g., Zeus/Jupiter) and searches must be made under both – or more – terms.

Vocabulary control also includes *co-occurrence*, where two things are happening at the same time (e.g., shear/stress), *cause and effect* (e.g., storm/flood), and *attribution* (e.g., paved/road). Differences in spelling really need to be taken into account when doing a computer search, for the machine is exact. Searches may need to be done under both British and American spellings (e.g., theatre/theater, colour/color). Similarity of function is yet another semantic relationship (e.g., nail/screw).

Material can be found under any one of these alternate headings. When searching for "nails," check also "screws," especially if one is looking for the function and not for the name of a nail manufacturer. Material about "storms" may also be found under "flood," and vice versa. A search for data on "Zeus" should be continued with "Jupiter" (or the synonym, "Jove"). These are not really problems so long as researchers remember that semantic relationships and hierarchical relationships do exist and are at the heart of vocabulary control.

Real problems in searching are derived from other people's habits and the weight of the past. For example, titles of articles can be

misleading. Some authors and editors title conference papers, journal and magazine pieces, and other publications with cute phrases
that are not exact in describing their content. Researchers really
don't know if the article has any relevancy unless they check the sub-
title, if there is one. I am reminded of an article called "Fists or Fingers," which described the difference between the binary and the
decimal notation systems. I had to read the article to find out that
"fists" referred to "2" (as in binary) and "fingers" referred to "10"
(as in decimal). While controlled vocabulary indexing systems
would pick up this article and place it in its rightful, hierarchical position (that was how I found it), no online computer system could possibly give it any meaning to anyone unless the terms "fists" and "fingers" were inputted in anticipation. And even then the researcher
would get a lot of health articles, pieces about demonstrators waving
their fists, and articles about people losing their fingers – not exactly
what was wanted.

Another problem is that the same word can have different meanings from subject field to subject field. This is quite common for
abbreviations (e.g., ms. = a disease, an American state, a manuscript,
a salutation), which a researcher would recognize by an appearance
in context but a computer might not, especially since many programs ignore the difference between upper and lower cases. Symbols, scientific nomenclature, conventions of usage – these will all
vary from field to field.

A third problem is historical inexactitude: classification and
indexing were evolving during the first part of the twentieth century,
and they barely existed before 1890. Many newer and more precise,
relevant terms have come into being for older concepts, especially in
the sciences, technology, and the social sciences. But when researchers take these contemporary terms and begin a search through the
past, they won't find these terms being used. Researchers are suspicious of any indexing done before 1950; there is so little demand that
there is no commercial worth in putting it all into a computer, not
even with scanning devices. One example of change: "World War I"
became known as that only when World War II started (and then
"World War III" became a heading to deal with speculative books
and articles related also to such terms as "Cold War" and "Iron Cur-
tain"). Subject material about the First World War, if a researcher is
looking for contemporaneous accounts, needs to be searched under

earlier terms such as "European War," "Great War," "World War" (but the latter only after the United States entered in April, 1917). Another example: the word "atomic" is now usually replaced by "nuclear" (since "atomic" used to refer to "fission" only), except in "ABC Warfare" (atomic-biological-chemical) where it is still mnemonically useful. Similarly, searching for material on environmental issues usually draws a blank before 1965 unless researchers also add the term "ecology," under which most environmental issues were classified at that time. Of course, "ecology" as a term came back to life in the 1980s. Historical research, or even any kind of searching beyond twenty-five years ago, can be a risky enterprise unless researchers are willing to place themselves in the perspective of the times.

A fourth problem is with languages, linguistics, and translations. How much knowledge of a foreign language does one need? Most of the material written about acid rain, for example, comes from Scandinavia, Germany, and northern Europe, where it is still a bigger problem than in Canada and the United States. Researchers who lack command of the relevant languages need to rely on translation or English-language abstract summaries. How exact or precise are these translations or summaries? Different new phonetic forms now in use in China affect vocabulary control and online access – is it Peking or Beijing? And when was the change made? Searches need to be made under the vernacular form as well: Firenze for Florence, Italy. There are some seventeen different spellings for Libyan leader Ghadaffi (Khadaffi and Qadaffi being the most common: G, K, and Q are the initial letters to look up in all sorts of indexes, but all seventeen spellings may be needed for online access). One searcher working for a database creator told me that she never looked under his name but rather searched for the terms "Libya" and "madman."

A fifth problem, if it can be so considered, deals with serendipity, finding information that one never knew existed. There is a real possibility of finding relevant material that one did not know one was looking for, and might never have thought of asking for in an online system. Researchers need to be alert, for the computer can only follow their instructions. Searching a printed index means just flipping the pages, and this sort of browsing can be productive. It is a little harder with a computer, since browsing is often difficult and expensive. A lot depends on how researchers think – left brain analytical or right brain creative – for this affects how they do research, how they respond to situations, and how their requirements can be fitted into (or even jammed into) the information chain. Perhaps some are not even cut out to be researchers!

A sixth problem is the time lag: organized communication systems are slow. Full-text online newspapers are ready within minutes of their initial publication, but it can be months before a print index gets set up and into a researcher's hands. This difficulty is compounded by those academics who want status by publishing only in prestigious journals. Some, like the quarterly *American Economic Review,* have a three-year or longer wait list for publication. "What's time to a hog?" seems to be the operative phrase in the humanities, where the information flow is cumulative. The science and technology sector, however, where the information flow is successive, needs to be quick in its dissemination of findings. Related to the time lag is the difficulty in keeping up with progress in one's own field. Not all researchers go to all relevant meetings or conferences, and many prepared papers found at these places are not recorded bibliographically, hence the papers drop out of sight (or out of cite). Researchers become more dependent on online systems as a way of keeping up to date.

Mastering a control of the vocabulary used to express searchable ideas is not difficult, so long as one remembers the hierarchical connections. But vocabulary control is essential even for elementary research.

BRITE

A starting point for any research into the unknown is through the BRITE strategy:

B = Background
R = Relationships
I = Issues
T = Terminology
E = Experts

This is for the deliberate hunting and evaluation of information.

Background

Read background material on the subject, using some kind of introductory source (encyclopedia, textbook) for an overview. This will provide a good idea of what is involved, the major and minor elements, and whether the search needs to be broadened or narrowed. This will also provide an introduction to the specific jargon of the subject as well as definitions of those terms, suggesting appropriate subject headings for use later on in the information centre listings, indexing services, or document research. Names of authorities and experts will also be mentioned at this point, either in the text or as footnoted references.

Relationships

Determine how the subject is related to other subjects through research guides and encyclopedias. Begin building references to other publications, checking out key parameters and topics tangential to the subject, and making lists of appropriate databases to search. Researchers will begin to recognize the names of more authorities and experts in the field as these names repeatedly appear in the references and begin to converge. A subject research guide will also suggest different strategies for finding specific data within the context of the subject area.

Issues

Determine the pros and the cons of issues within the subject. These can be found through the encyclopedia, the research guide, and the writings of experts whose names keep popping up in the references. Researchers should identify the main issues, recognize underlying assumptions and biases, understand any problems of communication, and relate the found data to ideas and issues. But they need to be aware of the danger of stereotyping and how easy it is to fall into its trap.

Terminology

Take the unique jargon and definitions of the subject and create a terminology of search terms. These can be subject headings of uniform words or phrases, or they can be catch phrases from an existing list. They can be whatever has been gleaned from background texts. These become thesauri for databases, and they can be hierarchically arranged for vocabulary control in a series of BT, NT, RT, and UT charts. Researchers pay attention to the terms used and how they vary. They follow through on the cross-references, watching out for breaks in the coverage periods of the index or for terminology changes.

Experts

Sift through the material that has been gathered and critically evaluate it, identifying the most important information that researchers can take to experts as a springboard, perhaps touching on the pros and cons of each issue. Don't forget that librarians are experts, trained to answer short questions such as who won a prize (and when), the address of a company, the amount of cheese exported from Canada to England.

Once the BRITE technique or strategy has been mastered, then beginning researchers make a plan, which is called the *research log*.

Research Log

All research problems fall into two broad categories: those that can be answered quickly and those requiring in-depth research (which may actually be a cumulative series of quick questions).

To solve either kind, researchers need a plan. In-depth research generally requires several steps and the need to tap a wide variety of resources ranging from brief background sources to obscure experts, quite often at the same time. This research, because it involves multiple sources of articles, books, indexes, documents, databases, microforms, primary materials, organizations, government agencies, and experts, calls for a log or a checklist for the researcher to keep track of in-depth research plans, which are the guidelines adapted to fit differing requirements of specialized research. Every research project will be different, but each can be planned using a common research log. And this will even allow researchers to handle several research projects at once.

A research log makes it possible to keep track of the specific steps taken in the search, as well as providing a place to record ideas and additional steps that one plans to take. It is especially helpful if the researcher is doing an exhaustive search, since over an extended period of time the sources, strategy, and ideas may become confused. Recording thoughts, observations, and interviews can also be useful in subsequent searches. Keeping a log will help researchers monitor their progress; they can review what has been accomplished at any step along the way. It helps also to assure an orderly search because one can record exactly which sources have been searched, the order of the search, what information was found, and where it was found, ensuring that nothing has been overlooked. Indeed, a research log could be compared to a shopping list or an errand list, although not everything will apply to each and every circumstance. If researchers work on several projects at once then the logs can be useful for ensuring that they only need to search a particular index one time for many projects, or access a computer database for many projects at one time and defray the costs over a wider range of research.

The research log helps to develop the habits required for getting information, and the discipline of recording those actions actually shows beginning researchers that the *process* of getting information is very important. One will know better how to approach sources: resource tools, documents, experts. The log permits imaginative thoughts about where to go for information – the trial-and-error technique of trying out the various routes imagined. It stops seasoned researchers from relying mainly on the same resource tools for every project. By searching from the point of view of what one already knows, one will be able to make free associations, particularly when the organizational side of finding information has been coded to a research log and does not interfere with creativity. *What* researchers are looking for will determine how the information is found, how the search is structured, and even how the "found" information is to be presented. Researchers remember that answers exist somewhere, and once they know that fact, then all they need to do is sit down and figure out the best approach to get at the answers. All data are available, but some of them are available more readily than others, and some of them must be privately obtained.

The research log can be a useful framework for clarifying unfamiliar terms, breaking the subject into simpler subtopics, determining primary sources needed, estimating the quantity and the quality of material needed, budgeting time, and evaluating the data received. In its simplest form, the log should have sections for:

- *needs* – some thoughts on what will be/is needed, including definitions, angles, leads, clarifying phrases, a narrowing of the focus, a widening of any subtopic.
- *search terms* – terms used, along the line of BT, NT, RT, and UT, plus terms that arc not going to be used because they are meaningless in the context of the current project.
- *sources used* – which ones are primary or secondary sources, which sources were found in which information centres, along with the relevant records of bibliographic data for titles, copyright dates, volume numbers, pages, so that one can refer back to those sources time and again.
- *names/addresses/phone numbers* – of people, interest groups, associations, information centres, likely prospects for interviews and verifications. These can be found through the sources, as well as from almanacs and directories. Also, this is a good place to record their response.
- *computer searches* – for the most up-to-date, recent information. Note the various services that have been accessed or used in the past, with an indication of their relevancy. This should cover the 1980s and 1990s quite well.
- *time log* – specifying dates, times, and actions on those days, as well as one's own reactions, thoughts, and feelings about research (different methods, techniques, false starts, dead ends, discoveries). Researchers can see where they are going and keep a record for billing purposes, for the fact checker, and for the taxman.

Each researcher creates his or her own style of log, depending on one's own approach to recording information. Here's one brief example. You are working on an in-depth story about the rising violence against abortion clinics, based on a recent local incident. Some of the sources you might use, as listed in your research log, include the secondary fact books of general reference tools. To discover how many abortions are performed in Canada, you'll need to refer to the *Canadian Global Almanac* or the *Canada Yearbook* (and their updating services). To trace violence against women's clinics, you might turn to *Canadian News Facts* and the American *Facts on File* (for a look at the United States). To locate potential sources for your story, you could use any number of directories, from the *Directory of*

Associations in Canada and the *Encyclopedia of Associations* to local telephone books, *Sources,* and the *Metro Toronto Community Services Directory.* By now you'll have set up various pages dealing with subject headings of controlled vocabulary (taken from indexed entries of your secondary sources), names and addresses of experts, ideas for places to look, plus dates of previous occurrences to check out. You'll look at books concerning the ongoing controversy over abortion; these offer helpful background information, provide the necessary context, and target expert sources through footnotes, listings, and the authors themselves.

To put your own local incident in context and to explore some of the component issues of the abortion controversy, you'll refer to newspaper and magazine articles. You could check the vertical files in the information centres, look at police records, consult various government documents and institutional sources. You should look at the *Canadian News Index* for printed material or the *Canadian Business and Current Affairs* database, or perhaps the online services of *InfoGlobe, Infomart,* and *CP Newstex.* For an American context, a quick check through *NEXIS* and the AP service on *DIALOG* should suffice, as well as the *New York Times Index* and *Reader's Guide to Periodical Literature.* For Canadian magazine articles, you should be looking at the *Canadian Periodical Index* or the *Canadian Magazine Index,* noting names of experts and writers, perhaps cross-checking for that embedded statistic, photograph, or illustration.

Building on the basic knowledge you've accumulated so far, you're ready to break your research into its component parts and use specialty sources. If you need background information on the medical side of the story, you could look at *Index Medicus* or *Medline* for pertinent articles. You can explore some of the legal questions through articles referenced in the *Index to Canadian Legal Periodicals. PAIS Bulletin* could steer you to articles dealing with abortion as a social concern, while the *Canadian Business Index* (also available as *CBCA* online) can give you articles on abortion as big business.

This search is based on specific questions that researchers formulate at the start of the search, and throughout the process as new data are uncovered. Breaking the research into component parts will guide the researcher to specialized references and sources, as she or he moves from the general to the specific, building up controlled vocabulary and names and addresses of institutions and experts.

Once the research log is mastered, the researcher will want to begin to use the collected information to pry data loose from another source. This type of log involves people as the main subject: the *paper trail*.

The Paper Trail

The paper trail is a phrase commonly used by journalists engaged in enterprise reporting (also known as "investigative journalism"): it means digging into documents to show links between people or between people and records. It involves doing things such as compiling a financial record on an individual, monitoring an elected official, and searching out answers in documents that, for the most part, are readily available for the asking (depending on the policy of the jurisdiction in the case of law and government). Catchy phrases include "follow the dollar," using fiscal records to show connections, and "forensic accounting," which is a highly skilled technique used mainly by auditors who are trying to link and verify every figure that appears in documents to stand up in court (in a business context the auditors are known as the "guys with ties").

There are paper trails on everybody, rich or poor, obscure or famous: relevancy will always depend on the amount of interest shown about these people's affairs. From birth to death, each person has a series of records in files: sometimes these are obtainable over the counter, and sometimes they are restricted. Various freedom of information and privacy acts have curtailed the release of much personal information, but data may still be available as aggregates, as embedded names, or as confirmations/denials. Certainly the data are there in the government and business files, and the information can also be privately obtained.

Here are some common everyday records that are on file somewhere about most adults; the only difficulty is to find out *where* each file is (for example, files may be scattered in court records or police reports) and then *how* to get it (in some cases, unethically).

- birth and death certificates – age, birthplace, place of death, names of parents, probate files.
- medical records (if applicable) – marital data, status of

children, serious diseases, sexual history, blood type, addictions, psychiatric history, hospital admissions.
- school files – learning habits, enrolment records, report cards and transcripts, yearbook items, social notes, school newspaper, alumni associations, sports records.
- law enforcement agencies – driver's licences, motor vehicle registration, police records, criminal records, traffic fines, accident reports.
- credit status – income, bank and department store credit cards, local credit bureau, bank accounts, loans, debts, charities, government loans and grants, bankruptcies, property and mortgages, zoning variances, building permits, landlord-tenant disputes.
- employment and employer records – job applications, work habits, promotions, layoffs, fringe benefits, internal memos, union contracts, occupational safety and health inspections, newsletters, government contracts, advertising, annual reports.
- insurance policies – life, automobile, home and contents, medical, personal property (e.g., boats, airplanes, horses).
- social welfare – foster care records, welfare payments, pension, unemployment benefits, child allowances, adoption records.
- utilities – electrical bills, telephone records, water bills, gas bills, cable television records.
- social habits – religious affiliation, memberships, marriage licence, divorce records, child support, political campaign contributions, voter enumeration, library records, video rental records.

As an example, a researcher could check out that phantom called Howard Hughes. Almost nobody saw him or talked to him for decades before he died. Yet Barlett and Steele, authors of *Empire,* found over 250,000 pages of documents about Hughes, drawn from the courts and government agencies. As they say in their book about Hughes: "Scores of civil and criminal legal actions involving Hughes, his companies, past and present Hughes executives and others connected with the Hughes empire were examined in two dozen different state and federal jurisdictions from New York to Los Angeles."

Paper trails seem to go on forever once the researcher has found the key. At some point the trail stops, but not before the researcher is able to seam together the fabric of the subject's life. Then, when interviewing the subject, the researcher will often know so much that inconsistencies and/or lies will easily be caught. There is a saying here: documents don't lie, but people do.

The best way to become adept at the paper trail is to practise it on yourself or on someone you know: remember what is available, how the files are organized, and what they mean. Carry a dictionary. Ask clerks questions for clarification. Note any irregularities.

Here's an example of how to find information links and to build a paper trail, using one piece of information to pry loose another. You're walking down a street after a rain shower when a car whizzes by and splashes mud all over your clothes. You are facing a $40 dry-cleaning bill and much inconvenience. What can you do? If you've remembered to jot down the licence plate number and note the make or colour of the car, then you can begin to assemble data about the driver. It does, of course, take a bit of time.

With the licence plate number (in Ontario, the plate number goes with the driver, not with the car), you can go to the local provincial transport ministry office for a *motor vehicle record search*, which is available to anybody. As of 1987, Ontario began asking for a reason why you wanted to know. You can produce the dry-cleaning bill or say you're interested in buying the car. You'll need to produce identification, and your name will be recorded. A computer printout, based on the plate number, will contain Mr. Driver's full name, his address (let's say, Scarborough), and his driver's licence number. The printout will also tell you that he once owned a 1980 Toyota Corona he purchased new in Bowmanville, and the name and address of that dealership are given. Many direct-mail agencies have access to licence plate number data; they compile mailing lists, usually keyed to a make of car that indicates wealth or a high level of consumerism. (I'll continue to use a male as an example, but differences will occur later on if the driver is female.)

Let's say you can't find his name in the telephone book and the Bell Canada operator tells you that he has an unlisted number. So you look up his name in the *city directory,* found in all public libraries; it is a good source for unlisted (by Bell Canada) phone numbers. And it even tells you his occupation – pharmacist for a multibranch firm. It doesn't tell you where he works, but many entries in the city directory do mention the name of an employer. (Also, there would be an indication of who else lives at his address.) So you can call the head office of the drug firm to see at which branch he works.

You might also want to find out about his driving record; in this case, you can file an application for a *driver record abstract* in person at the Ontario Transport Ministry office in Toronto (the headquarters), using information (name and birth date) from the motor vehicle search done earlier. This printout will be mailed to you, so you have to wait a while. When it arrives, it turns out Mr. Driver has a clean driving record and also that he is 185 centimetres tall (6′1″), has a general-class driver's licence, must wear glasses while driving, and that his licence expires this year (the specific date is, of course, his birthdate). If he had had any accidents, then these would be noted on the driver abstract, as well as any address changes within the previous five years. Any convictions under the Highway Traffic Act or the Criminal Code of Canada, any offences and a list of suspensions – they are all here.

To learn details of accidents, you can file for an *accident report search* (which will provide you with a copy of the police accident report). For this you will need the name and the date – both of which you would already have from the previous abstract. To learn details of convictions, check the court records.

Suppose, too, you wanted to explore Mr. Driver's *educational background.* Phone the government agency responsible for post-secondary education and get a list of places that educate pharmacists. Then phone the records office of the schools concerned and give his name. Be logical and start with the closest school. Every day these places do scores of employer checks for credentials, and while they give out little information over the phone, they usually confirm or deny existing data – e.g., did Mr. Driver attend pharmacy school in the late 1970s? (Remember, you have his birthdate, and most people go straight through school, so it sounds reasonable that his attendance would be when he was in his early twenties.) In this particular case, the records office confirms that he attended pharmacy school in the late 1970s, graduating in 1981 with a B.Phar. The following year he garnered an M.Sc. (the records office just threw this in – occasionally clerks will do this, especially on the telephone).

If you were searching for *Mrs*. Driver, you might reach an impasse here. It all depends on when she married and when she stopped (or started) using a maiden name, and whether a divorce was involved. She also might not have reported a name change to the records office at her alma mater. Her marital status and her personal name preferences will determine how easily you can discover her educational background. In many cases, a young woman uses her maiden name until she marries, starts using her married name, but then if she divorces, she reverts to her maiden name. Alternatively, she might keep her maiden name throughout the marriage and, of course, when the marriage ends. If she remarries, she may have another set of names. Occasionally, a married woman will use her maiden name until her husband predeceases her, then adopt his last name as a memorial. Other women might take their mother's maiden name, while others might legally change their last names by filling out forms with the government. Mrs. Driver (with all records up to now being in her married name) could have gone to university under her maiden name. If this is the case, then maybe the records office, which now lists her under her married name, will be able to supply the maiden name as well. Certainly the alumni association might have both names on file. In addition, many women take their maiden name as a middle name when they marry, so it's worth the researcher's time to make queries under that middle name. Other possibilities include a marriage licence (which would have to be obtained privately), a backsearch through a city directory, a search through property records. This is a little more complicated than searching for Mr. Driver, but Mrs. Driver's name can be found.

When you inquire about Mr. Driver's final grades, you are told that the school must have his permission before it can reveal the grades. So you can do a number of things. One, turn it over to a private investigator (you'll already have saved a lot of his fee by getting this far). Two, abandon the search for education and go on with other aspects (you've already got his address and phone number if all you wanted was to have the dry-cleaning bill paid). Three, type a letter from Mr. Driver without signing it, requesting a transcript of his marks, stating some urgency about the matter, and enclosing a stamped self-addressed envelope and five dollars.

Let's say you go with option three and send the typed, unsigned letter to the records office. Perhaps the office was swamped that day and sends off the transcript without bothering to check for a signature or to look at the address. Sometimes this happens: rushed clerks will err, sometimes in your favour, sometimes in theirs. The transcript covers all four years of the program; it tells you that Mr. Driver graduated from Grade 13 in 1978 and includes the Bowmanville mailing address he used when he applied for admissions. Grade 13 forms the so-called first year of university in Ontario, and most times the transcript will have Grade 13 marks included.

So now you know where Mr. Driver, in all probability, grew up, and you can continue searching in church and school records. Community histories and local newspapers will furnish some data; check out the local public library in Bowmanville. Many local businesses, churches, schools, and other institutions authorize the writing of histories about themselves. As well, there are miscellaneous community publications from churches, genealogical histories, newsletters of clubs, and so forth. Certainly in a small town like Bowmanville, Mr. Driver might have exposed himself to a wealth of media reporting. And the same is true for his family or parents, who should also be checked. Now that you know Mr. Driver went to a certain high school, you can continue your search by checking the school's yearbooks and/or student newspapers – look at these in the school library collection. Talk to former teachers, fellow students, and neighbours.

While you wait for the mail from the transport agency and the university, you can do a *property tax search*. Look at the tax rolls at City Hall in Scarborough, using his street address. This will give you the property assessment roll number, as well as the assessment on Mr. Driver's house. It reveals that he is a "Separate School" supporter, so more data about Mr. Driver may be available from the Catholic Church diocesan offices. This is useful when you begin to explore his childhood, for you can check at the local Catholic churches. With a few calculations, you can figure out how much property tax he pays (property assessment value times the mill rate) and what kind of house he lives in compared with his neighbours. But you will have reached another impasse if Mr. Driver is a renter, as most of Scarborough's residents are. However, you will find names of residents in the house if Mr. Driver lives with someone, or if Mrs. Driver uses another name.

With the assessment roll number, you can go to the Land Titles or Land Registry Office (for the moment, both systems are used in Ontario). Here you do a *title search* on the Scarborough home, and it turns out that Mr. Driver was married when he bought the house but was legally separated by 1985. A copy of the Land Transfer Tax form that Mr. Driver and his wife had to file when they separated reveals some details of their separation agreement, including the amount Mr. Driver paid to retain ownership of the house and the size of the mortgage he assumed. In addition, the tax form also has more biographical details concerning the spouse.

Most separation agreements ultimately lead to divorce; at least before 1986 in Ontario, partners needed a separation agreement before they could get a divorce. Court documents produce a wealth of details, and they are usually public records. *Divorce files* are kept at the courthouse where the original action was filed. Let's assume, since Mr. Driver spent most of his life in Bowmanville and Scarborough, that he got divorced locally. You check Family Court in Scarborough and find that the divorce was indeed granted there. You pull out the complete divorce file (about 7.5″ thick) and look at Mr. Driver's (virtually) whole life – date of marriage and divorce, where married and by whom, background data on the spouse, including her name, age, birthplace in France, her address, the grounds for divorce, the full separation agreement, no children, neither had been married before, name of their bank, names of divorce lawyers (this can be good for follow-up inquiries). And you can make photocopies from this file.

Along the way, you've spent $10 here, $10 there, occasionally fifty cents for a photocopy. You've visited many public record places. You've run a check on the plate number, taken that name to the city directory, used that occupation note for an educational check and that address for the assessment rolls and land titles, and then checked the courts for any automobile offences, civil litigation, or divorce. In other searches you may run into problems, such as changed names, people moving around inside and outside a local area, rental properties. Often this can be corrected by obtaining the information privately. By diligent searching, you can turn up alternate sources of information about names, addresses, phone numbers, marital status, and the like. Or, you can turn the whole matter over to a private investigator who will do the same work for a fee.

This latter course may be the best procedure when you need information from a number of private businesses, such as insurance companies, banks, and credit agencies. The investigator has his own sources of tips and contacts, and quite often information is traded back and forth between companies or even sold. This is how data can be "privately obtained."

Sometimes information crosses international boundaries; this is known as *trans-border data flow* or TDF. Canadian information can be found, for example, using the U.S. Freedom of Information Act or the U.S. Securities Exchange Commission records. The monthly periodical *Privacy Journal*, published in Washington, D.C., tracks issues like confidentiality of records, lie-detector testing, electronic surveillance, inaccurate credit reporting, invasion of privacy suits, and suppression of free speech. Although the journal is American, there are applications to Canada. Under our national and provincial privacy acts you can see what files the governments have on you. Legally, you can see only your own file. (Similarly, you can see your own files at a credit bureau and make changes if there are inaccuracies.)

There are three types of credit report systems. One is the credit bureau, which collects basic credit information on people who have consumer finance dealings; the credit bureau's information is usually limited to the city in which it is situated. Its credit history files include all details of loans, payment records, charge accounts, bankruptcies, judgements, change-of-name notices, and so forth. This results in a credit rating, usually from 1 ("pays on time") to 9 ("poor credit risk"). Area businesses and merchants are members: they contribute credit details and in return they get credit details. There is a national group, the Associated Credit Bureaus of Canada, which can be contacted for more details about credit bureaus.

Another credit report system is the private investigator working for employers who want to know the habits of a potential employee, or for an insurance company investigating a new policyholder or a claim. Types of data here include living habits, general health, education, relations with neighbours and friends. And the third credit report system consists of the information exchanges run exclusively by Canadian finance companies. These businesses trade information among banks, trusts, and finance companies, particularly about outstanding debts and repayment schedules.

Statutes in all provinces serve to protect individuals. Agencies have to use the best sources available for their information as well as try to confirm unfavourable data from another source. Agencies also have to record the full judgement against an individual if the file is thus noted, while no file can contain information that is prejudicial to human rights (e.g., race, colour, ethnic origin, politics). These statutes also restrict access to the files. Disclosure is usually limited to yourself, to financial institutions when you want credit, to potential employers, to insurance companies, and to landlords. This is one area where a lot of data can be privately obtained.

Members of any credit bureau have access to reports from more than 150 bureaus across Canada and more than 3,500 in the United States. They also have access to reports from Australia, Bermuda, Great Britain, Mexico, and most areas of Western Europe – for a fee, of course. For example, in Metro Toronto, the approximately 2,500 members can get data by telephone, fax, written report, or online computers. Such members include department stores, banks and other financial institutions, oil companies, apartment managers, builders, electrical contractors, doctors, and lawyers. In addition to the personal files on people, there are also commercial files on small businesses, with the names of principals, partners, officers, length of operation, credit history, current financial details, and items of public record. Further details are available in Steve Golick and Barry Goldberg's *The Canadian Credit Handbook* (McGraw-Hill Ryerson).

Other kinds of searches open to the public include bankruptcy, vital statistics, and personal property. For a bankruptcy search a government agency, the Bankruptcy Division, has records of company and personal bankruptcy. You must provide the full name of the individual or the company. They will tell you the date of the bankruptcy and the name of the trustee. The search can be requested over the telephone or in person.

Through the Registrar of Vital Statistics, birth certificates are not available except to the person concerned (or an agent), and marriage data are sometimes available depending on the circumstances. Uncertified death certificate searches are publicly available for a small fee, but you must provide the full name and must fill out a form in the office; the records are available within a few days. Only the next of kin (or an agent) can get a copy of the certified death certificate. The distinction here between "certified" and "uncertified" can be crucial. The uncertified document can indicate an official death but it cannot be used to collect CPP benefits or life insurance, or to open safe deposit boxes. The need for this certificate may be just to indicate that someone died and how, but not to go after the estate. A clerk who denies you the certified certificate will not deny you the uncertified document. The onus is on you to ask for the right piece of paper, or else you simply won't get it. Sometimes information on parentage is available with an application to the Search Index of Parentage.

With the name of a debtor in any purchase where credit is involved, searches can be made under motor vehicle registration numbers, business names, or birthdates. The provincial Personal Property Security Registration gives the debtor's name, the secured party, loan information, and the address given for the purpose of registration.

Many of these personal documents can be accessed in different ways. Any record on you held by a government can be looked at by you (or your agent) through the Privacy Act associated with the access to information legislation. Records on other people can be obtained in a variety of ways:

- through private investigators, who can privately obtain records by using their contacts;
- through lawyers, who can also be agents and who need the record for a court case;
- through looking at the court documents after the case has been completed and the materials filed away (e.g., a marriage licence in a divorce file);
- through willing clerks who take pity on you or interpret policy loosely;
- through contact people who actually create the file and are willing to leak data;
- through outright theft/photocopy/microforming, usually in the belief that minor laws could be broken in attempting to catch people who break major laws.

On a larger scale, when reporters are trying to find information not on Mr. Driver but on Mr. Big, there are many more complicated sources of documents, most of them on the public record. Some of these specific sources will be covered in Chapter 6, which deals with the subject fields of business, government, and the court system, but at this point some major elements of linkage need to be indicated. Can there really be evil lurking behind every document? Here are some themes of enterprise reporting using the paper trail, with an indication of specific topics:

- consumer fraud – scams, ripoffs, welfare abuses;
- conflicts of interest for government and business, or the appearance of a conflict of interest;
- law enforcement – corruption, informants, juggling of crime statistics, internal investigations, cutbacks;
- financial institutions – banking and trust company collapses, insurance company frauds, loan sharking;
- government mismanagement – environmental performance, hiring consultants, use of government perks;
- political corruption;
- lobbying – influence peddling, bribery, kickbacks;
- property values – land zoning, rezoning with variances, assessment, permits, fraud;
- organized crime – gambling, extortion, fraud, waste management, aggregate and construction industry;
- charities and foundations – corruption, disaster relief scams, administrative costs;
- white-collar crime – fraud, embezzlement, petty theft;
- labour unions – sweetheart deals, organized crime, political activities, management relations, occupational health and safety defects, pension funds.

Some of the relevant documents that could be checked, for example, in regard to political corruption include the following. For monitoring elected officials, you need to look at bank credit card payments, telephone bills, campaign contribution reports, public disclosure laws such as conflict of interest or blind trusts, corporation record tracing, assumed business names, planning and adjustment records, building permits, business licences and applications, government purchasing contracts and sub-contracts, auditing systems, retirement and pension funds. All of these are available in some form through court records, expense account filings, campaign records, and the like. Other useful items would include (in varying degrees of importance): professional licences and associations, landholdings, tax statements, freedom of information requests for spending patterns and slush funds, previous voting records, endorsations, political machinery, association with lobbyists, payoffs (check donors against later patronage appointments). Indeed, many other documents might also explain the enhancement of the elected official's lifestyle.

Top enterprise reporting in Canada has included Jock Ferguson's thirteen stories in the *Globe and Mail* about a chemical company polluting Lake St. Clair. He used court records, corporation records in Ontario and Michigan, hazardous waste records in Ontario, and approval certificates for waste disposal sites. He further used company and ministry records to document river and air pollution by chemical companies. He interviewed scores of people in government, business, and associations. A Montreal *Gazette* story by Robert Winters and Eloise Morin about Montreal middlemen getting renovation funds from the city was based on company registration records, land ownership records, bank records, city grant forms, and interviews with the principals.

A story for *Harrowsmith* by David Lees about waste management in Canada relied on many scientific, engineering, and social studies generated by the Ontario Waste Management Corporation. As well, transcripts of testimony by corporation officers at government hearings, Ontario Legislative Assembly debates, Ministry of the Environment memoranda, and clipping files of environmental groups and municipal governments were used, plus interviews with the principals. Robin Harvey's three major stories on reforms needed for nursing homes appeared in the *Toronto Star*; she had been on the beat for two years. Her documents included coroner's inquest reports, government inspection reports, court records, tax records, nursing home legislation, several reports on the aged and the health care system, along with interviews of the principals.

Elaine Dewar's massive story about the takeover of Union Gas by Unicorp (in two issues of *Canadian Business*) was a model for lots of document digging and background searching. The story required a careful reading of many documents: annual reports of major Canadian and American corporations going back more than ten years in some cases; notices of significant changes filed by American corporations with the Securities and Exchange Commission; forms disclosing significant changes in U.S. savings and loan corporations, obtained from the Federal Home Loan Bank Board; the findings of a U.S. federal court judge in a lawsuit between Brascan Corporation and Edper Investments; a report by the Office of the Superintendent of Insurance with regard to the sale and resale of a Canadian insurance company; filings by various interveners before the Ontario Energy Board hearing into the takeover; the report on the hearing issued by the OEB counsel; the report on the hearing issued by the OEB; the report into the purchase by Union Enterprises of Burns Foods Ltd. through the issue of new shares, as published by the Toronto Stock Exchange; a report into the same matter by Ontario's Director of the Corporations Branch; the transcripts of a hearing into the matter conducted by the Ontario Securities Commission, plus interviews with over fifty principals, a literature search of newspaper and magazine articles, and attendance at various regulatory hearings.

These reporters spend their days poring over transcripts, pictures, yearbooks, production charts, crime statistics, speeches, publicity releases, government publications, public records. This is a slow but cumulative process. Their success rests for the most part on voracious reading and then on applying serious thought to what they have read. Most of this work can be drudgery, with researchers spending endless hours sifting through mostly meaningless documents, looking for the few facts that can tie everything together. With creativity, serendipity, and logic, any good researcher should be able legally to intercept a paper trail at the bottleneck, then follow the dollar to see where the profits and losses go.

Forensic accountants, of course, have the advantage of being employed full-time to check the figures from the inside. They don't need to obtain data privately, but occasionally they are tipped off as to which direction to proceed in following the dollar. A firm such as Lindquist Avey Macdonald Baskerville (in business since 1975) will investigate white-collar crime and corruption. Some of their more notable cases have included a Trinidad kickback scandal, the Sinclair Stevens inquiry, and the Romanian Ceausescu financial investigation. Typical work involves shareholder disputes, pension fund fraud, stock market manipulation, real estate fraud, money laundering, patent infringement, and world-wide funds tracing.

For the rest of us, here are some tips for investigative work.

(1) Acquire an *overview* so that you look for the right details in the right document or with the right source. For example, a lot of the same information is kept in several different government agencies. If you understand government and how it works, then you will know this and can try different angles to get at the information by checking as many places as you can. One agency may classify something, another might not. A report on the dangers of an atomic reactor's pile may be classified by Atomic Energy of Canada Limited, but not by Ontario Hydro. Sometimes material is already public but few people know about it, including government personnel themselves.

(2) Build a *chronology*. Organize all the paper with a systematic plan for the records, documents, invoices, and vouchers, anything with a date. You should be able to show links by checking dates. Don't confuse the years, and remember the differences between the American (month/day/year), British (day/month/year), and metric (year/month/day) systems of dating. This has implications for computer searches.

(3) Cultivate *contacts*. Occasionally you can threaten to use freedom of information legislation to pry loose some documents, and your contacts might just decide to give you the material and save you and them from the hassle of filling out forms. Occasionally, you might get a brown envelope, particularly if someone on the inside sees you working hard at your research. Sometimes you might be able to find the author of a report and convince him or her that you should be given the document. Get your contacts to explain documents to you or to steer you in the right direction. Make friends with the people who run the offices in which you search.

(4) *Evaluate* and *verify* your written sources. Check for bias, material out of context, conflicting or irregular data. Seek the advice of sympathetic clerks.

(5) Follow through on *referrals,* for one source will lead you to another. One piece of information can be used to pry loose another. Keep in mind the mosaic theory developed in the previous chapter, and the jigsaw theory (if you fit one piece into place, then it enables you to fit another piece in somewhere else). Sometimes you might find a document that contains a listing referring to other documents that might still be marked "classified." Bureaucrats are often not thorough in obliterating cross-references; they themselves don't always "follow through." With the name of a cited document, you have the beginning of a paper trail. You can go to an official and say "I want *this* piece of paper," and he cannot say that it does not exist. He may give in if you can prove it is listed somewhere, so always try to look at the index and footnotes in a document.

(6) *Protect your notes.* Whatever you have obtained legally should be certified, copied, or even faxed to another location, in case your files mysteriously vanish, burn, or get subpoenaed. *Never* keep your notes mounted only on a computer; make lots of backups and paper copies.

Search Strategies

In any search strategy, which is a step-by-step system of procedures to dig out information, the *process* of getting the information is important. It is best to know where to go for a fact rather than to know the fact itself. Many researchers simply never bother to memorize information they can find elsewhere, particularly since the data are transitory and only relate to the current project while the technique stays forever. In an apocryphal story told about Albert Einstein, when he was asked for his phone number, he said he'd have to look it up in the directory. Since it was listed he didn't try to memorize it. Ultimately, there are no hard and fast rules for deciding search strategies. Most information is uncovered by trial and error. There are a number of guidelines and suggestions about pitfalls, and tips for enhancement, but most of these relate to individual, narrow topics. (These will be discussed in Chapter 6.)

For now, the absolutely *basic* strategy is simply: (1) *What do we want?* Clarify needs for the most efficient, time-saving search. (2) *How do we get it?* Identify the proper sources for the most effective, best-quality search.

The rest is merely a system, a follow-through, with necessities of detail for the novice researcher. And we are all novices when we begin searching for data in subject fields foreign to us. We don't know the vocabulary (but we do know the rules of control); we don't know the background (but we do know where to go for this); we don't know the specifics of the problem (but we'll narrow our focus in terms of the vocabulary and the sources). Once we've analysed the search problem and have identified the proper source, then we follow the known rules about

- translating the need into the vocabulary of the source;
- planning a logical series of steps;
- locating the sources (multiple ones are needed for verification);
- conducting the search, and accepting and rejecting data as the search moves along.

Often I use the analogy of a bridge contract. The bidding is the clarification of the need, and the contract settlement is the identification of the proper sources. Any bridge player, having reached a thought-out contract, will know where all the major cards lie. And in a slam or grand slam contract, the contract player will know where *all* the cards lie. There is a saying in bridge that bidding is 90 per cent of the game: it only remains to play it out after the contract has been arrived at. Finding answers is the same.

Researchers need to know, among other things, how information is put together, where the sources lie, how needs can be formulated in terms of the sources, how the systems work in specific subject areas, and what kinds of parameters are useful and when. Once these patterns are learned then the finding of answers is easy. Previous chapters have dealt with the nature and linkage of information; the next chapters will look at some parameters and systems.

Researchers need to decide on the order in which each of the various resources available will be consulted, which to skip over for the moment, and when to return. This is part of the research matrix of moving about: points of entry will be determined by one's previous knowledge of the subject field. The researcher's instinct will lead along the most likely path to the data, sometimes without any realization that it has occurred. This trial-and-error approach has been characterized as being a rapid subconscious review of what is known about the subject field and what decisions to take. Strategies will vary according to the limits of the subject field, the nature of the researcher's thought patterns, and the type of need. But at the heart of searches, regardless of which strategy is chosen, purpose comes before action:

- Know what is being looked for (focus).
- Know that it is available (confidence).
- Know where it might be (strategy).
- Know how to use the resource (technique), whether it is a book, a library, an institution, a document, or an expert.

In other words, "look before you leap." Success depends entirely on how well researchers are prepared, and such preparation can save much wasted time and unnecessary work. This means developing a "search behaviour" pattern that is formed only by doing research many times. Behaviour includes automatically describing information needs into a controlled vocabulary and thesaurus, generating synonyms, and thinking in terms of subject headings, as well as alphabetizing terms and directing one's will toward a goal. Material is then found through patterns, routines, or trial and error. And it will vary. No researcher has a clear idea of what is totally and exactly needed when research is about to begin. Fine tuning is customary, and the research matrix is designed for it. Using deductive and inductive logic, broadening or narrowing a focus or search term, finding background data in a textbook or encyclopedia, generating search terms – all of these variables depend on the researcher's previous knowledge, attitude, and current subject matter. With a research log, a researcher can codify what has to be done so that nothing is overlooked and items and searches can be returned to. Such simple, quick checks include the following:

- Verbalize topic.
- Obtain overview.
- Focus topic (broader, narrower).
- Formulate questions.
- Plan research.
- Compile references.
- Find sources (databases, institutions, experts).
- Analyse sources.
- Evaluate sources.
- Take notes.
- Organize information.
- Evaluate evidence.
- Establish conclusions.
- Outline final product.

Along the way, the researcher will be constantly moving in the research matrix. For example, if there are too many subject headings, then he will cut back; if too few, then he will enlarge. If material is too old, then he will update or replace it. If certain kinds of information are missing, then he will go back and find more. He will also do this if certain data cannot be verified or properly evaluated and attributed. If the subject (or even a sub-topic of the subject) is too new or vague, then he will obtain an overview to get his bearings. All of these choices will determine how much research is generated. Because the researcher may decide later to change direction (based on the kind and amount of data found), he won't make a definite decision on a searchable subject. Instead, he'll make a decision on what to begin with: to find a marker that can be explored and later modified. Research has to begin at some point.

The basic method of answering queries is to break them down into their parameters (more on this in the next chapter) so that specific resources, which possibly contain answers, can be suggested. The formula is: a "need for information" is rephrased as a specific query, which in turn is generalized to a general query to suggest a general source, which in turn is rephrased as a specific source or sources with the answer and (perhaps) the verification. For example, a need-turned-query such as "How many houses were built in Vancouver in 1987?" or "How many cars were built in Toronto in 1990?" can be rephrased as a general query: "How many of any product were built in any place in Canada in whatever year?" This suggests general sources dealing with statistics (how many) or products (houses, cars) or industries (housing, automobiles) or geographic location (Vancouver, Toronto) or chronology (1987, 1990). These general sources in turn become a specific source with the answer/verification (housing statistics from Statistics Canada, automobile yearbooks, Vancouver or Toronto chambers of commerce, general yearbooks for 1987 and 1990). The same answer, then, would lie in different resources, so if a book on the construction industry in Vancouver is temporarily unavailable, then the researcher need only move on to find the same answer in other tools, which he needs to look at anyway for purposes of verification.

All queries have a number of different parameters that allow researchers to get a handle on names, places, dates, and things related to the five Ws: who-what-where-when-why. The research matrix operates by applying these parameters to individual subject fields, and sometimes these subjects determine the usefulness of the parameters. For example, to answer queries about working mothers:

(1) How many working mothers are there? Look at a source dealing with government labour statistics or welfare statistics (Statistics Canada, *Canada Yearbook*).

(2) Do working mothers feel guilty about leaving their children in the care of others? Look at research studies for the larger issues (*Psychological Abstracts, Sociological Abstracts*, Canadian associations dealing with psychology and sociology) and look in popular literature for personal accounts, checking business, women's, and feminist magazines (*Canadian Magazine Index, Canadian Periodical Index, Canadian Business and Current Affairs*).

(3) How do businesses view working mothers and maternity leaves? Look in business magazines, popular magazines, scholarly journals (*Canadian Business and Current Affairs, Business Index, ABI Inform*).

(4) What kinds of support groups are there? Look in newspaper articles (*Canadian News Index, InfoGlobe, Infomart, NEXIS*) or look at organizations for contacts (*Directory of Associations in Canada, Encyclopedia of Associations*).

Every subject field has parameters, which can be modified according to the needs of the topic, and the research log helps to determine the modifications needed. Experienced researchers know where they are at every moment of their research.

In addition to the basic search strategy and research matrix, researchers also employ some techniques that are extremely useful in pulling together a comprehensible report or a piece of understandable expository writing. Almost every written report should make use of at least some of these, which means actively searching for them in the databases used. These techniques help clarify the perspectives and viewpoints of the final report.

(1) *Definitions.* All reports need explanations, and several definitions can be consolidated for identification purposes and so audiences can understand. Most of the definitions come from dictionaries, encyclopedias, and textbooks.

(2) *Context.* The circumstances of each situation and/or subject field will dictate approaches, but background and perspective are important for understanding subject material.

(3) *Analogies.* Differences can be contrasted and similarities compared. As alternative or verified sources are being searched, the researcher can also gather material for analogies. A useful strategy here when searching is to generate antonyms in addition to synonyms. Serendipity or prepared browsing may also be a help.

(4) *Classification.* This technique puts things, people, places, and other parameters into *lists,* such as wines by region, music by type, companies by size. Specific resources can do this in all subject fields. Computerized databases are exceedingly useful here.

(5) *Statistics.* These are extremely useful if they have some meaning, perhaps as interpreted from authoritative sources, but this is a minefield that needs careful treading. Statistics require selective handling so that they are not misused or overused.

(6) *Example.* Add the specific to the general: all research reports should have examples, which can be culled from the popular press through magazine and newspaper indexes. The media are rich sources for finding situations to support points being made, especially on a regional basis.

With these six techniques, it should be easy to justify analysis or persuade readers of conclusions; the material is easy enough to find in the information resources.

Summary

In discussing the linkage of information (showing how one source leads to another), this chapter suggests a system: a research log for project management and record-keeping. The structure of information controllers (union lists, bibliographies, indexes, abstracts, lists, and directories) and the bibliographic trail (subdivisions of topic analysis, citation indexes) are examined. At the heart of "control" is vocabulary control, with its hierarchical arrangement and principle of unity. Thesaurus structures here include the semantic relationships between words as well as the problems of cute titling, jargon, historical inexactitude, language translations, serendipity, and time lag. The basic BRITE strategy is introduced (background, relationships, issues, terminology, experts), leading to the checklists of the research log (sources used, sources not used, experts, computer searches, time log) as prime examples of the process, of information as its own "system."

The paper trail uses methods of forensic accounting and linkage of documents obtained both openly and privately. Stress here is on acquiring an overview, building a chronology, cultivating contacts, evaluating source material, following through on referrals, and protecting notes. General search strategies are developed to generate parameters producing sufficient handles or angles to manage the flow of information. Asking "What do I want?" clarifies the need, while asking "How do I get it?" identifies the resources. Researchers are advised to know what is being looked for, to know that it is available, to know where it might be, and to know how to use the resource. Trial and error play a major role here in planning a proper thesaurus, locating sources, conducting the search, and evaluating the results. This chapter concludes with a discussion of some writing techniques (definitions, context, analogies, classification, statistics, examples) that will help the researcher present his findings more cogently.

PART 2

THE PRACTICE

SEARCH STRATEGIES

Knowledge is of two kinds: either we know a subject ourselves, or we know where to find information on it. – Samuel Johnson

You could look it up. – Ring Lardner, Jr.

This chapter looks at the key parameters for access to information; these can be applied to any subject area and any situation. It presents material on:

- background;
- definitions;
- addresses;
- biographies;
- geography and travel;
- current events;
- reviews (product evaluations);
- multidisciplinary topics;
- statistics;
- polls and surveys.

Key Parameters

The reference collection in any home or library provides the fastest answers to short, common questions. Some other more detailed or obscure queries will need more time or larger reference libraries, but even so, they can be answered relatively quickly – provided one can wait for turnaround time. Researchers cannot always visit a huge library whenever they need a quick answer, but they can phone during open hours, and they can also access various databases and hypertext boards to find common answers.

The reference materials (whether in a library or at home) can do a number of things well: they provide needed definitions; they describe and identify people; they explain unfamiliar concepts; they supply additional background information; they verify the accuracy of facts that other people give; they provide statistics. Their arrangement of information is usually arcane, for they are designed to be consulted for definite items of information rather than to be read consecutively. Facts are brought together from many sources and arranged for convenient and rapid use, being designed to be referred to.

Reference tools, then, provide the parameters: they allow the researcher to get a handle on names, places, dates, and forms of information. Focusing on their actual need allows researchers to know what type of resource to use, depending on the subject field and the tool's appropriateness at the time of use.

- If you need *background,* then use an encyclopedia.
- If you need a *definition,* use a dictionary.
- If you need an *address,* use a directory.
- If you need *personal* data, use biographical sources.
- If you need a *geographical* fact, use an atlas or gazetteer.
- If you need *current events,* use a news digest or similar tool.
- If you need a *review,* look at product evaluation indexes.
- If you need *multidisciplinary* information, use a computer database.
- If you need a *statistic,* use an almanac, yearbook, or statistics source.
- If you need *opinions,* use a poll, survey, or news database.

Researchers use the parameters of journalism: *who* (biography), *where* (geography, address), *when* (current events), *why* (background), *what* (definition), *how* (reviews, opinions: motives, intentions, explanations).

Some of the top reference works used by librarians, researchers, reporters, and students that will answer most queries quickly include:

1. An unabridged dictionary (from Oxford, Merriam-Webster, or Random House; the latter has useful supplements and maps).
2. The city directory, the area telephone books, and the government phone books for all levels.
3. A world atlas for maps.
4. A geographical dictionary for location and gazetteer data.
5. Local, provincial, and Canadian road and street maps.
6. *The Canadian Who's Who.*
7. *The Canadian Global Almanac.*
8. *The Canadian Encyclopedia* (4 volumes).
9. *The World Book Encyclopedia* (22 volumes).
10. A style guide, such as Fowler's.
11. A quotation book (Oxford, Bartlett, Home).
12. *Roget's Thesaurus.*
13. *Corpus Almanac and Canadian Sourcebook,* or *Canadian Almanac and Directory.*
14. *Canada Yearbook.*
15. *Statesman's Yearbook.*
16. *Canadian Parliamentary Guide.*
17. A directory of special libraries.

Added to these, of course, is access to a computer database such as *InfoGlobe, CBCA,* or *Infomart.*

These all become "first places to look" by virtue of their comprehensiveness and the fact that they are easily accessible, for most have a highly developed indexing system. These general tools cover the breadth of human knowledge. What follows next in this chapter is a short guide to the ten major parameter sources of information listed at the head of this chapter.

Background

Encyclopedias are best for background. They are concerned with subject matter, providing an overview of a topic, defining, describing, explaining, and summarizing, with how-to material and suggestions for further research and new leads. They provide names of contacts, illustrations, and thesaurus descriptors for further searching.

Encyclopedias are known as "first aids" because they provide a methodical, though superficial, summary of much of human knowledge. They are good beginning points for investigation or verification research; however, they are only a beginning and should not be viewed as comprehensive one-stop sources of information. Their major difficulty is that they are not revised quickly; for current or updated information, researchers need to check a yearbook, almanac, news database, or an encyclopedia that is online and has been updated.

Since encyclopedias are arranged alphabetically with cross-references to other related topics, and since they have indexes with about forty times as many entries as in the main text, then there are only two access points: the text heading and the index heading. Researchers always use the index first, searching alphabetically by choice of search term, to discover the range of material available on subject fields. This approach by index is more fruitful because one can see at a glance the specific terms included with the general topics, and also that these terms are scattered throughout the encyclopedia. Researchers are able to pinpoint locations of illustrations, maps, figures, and the identification of minor items. This principle of "index first" applies to all reference books. Initially, it may seem time-consuming, but it does guarantee that beginning researchers will find answers.

Some types of encyclopedias will prove more useful than others. The most common ones are the multi-volume sets such as the *Encyclopaedia Britannica*, *Encyclopedia Americana*, *Collier's Encyclopedia*, and the *Academic American Encyclopedia* (the latter is online and is also available as a CD-ROM, known as *Grolier Encyclopedia*). The one-volume books are useful for brief identification (e.g., *New Columbia Encyclopedia*), while sets for young adults (e.g., *World Book Encyclopedia*) are useful for uncomplicated explanations of technical subjects, for colour illustrations, for simpler ideas in general, and for being more up-to-date (they are sold to the education market). There are specialized subject encyclopedias, such as *The Canadian Encyclopedia*, which deals only with Canada and a Canadian interpretation of the world, and the *Worldmark Encyclopedia of the Nations*, which deals only with geopolitics. These are useful sources for specific statistics, concepts, and identification. Foreign-language encyclopedias are useful for non-North American facts and figures, maps, illustrations, and anything else that does not need much translation. Most foreign works have many shorter, fact-specific articles, and they are easy to use. Older encyclopedias of any type are useful for information about their own and earlier times, which may not have been brought forward into modern encyclopedias, especially historical illustrations and older statistics. Other background and introductory material can be quickly found through the larger dictionaries, some almanacs, biographical sources, and handbooks.

Definitions

Definitions and usage are most commonly found through dictionaries. These books list the words of a language or of a subject area; they are arranged alphabetically (hence the term "dictionary arrangement"). Unfortunately, some dictionaries are poorly put together, with obsolete information. These should be avoided. (Kenneth Kister's *Dictionary Buying Guide,* published by R.R. Bowker, provides detailed evaluations of dictionaries and can be of great help in weeding out the unreliable ones.) Depending on the size and level of the dictionary, it should cover not only meaning and usage but also derivation, style, spelling variants, synonyms, antonyms, pronunciations, syntax, current status in the language, and syllabication. Dictionaries may describe the usage of words, or they may prescribe usage by setting standards. They may also be graded for expertise, ranging from school dictionaries to college level. And many dictionaries have non-word appendix information, such as maps or lists or charts. All of the larger dictionaries are updated by supplementary services. There are the online database *OWLS* (Oxford Word and Language Service), the Language Research Service of Merriam-Webster, and the quarterly journal *Barnhart Dictionary Companion.*

For word dictionaries, size is everything: bigger is better. The major unabridged English dictionary is Oxford's *New English Dictionary on Historical Principles* (often abbreviated as the OED), which shows every use of about 600,000 English words through 2.5 million quotations, from the time the word entered the language through to its exit. The unabridged *Webster's Third New International Dictionary* inventories American usage, but without the extensive quotations. It can be matched by the *Random House Dictionary of the English*

Language. All three publishers have portable abridgements for home or college use.

Specific dictionaries for the United States also include the *Dictionary of American English on Historical Principles* and the *Dictionary of Americanisms on Historical Principles,* both of which explore the historical meanings of American English. The former deals with the changes in the English language in the United States, while the latter deals with the new words that are entirely American in derivation or meaning. The *Dictionary of American Regional English* explores the meaning of words found in local areas in the United States. The *Barnhart Dictionary of New English* defines new words of post-1965 origin. For Canada, the *Dictionary of Canadianisms on Historical Principles* introduces the derivation and meaning of words uniquely Canadian, while the *Gage Canadian Dictionary* has currently used derivations and adds Canadian meanings and pronunciations where they differ from English and U.S. usage.

There are also many usage and style books. The *Oxford Dictionary of English Etymology* shows the original meaning of words. Morris's *Dictionary of Word and Phrase Origins* presents a history of unusual words. The *Dictionary of Slang and Unconventional English* does for England what the *Dictionary of American Slang* does for the United States. Nicknames, solecisms, and vulgarities are also included. Both cover only the pre-1950 period, so more specific dictionaries must be used to find data about, say, rock music, drug culture, or corporate business slang. Fowler's *Dictionary of Modern English Usage* is an arbiter of style for England, while Follett's *Modern American Usage* does the same thing for the United States. Both analyse how words should be used, as well as points of grammar, syntax, and pronunciation. *Webster's New Dictionary of Synonyms* presents the synonyms in an alphabetical format, while *Roget's Thesaurus of English Words and Phrases* gives the words a classified format. The *Acronyms, Initialisms and Abbreviations Dictionary* presents over 100,000 shortened forms, explaining their meaning. There is even a *Reverse Acronyms, Initialisms and Abbreviations Dictionary,* arranged alphabetically by the original longer version of the word or phrase.

Every subject area has its own "special term dictionary," such as the *Dictionary of Canadian Economics.* Some of these will be looked at in the next chapters. They are extremely useful for tracking down jargon or local meanings of words. They can be found for any subject by checking the subdivision "Dictionaries" under the main subject term in databases. Also, many specialized texts contain glossaries of technical terms at the back of the book. Translation dictionaries are another specialized type: some are monolingual; others are bilingual.

Addresses

If an address is needed, then look at a directory or at tools that contain directories. Directories are lists of people, places, and things, tied to an address and/or telephone number. Addresses, of course, are needed when tracking down experts, consultants, or associations. Most new projects that researchers undertake require directories to locate new sources. For strategy in finding a human resource, think of the project's subject matter and search directories using that vocabulary. Most current biographical directories give data on where to write to an individual, so the appropriate person can then be contacted for facts, figures, and verifications.

Directories can be found in information centres (they pride themselves on providing access to a wide range of directories) by simply looking up the name of the subject, the name of the country, or the name of an occupation, followed by the subheading "Directories." Listings can also be found by shooting the word "directory" through a computer database. Here are the essential directories:

1. City directories – for location of local businesses, characteristics of residents and neighbourhoods, addresses when there is a phone number, phone numbers when there is an address, unlisted phone numbers (sometimes).
2. *National Directory of Addresses and Telephone Numbers* (U.S.).
3. Electronic Yellow Pages (online) and *Phonefiche* (telephone directories on microfiche).
4. Government organization manuals and telephone directories.
5. *Directory of Information Sources in Canada,* a directory of 1,500 Canadian directories, including handbooks, membership lists, and phone books; the American counterpart is

Directory of Directories. For other countries, try *Current British Directories* and *Current European Directories.*

6. *Public Affairs Information Service Bulletin,* an extremely useful print and online journal index that has "Directories" as a unique subject heading.
7. Almanacs such as the *Canadian Almanac and Directory, Corpus Almanac and Canadian Sourcebook, World Almanac.*
8. Yearbooks and encyclopedias also have listings.

Remember to check the directory's prefatory material, so as not to miss anything in the physical arrangement of the directory.

Biographies

Personal information is pervasive; it can be found everywhere, for all types of information resources contain some biographical data, no matter how minimal. The problem is often one of sorting out all of the available resources so that the greatest amount of information can be retrieved quickly and efficiently. Some of the more personal details about people were explained in the previous chapter as the paper trail.

The major and most common problem in biographical searching is that there is just the one access point: the person's surname. (Occasionally, researchers are actually searching for the name of a person who occupies a certain position.) Many details must be ferreted out, such as identification (name changes and variations), disputed facts, obscure details about famous people. The information found in the area of biography may be more subjective and contradictory than almost any other kind. Information needs can be categorized into two forms. (1) What *kind* of information is needed? Is it a date? membership? marital status? photograph? age? address? background? (2) How *much* information is needed? brief? summary? exhaustive? contemporary? previous? critical? evaluative? factual?

Most of the common large biographical sources can be split up according to type and quantity. Some tools are for non-living people only, some only for the living. Others are useful along a nationality basis, while still others give a wealth of critical description in addition to basic identification. Thus, for Canada, there is the *Dictionary of Canadian Biography,* which is concerned with evaluations of non-living Canadians. For Great Britain there is the comparable *Dictionary of National Biography*; the United States has the *Dictionary of American Biography.* The *Canadian Who's Who* gives identification for living Canadians; the appropriate British and Commonwealth tool is *Who's Who,* and the American tool is *Who's Who in America.* Brief identification for dead Canadians can be found in the *Macmillan Dictionary of Canadian Biography* (for Britain and the Commonwealth, try *Who Was Who*; for the United States, try *Who Was Who in America*). Sources covering the whole world's past include *Webster's New Biographical Dictionary, Chambers' Biographical Dictionary, New Century Cyclopedia of Names,* and *McGraw-Hill Encyclopedia of World Biography* (at twelve volumes, this resource tool also describes and evaluates people). For living persons, there are the *International Who's Who* (identification) and *Current Biography* (descriptive), although since the former started in 1935 and the latter in 1940, both of their older editions can be searched for non-living persons of the twentieth century.

Another category is the obituary index. Obituaries often appear as necrology surveys in yearbooks, newspaper indexes, and separately published books. Most obituaries are drawn from newspapers, so researchers can simply shoot a name through post-1979 newspaper databases. For earlier listings, they should look for *New York Times Obituaries Index,* 1859-1978, *Obituaries from the [London] Times,* 1785-, *Obituaries on File,* 1940-1978. Newer print tools include *Annual Obituary,* 1980-, and the *Canadian Obituary Record,* 1988-.

Special biographical indexes, which provide access to millions of names, include *Biography and Genealogy Master Index* (about five million names of non-living persons) and *Biography Index* (which analyses magazine articles and books for biographical data about both the living and the non-living). The latter, which has been published since 1946, has an occupational and subject listing so that researchers can find names of people who satisfy a particular set of criteria. Indeed, if researchers require the name of someone who has a certain job, then the best search is probably through the computer using the name of the job as the search term. Look through the online version of *Biography and Genealogy Master Index,* the American *Who's Who* series from Marquis (and this includes the regional and subject *Who's Who*), and the citation indexes from the Institute for Scientific Information. Only a few print materials have this capability, namely those with membership rosters or those organizations with phone books. The *Financial Post Directory of Directors,* for example, will give the name of company directors. From there it is a simple matter to look up that surname in the main text.

Biographical directories are lists of names such as telephone books, voter enumeration lists, magazine subscriber lists, and professional association memberships. Such directories are most useful for finding addresses and phone numbers and verifying career progressions. Many association memberships can be found in information centres catalogued under the name of the association or the subject matter. *Directory of Information Sources in Canada,* as noted above, lists Canadian directories, most of them biographical.

The basic steps, then, in finding information about a living person should include the following:

1. Check the city directory, the phone book, library files.
2. If the person is prominent, check who's whos, business directories, news databases.
3. Make phone calls to friends, and to the individual's friends, neighbours, enemies, associates.
4. Get a curriculum vita/résumé from his/her place of employment or affiliated organization.
5. Through licensing commissions and/or professional associations, get licence or corporate records for performance standards, as well as previous employment records and salary ranges. This applies to lawyers, doctors, teachers, accountants, architects, engineers, psychologists, social workers, insurance agents, real estate agents, morticians, taxi drivers, hazardous waste handlers, dairy product handlers, electricians, plumbers, barbers, auctioneers, nurses, ambulance drivers, and scores more.
6. Do public record searches, such as motor vehicle and driver's licences, voter enumerations, vital statistics (birth, marriage, death), non-specific debt searches, courthouse files (bankruptcies, land titles, tax disputes, liens, sales records, property taxes, appeals), probate, divorce, litigation, immigration files.

Finally, researchers who are really stuck on an obscure person can always try to do a news database search under the surname and hope that something turns up.

The basic pattern of a life is familiar no matter how unusual the details. Biographical research is relatively simple to structure, with defined outlines that pay attention to events, ideas, developments, and theories. By locating data about little-known people, a researcher may be able to study a profession, a social problem, a movement, a point in time or place, or a specific institution or organization. And the reverse is also true: by locating data about these things, a researcher will find information about little-known people. Additional biographical sources, better located through a library that accepts manuscript donations, include biography books, autobiographies, journals, diaries, notes, and letters.

Geography and Travel

Usually, geographical sources deal with descriptions of places or spatial relationships between places. Sources for looking up such information can be divided into three categories.

(1) *Maps and atlases* are used for visual and spatial identification. Maps are separate sheets; atlases are bound volumes of maps. The four types of maps include locational (identification, determining distances, boundaries, roads, with colours and lines), morphological (geology, relief, soil), thematic (subjects such as the *Atlas of the Bible* or statistical, such as the *Ontario Economic Atlas*), and topographic (surveys, surface of the land, rivers, roads, vegetation, such as the *Canada Land Inventory*). With atlases, "bigger is better": the larger the plate, the larger the scale or detail. The more extensive the index, the more depth. The most respected is the *Times' Comprehensive Atlas of the World,* with multiple maps for several countries (125 double-paged, eight-colour maps by Bartholomew of Edinburgh, with fourteen different typefaces and 113 symbols for lighthouses, reefs, glaciers, salt flats, pipelines, cemeteries, race tracks, tunnels, bridges, churches [four kinds], and so forth). It has a quarter-million entries in the index-gazetteer. Other excellent world atlases that are useful for vernacular names include the German *Der Grosse*

Bertelsmann Weltatlas, the Russian *Atlas Mira,* the French *Atlas International Larousse Politique et Economique,* and the Italian *Atlante Internationale.* National atlases for specific countries offer more detailed, larger-scale maps covering climate, history, flora, and fauna. The *National Atlas of Canada* has over 300 maps, some in sixteen colours, showing agriculture, population, fisheries, forestry, pipelines, metals, and transportation routes, with excellent explanatory notes and cited sources. The *Canada Gazetteer Atlas* has about fifty-five colour double-paged maps showing many roads, military establishments, railways, transmission lines, churches, schools, airports, lighthouses, trailer courts, and parks. Its gazetteer-index covers the place names of all locations with more than fifty residents. More maps can be located through the *Map Sources Directory,* which has names and addresses for commercial map publishers, government agencies, tourist bureaus, and municipal organizations. Researchers are aware that maps can be difficult to interpret. They pay attention to the keys and legends, relief notation, vernacular names, scales, index, and recency.

(2) *Gazetteers* identify and briefly describe places and physical features such as towns, rivers, and mountains. They provide geographic information in a dictionary arrangement, along with some basic economic and political facts. There are pronunciations, cross-references from variant spellings, and some statistics. Most common data can be found in encyclopedias, but if researchers need pronunciation they might want to look at *Webster's New Geographical Dictionary* with its 50,000 entries, brief identifications, spellings, and pronunciations. It has valuable special lists such as names of the Alp ranges, rivers of the world, canals, waterfalls, dams, parks, volcanoes, capes, and bays. *Geo-Data: the world almanac gazetteer* also gives demographic information on countries, while the *Macmillan Book of Canadian Place Names* covers 2,500 urban areas, lakes, rivers, mountains, and so forth, describing how they got their names.

(3) *Guidebooks* are for longer descriptions from the traveller's point of view. Beyond basic geographic data there is handbook-type information about museums, sights, hotels, and restaurants. Leading guidebook producers are Michelin, with the "green guides," Fodor, and Fielding. More can be found through *The Travel Book,* an annotated guide to the travel guides. Other sources for travel information include the Alliance of Canadian Travel Associations

(ACTA) in Ottawa, specialized bookstores, tourist boards (listed in the white pages by country), national clubs like TRANZAC (Australia-New Zealand), travel clubs found through community centres, travel magazines (indexed in the *Travel and Tourism Index*), and local travel agents.

In addition, current events sources include such publications as *Background Notes* from the U.S. Department of State, *Area Handbooks and Country Studies* from the U.S. Army, *Deadline Data on World Affairs*, plus country sheets from the various world trade centres (see the next chapter), online versions of *BBC Summary of World Broadcasts*, *EURNOR*, *World Information*, *Africa News*, *Mideast File*, *Latin American Newsletter*, and *Current Digest of the Soviet Press*. All of these, in addition to foreign news services such as Agence France Presse and Xinhua (China), can provide a monitor to the world situation. But researchers do need to keep an eye on agenda setting and bias in the treatment of coverage here.

Current Events

One of the greatest problems in information work is currency, but as time goes by the problem is being resolved. The electronic newspaper and the electronic encyclopedia as computer databases mean that information could be no more than hours old. The most time-consuming and futile type of information search is plowing through newspapers and magazines for unindexed recent events. Whatever data exist should always be updated. A typical strategy for the academic professor, just before delivering a lecture or speech, would be to check his thesaurus terms in the online systems to see what is "new." A similar strategy for the businessman, just before making a presentation to colleagues or to a client, would be to check the online systems. A researcher, just before handing in a story or report, would also do a check of the news databases for recency.

It is always wise to check copyright dates of articles and books, for then an update need only go back to include that year. Researchers are aware that articles take months and books take years to be written, published, and disseminated. Some information, of course, appears only at regularly scheduled intervals, such as the census (after years ending in "6" and "1" in Canada, and "0" in the United

States) or Olympic records and American presidential elections every four years.

In a time frame for indexed information about today and yesterday, there are the online news databases: well over 100 in North America, accessible through Knight-Ridder's *DIALOG*, its own *VU/TEXT, NEXIS, Datatimes,* and *Infomart* in Canada, as well as individual papers such as *InfoGlobe, Wall Street Journal, New York Times, Washington Post,* plus the various news services of UPI, AP, CP, and those in foreign languages.

Broadcast radio and television, while certainly current, are not yet indexed for daily retrievability. *Burrelle's Broadcast Database* (for U.S. commercial networks and NPR) has a two-day delay. Older transcripts to the *MacNeil-Lehrer News Hour* are available from *NEXIS,* while PBS's *Wall Street Week* transcripts come from the Dow-Jones News/Retrieval Service. *CBS News* is indexed by Vanderbilt University in Tennessee. *The BBC News* is available through the *BBC World Reporter* database. For the moment, there is no retrospective access to national news broadcasts in an online mode in Canada. Transcripts can be requested, but these take time. One strategy is to use *Burrelle's* to get at NPR, which rebroadcasts some CBC radio documentaries; such Canadian items, then, become available only through a circuitous route of trans-border data flow.

Daily business newsletters and daily reports of research-in-progress, as well as internal communications on bulletin boards and networks, attempt to keep up with daily affairs. All of these can be faxed and/or be online. Certainly, if currency is needed, then online news databases should be accessed (the additional advantage is that this can be done without leaving the home or office).

For indexed information of the past two weeks, quick current data can be found online with the *New York Times Information Service, NEXIS,* the Sunday editions of newspapers with their world roundups, newsmagazines, and various news summary services. All of these save time by sorting through the material and setting their own news judgement of what is important, separating the wheat from the chaff. Some typical services include the news digests of *Keesings' Contemporary Archives,* 1931-, *Facts on File,* 1940-, *Canadian News Facts,* 1967-, *Editorials on File,* 1970-, and *Editorial Research Reports,* 1924-. Most of these are online. And since today's news is tomorrow's history, one can search these news summaries back to their beginnings to get a view of contemporary history.

Both these summaries and "newspapers of record" such as the *New York Times* or the *Globe and Mail* may contain texts of speeches, treaties, and other important documents. By doing a content analysis, one can sift through the news and arrive at trends of present or past opinions. One word of caution: do not confuse the date of reportage with the date of the event. Check out all the antecedents ("yesterday," "three days ago") in the text and cross-verify with another paper if possible.

There are over 1,000 local newspaper indexes in North America, produced by the newspapers, libraries, or commercial firms. Many of them are historical, but all of them cover a variety of subject matters, from local births and deaths to international catastrophes. Important indexes for checking data are the *Times of London Index*, 1790-, *New York Times Index*, 1851-, *Christian Science Monitor Index*, *Wall Street Journal Index*, *Washington Post Index*, *Canadian News Index*, *InfoGlobe*, *Infomart* (the latter covering *Toronto Star* and the Southam newspapers). The online indexes only go back to just before 1980, so it is good to know which library has the printed indexes for the pre-1980 period.

Other current information of the previous year can be derived from magazine articles, newsletters, and conference proceedings. Articles tend to be short and specific, and the better ones are abstracted in another information tool. Academics and librarians automatically think that a publication that is indexed is more important than an unindexed publication. Hence, a good guide to the quality of data in a magazine would be the fact that it was indexed. The smell of money has created duplication of indexes, which is unfortunate. Magazine indexes all look the same, using the same principles of retrieval. Their only variance is whether they cover Canadian or American magazines – or both. Here are the top ones:

1. *Reader's Guide to Periodical Literature* (1900-) covers about 250 American magazines.
2. *The Magazine Index* (1959-) covers about 500 American magazines and is available on compact disc for the period from 1959 to the present.

3. *Canadian Periodical Index* (1924-) covers about 200 Canadian magazines.
4. *Canadian Magazine Index* (1985-) covers about 100 Canadian magazines, plus twenty top American magazines. It is also part of *CBCA*.
5. *Canadian Business Index* (1975-) and *Canadian News Index* (1977-) are available separately in print or together online as *Canadian Business and Current Affairs (CBCA)*.

All of these indexes are searchable by computer from home or are available in print at most public and academic libraries. As well, some are available as compact discs. Researchers should be aware that online availability only became general around 1980. There are hundreds of specialist indexes for academic and scholarly materials, for research, for business and technology. All of these are relatively current within their respective subject fields, and most are available online. Some examples of the use of news databases include the following.

– A researcher in California sought *Philadelphia Inquirer* stories on coverage of chemical spills in New Jersey.
– Reporters at the *Globe and Mail* used their library's search services to check a quotation by a prominent politician, to discover the amount of money paid by an insurance company on a widely covered incident, and to find articles about the potash industry.
– The Canadian bureau chief of the *Los Angeles Times,* based in Toronto, used *InfoGlobe, Infomart,* and his paper's own database to bring the world into his office.
– Investigative reporters in Seattle, looking at a local crime figure, fished for stories that had been published in communities throughout the United States.
– An English-language researcher wanted to sense the pulse of French Canada on a series of issues; she used the *Québec-Actualité* database for quick retrieval.

Some other important databases for doing current research include *ABI/INFORM* (for business), *PAIS International* (public affairs), *Congressional Information Service* (American federal government documents), *Trade and Industry ASAP Index* (texts of articles),

Marquis PRO-FILE (biographical texts about professionals, derived from the *Who's Who* print series), *McGraw-Hill News* (texts), *Reuters* (texts), *DISCLOSURE* (business data texts), *FINDEX Reports* (market texts), and *Magazine ASAP Index* (texts of articles). Others can be located through the *Database of Databases.*

For information from the past year or so, such as annually released figures, sports achievements, and election results, a broad range of annually printed tools exists, including *Guinness Book of Records, Awards, Honors and Prizes* (for North America), and *Deadline Data on World Affairs.* These sources are usually divided into either almanacs/yearbooks or annual reviews.

The almanacs/yearbooks cover miscellaneous information (names and addresses, tables of nutrition, lists, political events, simple geographical and economic information, coloured maps, survey articles, chronologies of past years, legal holidays, perpetual calendars), with annual statistics and sports records in tabular form. Leading ones include the British *Whitaker's Almanack,* the American *World Almanac and Book of Facts* and *Information Please Almanac,* and the *Canadian Global Almanac.* Most libraries keep previous editions of these, so history becomes more searchable. Other yearbooks, which often cover more than one year, include *Statesman's Yearbook* and *Europa Yearbook* (both good for politics and economics), *Quick Canadian Facts, Commonwealth Yearbook,* and *Political Handbook of the World.* Usually, the date on the cover is the year for current usage, not the year of coverage.

Annual reviews cover only the year listed in the title. Typical reviews include encyclopedia yearbooks such as *Britannica World Data Annual, Americana Annual,* and *World Book Year Book*; all of these cover the events of the previous calendar year in a brief, concise style, alphabetically arranged. These are good for noting trends, for lists (such as archeological finds in any one year), for summaries of changes in politics, science, entertainment, for statistics, for chronologies, for illustrations from that year, and for obituaries of famous people, usually listed and described under "O" (Obituaries), "D" (Deaths), "N" (Necrology), or set off separately at the end of the review. Other annual reviews include *Yearbook of the United Nations, Annual Register; a record of world events* (which has been publishing since 1758), *Canadian Annual Review of Politics and Public Affairs,* and specialized subject materials, mostly in the sciences, with titles that begin "Annual Review of," "Progress in," "Year's Work in," "Yearbook of," "Advances in." Over a period of time, these reviews are fascinating documents through which to do historical or background research.

Other materials dealing with "currency" can be found listed in the sections below on reviews and statistics.

Reviews and Product Evaluations

The question of how things work intrigues most people, but often they are too busy to see for themselves what the world is up to. "Reviews" or "product evaluations" are notes within a critical context: they summarize, they evaluate, they give comparative data, they note strengths and weaknesses, and they sometimes indicate future needs. Reading reviews will always save people money and time; both can be wasted if the product is unappealing or not as advertised when tried. Reviews of films may indicate whether or not one will like the movie, based on a knowledge of reviewer preferences; the same is true for any other product. Self-proclaimed experts have their own agendas, but as long as these are taken into account, one can be guided by the expert's tastes. A restaurant reviewer may be severe on supercilious service but tolerant of hot seasonings. A wine reviewer may appreciate heavily oaked white wines or massive red wines and pooh-pooh fresh and fruity wines. Once the bias is known, then the critique can be used in the context of one's own preferences.

For the researcher, product evaluations are a godsend. Because of evaluations, opinions, and summaries, much work may have already been done for the researcher. It then becomes mostly a case of assimilation and verification. For instance, it should be no problem to shoot the name of a film or of a travelling art exhibit through news databases and retrieve scores of reviews. And if the researcher deals with consumerism and consumer advocacy, then what better way to measure acceptance or rejection then by comparing reviews?

As a parameter, the word "review" or another thesaurus term can be shot through the system and tagged to the name of the product; depending on what is retrieved, the search can be modified. Bear in mind that the retrieval of product evaluations was limited before computer access began around 1980, since indexing was restricted to such items as books, records, films. Now, however, products are also covered in annual reviews. Many of these annuals, noted above, will comment on or review new products as part of trends or developments. Here are some types.

Books seem to be the best-organized product evaluation. Once the researcher has a book title, he or she may wish to check on the reliability of its data. Reviews by experts give an indication of the value of a book's contribution to knowledge, and at the same time the reviews usually summarize. So it is possible to find information through the review without actually having to read or even to see the book. There are three major categories of tools for finding book reviews – indexes and abstracts limited to book reviews, specialized indexes and abstracts, and general indexes – each with different internal arrangements. Note, too, that book reviews are often indexed separately from the main index, so be sure to read the prefatory material in each tool.

Some indexes and abstracts are concerned only with book reviews, such as *Book Review Digest, Book Review Index, Canadian Book Review Annual,* and the *Masterplots* series. Specialized subject indexes and abstracts that list book reviews include *Alternative Press Index, Art Index, Film Literature Index, Humanities Index, Music Index, Social Sciences Index, Index to Canadian Legal Periodical Literature, Business Periodicals Index, Canadian Business Index, Biological and Agricultural Index, Psychological Abstracts, Economic Titles and Abstracts, Historical Abstracts, Sociological Abstracts, Canadian Educational Index,* and *Applied Science and Technology Index.* General indexes, such as *Canadian News Index, Canadian Magazine Index, Canadian Periodical Index, Essay and General Literature Index, New York Times Index, Reader's Guide to Periodical Literature, Magazine Index,* and *General Science Index,* also include book reviews. Computer availability of the review's text will vary from database to database, but certainly there will be enough indexed citations to seek out.

Drama reviews from Broadway can be found through the *New York Times Index* and the *New York Theater Critics' Reviews,* which covers newspapers, magazines, and broadcasts in the New York area. Drama elsewhere can be located through news databases, such as the London *Times,* magazine indexes for drama magazines, and scholarly indexes for specialist reviews.

Film reviews can be found through the news and magazine databases, as well as in *Magill's Survey of the Cinema, Film Review Annual,* and *Film Review Index,* plus any number of popular book listings – if all that is wanted is a year, a director, or a cast list. The *New York Times* is particularly good for listing credits. The *International Motion Picture Almanac* gives industry reviews as well.

Other reviews and product evaluations can be found in the following indexes and other sources:

- *Records and compact discs*: news and magazine databases, plus *Index to Record Reviews* (for classical music), *Annual Index to Popular Music Record Reviews,* and *Music Index.*
- *Music*: general indexes and *Music Index.*
- *Dance*: general indexes and *Dance Index.*
- *Sports*: general indexes and *Sports and Recreation Index.*
- *Art exhibits*: general indexes, plus *Art Index* and *World Painting Index.*
- *Television*: news databases, communications indexes, and the *International Television Almanac* with its industry reviews.
- *Durables*: *Consumers Index* (covers 126 periodicals) and *Product Evaluations* (covers 400 periodicals) are quarterly indexes to reviews, including the well-known *Consumer Reports.* Leading durables include appliances, kitchen equipment, home cleaning items, audio and video equipment, business office equipment, children's equipment, computer equipment, home heating, motor vehicles, sporting goods, photography. Useful specific indexes include *Buyers Laboratory Test Reports, Microcomputer Index,* and *Auto Index,* plus, of course, most product books with the word "guide" in their title.
- *Restaurants*: newspaper and magazine indexes.
- *Wine*: news and magazine indexes plus *Wine Index* database.
- *Food*: general indexes plus *Recipe Index.*
- *Nutrition*: general indexes plus *Nutrition Abstracts* and other medical sources.
- *Travel*: general indexes and *Travel and Tourism Index.*

- *Crafts and Fashion*: general indexes plus *Craft Index* and *Hobby Index*.

Researchers should keep in mind that product evaluation is a useful parameter even if they do not need an evaluation: lots of other useful data are here, such as dates, names, addresses, prices, opinions, story ideas, consumer follow-up, and so forth.

Multidisciplinary Topics

This parameter simply serves as a reminder that much data can be found *outside* a known discrete subject field. The researcher must cast his net widely. Libraries do a poor job of covering topics that can be labelled "cross-disciplinary," "interdisciplinary," and "alternative." Materials and subject fields here fall through the cracks of the classification and subject heading schemes, mostly because the search terms are too new or because the subject matter cannot be handled in the traditional manner of hierarchical searches. In some cases, the researcher must travel through a half-dozen or more subject areas simply to pull together the prime research materials. For instance, material needed on "international trade" covers geography, economics, and politics. The "drug trade" also involves medicine, law and crime, and perhaps even foreign aid. "Coping skills" is another nebulous area, dealing with family, aging, children, free time, home-job relationships, and money management.

Computers are the most effective approach here. Their thesaurus system means that the researcher can simply shoot a phrase through the entire system and see what comes up. For example, searching for material linking crime to disasters (such as "looting"), the researcher might want to search all relevant current event sources as well as such online databases as *National Criminal Justice Reference Service, Criminal Justice Periodicals Index, Psychological Abstracts, Sociological Abstracts, GEO-REF, GEO-ARCHIVE,* and *Meteorological and Geoastrophysical Abstracts.*

For material on "gentrification" (the displacement of the urban poor from older neighbourhoods that are being renovated), researchers will need to find resource tools, experts, and documents in the fields of economics, architecture, insurance, banking, housing, city planning, demographics, race relations, urban affairs, construction industry, and tax policy. For material on "child abuse," typical data to be found include aspects of the law, such as complaints and arrests and occurrences. The variety of subject fields include sociology, anthropology, social work, family counselling, law, criminology, and psychology. There is even a specific resource tool, *Child Abuse Abstracts*. Who is to be interviewed over what subjects will be determined by what the researcher learns. There is a fair amount of cross-referencing here, with work across several disciplines.

Guides and handbooks are extremely useful. Esther Stineman's *Women's Studies* pulls together hundreds of disparate sources, while the *Handbook of American Popular Culture* (in three volumes) covers over sixty areas of multidisciplinary work, such as popular music and mystery novels. Yearbooks and annuals present a record of current developments in multidisciplinary areas, often with compilations of statistics. These sources are useful for indicating trends. The *Progressive Periodicals Directory* details some 600 magazines and newsletters in categories such as civil rights, culture, environment, labour, and peace. *Bibliographic Index* will pick up minute, out-of-the-way, additional sources for reading, usually derived from magazine articles.

Large, sprawling terms that have been around for some time but that show few signs of being tidy in the classification schemes of knowledge include "urban affairs," "Third World," and "alternate lifestyles." "Energy and the environment" is another large multidisciplinary term. Here, the researcher must be made aware of the close relationship between the various energy technologies, their environmental impact, and their use of natural resources (renewable and non-renewable). The researcher needs to be aware of the policy and legislative decisions at the local, regional, provincial, national, and international levels that will have a direct impact on energy-related environmental questions. Through all this, the researcher becomes aware of uneven regional impacts. Thus, for energy-related environmental issues, she or he needs to check specialized subject databases and specialized format databases. Some examples of the subject databases are: atmospheric and climatological sciences, business and industry, electric power, land-related resources, legislation and government policy, nuclear power, oil and gas, toxicology, transportation, and water resources. Examples of the format databases include: patents, procurement and contracts for government, statistics, government documents, and newspapers.

And, after all this, there are still more multidisciplinary sub-parameters to impose. For instance, looking into the catchword "Temagami" (the locale of a bitter controversy between Native peoples, environmentalists, the logging industry, and politicians in northern Ontario) demands an analysis of several different topics, with different approaches. Several layers of government are involved (the federal Department of the Environment, Energy Mines and Resources, Indian and Northern Affairs Canada, Supreme Court of Canada, Ontario Ministry of the Environment, Minister of Natural Resources with responsibility for Native Affairs, Ministry of Northern Development, opposition political parties, and local municipalities), as well as the intergovernmental Indian Commission of Ontario, associations (Native Council of Canada, Union of Ontario Indians, Native Canadian Centre of Toronto, Ontario Forestry Association, Ontario Forest Industries Association, Canadian Nature Federation, Conservation Council of Ontario, and Federation of Ontario Naturalists), plus several specific *ad hoc* groupings. Failure to contact any of these areas after searching for background details must be seen as a major defect in the search strategy.

Statistics

If one can count it, then one can measure it: *how many* is a valid parameter. Statistics are a prominent feature of most yearbooks and annual reviews. In fact, many of these contain little more than statistics. Statistics are also buried in articles, but not indexed as statistics. Thus, when one looks for statistics, one should be sure to check all the current event sources, for the articles from newspapers and magazines are bound to have some statistics.

Statistics are often collected from non-governmental bodies, such as universities and industries. The differences between these and governmental bodies are slight; there is a greater difference between authoritative and non-authoritative statistics. It all depends largely on who is responsible for issuing the statistics. For instance, the

Statesman's Yearbook (privately published) is more reliable than statistical yearbooks from certain Third World countries.

Obviously, very recent figures are usually sought but most sources are two to three years out of date. Published statistics can never be up to date since they must first be collected, sorted, manipulated, and then published. Official sources in the government will issue "interim" figures on a weekly or daily basis, but researchers need to be prepared to make phone calls to get the latest figures and estimates from experts.

Sometimes statistics that are located are not in exactly the form that a researcher needs. So one should be prepared either to look further or to recalculate the figures. This is usually more tedious than it is difficult, and one should always carry a pocket calculator. Correct terms should be known so that interpretations and recalculations make sense: know about base numbers, ratios, percentages and percentage points, and types of averages (median, mean, mode). Watch out also for varying degrees of coverage over a variety of sources. This means reading the footnotes, the headnotes, the prefaces, and any other caveats that explain the time frame, the geography spread, and the definitions used.

Some statistics are seasonally adjusted: seasonality affects different economic activities to varying degrees. This must either be explained or factored into any use of the statistics. Also suspicious are dressed statistics (with pictures, cartoons, colours), often seen in newspapers because they have a stronger impact on the reader. With a bar graph, line chart, or pie graph even the average reader can see how the figures differ from each other. If the researcher does not understand some figures, then he should keep asking questions about them. Remember: statistics, like documents, do not lie – people do. Researchers need to be careful to verify and cross-check all statistical information used and should not adjust or manipulate statistics ("fudge the figures") to fit a report.

Here's one example of this fudging. A recent report from the Social Planning Council of Metro Toronto dealing with the homeless suggested that 8,000 to 10,000 persons were without a home in Toronto. Not so, said the United Way: make it 34,000! Where do these numbers come from? Two thousand live in hostels, 2,000 sleep on the streets, and 4,000 to 6,000 are casual transients. To this number, the United Way has added 24,000 people who are "without a permanent address" (e.g., families sharing homes with others, siblings living together because of a lack of separate accommodation). The Planning Council is not a political body, so it chose the lower, more acceptable figure; the United Way, in its drive to collect more money (virtually none of which would go to the extra 24,000 who had roofs over their heads), sent out the higher figure with its information kits to schools. A reporter caught the discrepancy and got a story out of it. The value of any statistical data is limited by the quality of the raw data collected. The only way to estimate the accuracy of raw inputs is to cross-check against other independent data. The right approach to all statistical data is to regard figures as estimates rather than measures.

Researchers who use statistics a lot need to understand the quantitative methods employed by social scientists. They use computers to count and measure, along with practical statistical tools such as factor analysis, multiple regression analysis, deviation and bias, interval and ratio measurements, probability, social and economic indicators, computer modelling and econometric analysis, and other quantitative methods. Errors usually creep in when researchers are careless: transposing numbers, dropping lines, keyboarding improperly, sampling inadequately, making inappropriate comparisons, miscounting, lacking logic in writing style, failing to understand statistical jargon.

Statistics are needed to colour or justify almost any report. Quantifying statements are, simply put, more credible: many people are interested in the number of unemployed in British Columbia, how much television young adults watch, and the level the Consumer Price Index (compared to last summer, last year, and last decade). There are whole resource tools devoted to statistics.

To move into the unknown, try *Statistics Sources* (Gale Research Publications). This is a subject guide to data on industry, business, and social issues for most countries. Around 12,000 subjects are covered (wages, health, iron and steel, helium, leather, herring, cocoa, housing, corn, hepatitis, beef) through a selection of government and non-government sources for statistical publications. Other statistics tools are found in complementary Gale books (*Statistics – America, Statistics – Africa, Statistics – Asia and Australia, Statistics – Europe*), although the social and economic statistics are designed to facilitate market research.

Statistical indexes (all monthly, all online) include *Canadian Statistics Index* (to StatsCan materials and to magazine articles), *American Statistical Index* (to federal and state official statistics), *Statistical Reference Index* (to articles and to non-governmental sources in the United States), and *Index to International Statistics* (to over forty United Nations agencies and international organizations). All of these indexed statistical documents are available on microfiche, usually from the vendor of the index.

Computerized online searching for statistical information can be useful if the strategy is carefully worked out. One needs to decide on what (subject matter), when (as a period of time), and where (in what place). Many statistical databases are online, including the economic time series *CANSIM* from Statistics Canada, and there are also many textual databases with figures buried in articles and documents.

Books often have statistics. These will not be up to date, but they may be the latest available. Almanacs contain charts and figures, some with sources in the footnotes that will lead to other resources. Specific professional and trade associations have statistical reports (some of these are noted in *Statistics Sources*), while Ph.D. dissertations are frequently filled with statistical information. Books of trivia will have data and rankings, such as *The People's Almanac* and *The World Book of Odds*.

Statistical yearbooks for countries often provide specific information not always available in more general resources. For Canada, there are *Historical Statistics of Canada, 1867-1980, Canada Yearbook, Canadian Statistical Review,* the census, *Ontario Statistics,* and *Annuaire du Québec.* For the United States, there are *Historical Statistics of the United States Colonial Times to 1970, Statistical Abstract of the United States, Economic Indicators, Survey of Current Business,* and *Business Statistics.* For Great Britain, there are *British Historical Statistics, Annual Abstract of Statistics,* and *Monthly Digest of Statistics.* On an international basis, there are *European Historical Statistics, 1750-1975, International Historical Statistics – Africa and Asia, Statistical Yearbook of the United Nations, Monthly Bulletin of Statistics* [UN], *Demographic Yearbook of the United Nations, Yearbook of International Trade Statistics,* and *Unesco Statistical Yearbook. Statistical Yearbook of the United Nations,* for example, would be used to find out how much tea is grown in China or coffee in Brazil, how many television sets are made in Japan, how much sugar the Nepalese eat, livestock figures, employment, exchange rates, gold reserves, and production of paper, tobacco, books, or tractors.

A quick checklist for finding statistics is:

- determine geographic area, time, and subject;
- begin with the *Canada Yearbook,* if the topic is Canadian;
- search the *Canadian Statistics Index,* if the topic is Canadian;
- search information centres under subject terms and the subdivision "statistics";
- for really obscure data, check online databases;
- read all the footnotes and explanatory annexes.

Every major country does a census at the national level, a sort of inventory on one particular day. But census materials cover much more than just people. Under "population" one can find distribution by race, age, sex, household size, education, national origin, labour force status, marital history, occupational status, religion. Under "housing" one can find information on structures, vacancies, plumbing facilities, rooms, rents, telephones, mortgage status, and air conditioning. Under "agriculture" are farms, acreage, crops, produce, sales, land use, livestock, market value of land and buildings, use of fertilizers and pesticides. Under "construction," information covers employment, number of companies, payments for materials, machinery, equipment. Under "retail trade" there are sole proprietorships and partnerships, payrolls, sales by kinds of businesses. Under "wholesale trade" can be found sales, payroll, operating expenses, inventories, kinds of business. Under "service industries" there are payroll receipts and number of sole proprietorships and partnerships. Under "manufactures" and "mineral industries" are given the quantity and value of products shipped and materials consumed, capital expenditures, assets, rent, inventories, employment, payroll, hours worked, number of companies.

Statistics Canada is responsible for the Canadian census. On behalf of the federal government, StatsCan publishes a broad range of materials on the primary industries, transportation, communications and utilities, labour, education, culture, and health. All of it is indexed by both StatsCan and the *Canadian Statistics Index.* As well, StatsCan has many expert statisticians available either to supply needed figures or to give directions on how to get the data. These experts are found through *Data Users Directory: who to dial at Statistics Canada.* Their CD-ROM index *STATSCAN: Reference Disc* database has about 3,000 titles, including catalogues, yearbooks, and conference proceedings, a terminology reference list, and a phone directory, as well as data about *CANSIM* (Canadian Socio-economic Information Management System), which is StatsCan's number-crunching databank of economic time series. The heaviest users of *CANSIM* are businesses seeking market research. They also use Reuters Canada Holdings, the world's largest vendor of online statistical tables, such as *CHRONOS,* which is European macroeconomic statistics; *Consumer and Producer Price Index,* from the U.S. Bureau of Labor; and *International Financial Statistics,* produced by the International Monetary Fund. The Reuters tables can be accessed directly or through information brokers, both for a fee.

Many of the StatsCan printed publications are available at public and academic libraries. However, StatsCan does have regional Advisory Services offices, which also house libraries. These can be consulted for free, but research time is fee-based. These services are invaluable because they have three layers of data (print, microfiche, and computer), which are progressively more dense, with more breakdowns. Thus, a printed table may indicate quantities of goods by province, while the microfiche can break these data down to counties or regions and the online version can break down to municipalities or postal codes. Herein lies the business use for market research. And this helps to pay StatsCan's bills. Its Advisory Services provide great help to researchers. Besides those regional offices, there are also phone lines to provide assistance with regard to the most recent information on the consumer price index, the labour force survey, and demographics.

Other big producers of statistics at the national level include the departments of Employment and Immigration and of Labour, as well as the Central Mortgage and Housing Corporation.

Here are some typical examples of the research areas of statistics sources.

(1) *Transportation statistics.* Any book will cite Statistics Canada as a source, but associations (*Directory of Associations in Canada*) and their information centres also have data. Business libraries have directories and books on transportation, goods distribution, and warehousing, providing data on tariffs, handling charges, and port

and warehouse facilities. Associations publish their own reports and statistics, verifiable through StatsCan's publications, such as *Aviation Statistics Centre Service Bulletin*, *Air Carrier Traffic at Canadian Airports*, *Air Passenger Origin and Destination (Domestic and Foreign)*, *Railway Carloadings*, *Railway Operating Statistics*, *Railway Freight Traffic*, *Shipping in Canada*, *Trucking in Canada*, *Canadian Travel Survey*, *Tourism and Recreation*). Resources for warehousing facilities, dockage, wharfage, port charges, cargo handling rates, and the like include *Canadian Highway Carrier's Guide*, *Chilton's Distribution for Traffic and Transportation Decision Makers*, *Ship by Truck*, *Guide to Public Warehouses and Distribution Centres*, *Canadian Transportation and Distribution Management*, *Containerization International Yearbook*, *Greenwood's Guide to Great Lakes Shipping*, *Canadian Ports and Seaway Directory*, *Ports Dues Charges and Accommodations*. If the project concerns an urban area, such as Toronto, then sources from government agencies, or consultants, include *Ontario Exit Survey: Metropolitan Toronto*, *Ontario Travel Survey*, *Visitor Survey Annual Summary* (from the Metro Toronto Convention and Visitors Association), *Canadian Lodging Industry*, *Food Service and Hospitality Fact File*, and the *St. Lawrence Seaway Traffic Report*. Associations in this area include the Toronto Harbour Commission, the World Trade Centre, the Ontario Trading Association, and the Canadian Warehousing Association; agencies include Ontario Ministry of Tourism and Recreation, Ontario Ministry of Transportation and Communications, Metro Toronto Convention and Visitors Association, and the St. Lawrence Seaway Authority.

Occasionally, a researcher will find that two studies purporting to measure the same variable show different results because they used different methodologies, samples, or definitions. Thus, percentage occupation of hotels will vary, as will tonnage at Ontario ports, due to different physical definitions or the use of different source documents. Definitions are usually pointed out in footnotes, but source documents must be correlated for verification.

(2) *Vital statistics.* These are numbers related to life – births, deaths, marriages, divorces – in a given period of time and particular place. They can be found in almanacs and yearbooks such as *Historical Statistics of Canada*, *Canada Yearbook*, *Ontario Statistics*, and *Demographic Yearbook of the United Nations* (with its special tables on abortions, fetal deaths, and others). The StatsCan print series

includes *Quarterly Demographic Statistics, Marriages and Divorces, Births and Deaths, Causes of Deaths by Census Division,* and *Life Tables (Canada and the Provinces).* This information is also available through StatsCan's online *CANSIM.* The World Health Organization publishes *World Health Statistics Annual,* with birth and death rates, infant death rates, and infectious diseases. *International Statistics Yearbook on Large Towns* has vital statistics for major cities of the world. Statistical rates are extremely useful when researching social topics, such as teenage suicides, the drinking habits of native people, WASP divorces in inner cities, and visible minorities. Those who are responsible for improving the health of a population use vital statistics to assess that population's current state of health. Each province maintains a vital statistics office where one can get figures and even information on individuals (such as whether or not someone has changed his name, had children, married, died, or was ever born in that province). Such data are not always easy to obtain unless they are needed for a court case, for one's own family (e.g., a death certificate), or for personal reasons, such as looking into a lover's marital status. Access is quirky: much can be privately obtained, other data can be given out for a school project, while some types of information will be given a verbal confirmation only, such as answering a query about whether or not someone is married by responding "yes" or "no" and not revealing any specifics.

(3) *Crime statistics.* Canadian criminal statistics can be obtained from Statistics Canada. The annual *Crime and Traffic Enforcement Statistics* gives all crimes reported by Canada's various police forces, the conviction rate, provincial comparisons, crime rates, trends, and breakdowns of crime categories: crimes of violence, which include murder, attempted murder, manslaughter, sexual assault, wounding, assaults, and robbery; property crimes, which include breaking and entering, motor vehicle theft, theft under and over $200, possession of stolen goods, and frauds; Criminal Code violations such as prostitution, gambling, offensive weapons, arson, bail violations, counterfeiting, indecent acts, kidnapping, trespassing; drug-related offences; and violations of provincial statutes, such as liquor legislation and municipal by-laws. More specific publications are available for statistics on homicide, car theft, and young offenders. The annual *Justice Statistics Ontario* provides greater local detail and

comparisons between districts, towns, and cities in Ontario. Each province produces a similar annual.

Located in Ottawa as a division of Statistics Canada, the Canadian Centre for Justice Statistics provides governments with crime figures. Each police force in the country supplies the CCJS with monthly crime statistics under the Uniform Crime Reporting System. This compulsory reporting, from over 600 Canadian communities, is sorted nationally, provincially, and municipally, and also by the age and sex of the perpetrator. Charts show "occurrences" (reported crimes), "clearances" (occurrences that result in charges), and "occurrences not cleared." Major police forces release their own annual reports, which contain basically the same statistics (yet the 1987 CCJS reported 207,647 crimes in Metro Toronto while the Metro Toronto police reported 234,693 in the 1987 survey). The local reports do more comparative analysis in an attempt to prove how good they are or how much more staff they need. When reports are released, researchers can pick up on trends to evaluate the effectiveness of the police force. Rigorous analysis of the statistics issued by the police and by politicians is useful in exploring such questions as the following. Is Hull the crime capital of Quebec? Is drug trafficking a $10-billion-a-year business? Should parolees be blamed for rising crime? Why do more bank robberies occur in Montreal every year than in the rest of the country put together? Do the police honestly report all the charges, or do they fudge the statistics at certain times of the year in order to deflate (or inflate) figures? And where does the geographic coverage differ? (For example, Statistics Canada now includes Peel Region as part of Metropolitan Toronto, but the Metro Toronto police force does not.)

Crime statistics can be accessed online through articles in the *QL Systems* and *Canadian Business and Current Affairs* databases. These show how writers have interpreted the statistics. Other statistics are available through the local police forces, record bureaus, the provincial police forces for Ontario and Quebec, the RCMP, the Centre for Criminology Library at the University of Toronto (which also has a wide range of original research papers), the various provincial correctional services libraries, and the libraries of the provincial attorneys-general.

Polls and Surveys

Polls and surveys are statistics of another kind. Most are entirely speculative, since they deal with attitudes, opinions, behaviour, future intentions, "what ifs," and a sampling basis imposed on a national stream. As a parameter, they provide the "public opinion" aspect to any searchable topic. Surveys, sampling, and polls usually mean the same thing; there are three major categories.

(1) *Public polls* are conducted by such private polling firms as Gallup and Harris and by media organizations such as CBC/*Globe and Mail,* CBS/*New York Times,* ABC/*Washington Post.* Each week the Canadian Institute of Public Opinion (Gallup) surveys the opinions in a sample of 1,000 Canadians. It uses statistical inference, estimating the attributes of an entire population from one sample. Many questions are asked and they vary from poll to poll, but the same questions are asked over a period of years, allowing the evolution of public opinion to be traced. Sampling is determined by both the quota-stratified method (characteristics of population) and the area-probability method (dividing the country into rural areas, urban areas, renters, owners, apartment dwellers, etc.). Sample size and make-up are very important for determining an outcome. Sponsorship of this kind of poll comes from the media, who subscribe to the results and present the stories. Occasionally there are omnibus polls, in which a lot of questions are asked of a wide sample on a number of issues and products. This spreads the cost around, so that a national poll can be done once for many clients. Voting intentions, dog food, toilet paper, drinking preferences, government policy: they are all in the same survey. But the attention to detail and question modification and pre-testing are not as well thought out as they are for issue- or product-related polls. Omnibus polls are merely an inexpensive shot through the public opinion system.

(2) *Political polls* are conducted by such groups as Decima Research and Angus Reid in Canada and Louis Harris in the United States. There are two types here: one is the poll conducted by a party in or out of power to determine the current public reaction to that party's policy. This is a kind of market research poll, and it is quite often conducted at the government's expense if the party is in power. These polls (about 200 a year) are usually available through the

Access to Information process, and of course each province has its own set of polls, which may be accessed through existing provincial laws. The other kind of poll is the one held during an election campaign, which assesses the popularity of the parties and the leaders running for office. Researchers have claimed that this polling strongly influences the opinions it seeks to measure. Polls can cause voters to change their minds, so they can be on the winning side, but the polls can also benefit weaker parties (the "underdog" effect) and discourage voting by many of the electorate, who feel that the results are foregone.

(3) *Market research* is conducted by such organizations as A.C. Nielsen, Decima Research, and Canadian Facts. New techniques of motivational and mass-attitude analysis are deployed at both national and local levels in determining the commercial acceptability of a new product or service, or even of a government policy. These surveys are conducted not only by conventional polling specialists but also by sociologists and social psychologists. These methods are costly, but then the rewards are great. Still, companies make mistakes, such as the Coca-Cola formula change based on inappropriate polling. In addition to telephone and in-home interviews, these firms use mall intercepts. Canadian Facts has storefront locations in four suburban Toronto shopping malls, where shoppers can be steered in to see product samples. Public relations personnel need to know what people are thinking (the consumer's behaviour) and how to marshal all that material to their clients. The biggest users of public opinion research – for marketing, promotion, and advertising campaigns related to products and programs – are business and industry, followed by government. Polls are not exact, however, and they suffer from methodological problems.

(1) *Margin of error.* Random sampling is prone to errors, depending on the size of the sample. For example, 1,500 telephone interviews with Canadians aged eighteen or over from just the ten Canadian provinces will produce accurate results within 2.5 percentage points, in nineteen cases out of twenty. If the number changes to 1,000, then accuracy drops to 3.6 percentage points in deviation, while 500 interviews produces a 4.5 percentage point spread. There can also be deviations based on age, sex, income, province, and so forth. To maintain the integrity of the sample, pollsters make at least four attempts at "callbacks."

(2) *Wording*. Questionnaires are standardized forms containing researched and supposedly well-thought-out simple questions. These questions should be worded in such a way that the respondent's answers won't be biased. Of course, if the pollster wants to elicit a certain response, then the questions can be asked in a way that would ensure a desired answer from an unsuspecting respondent. Questions need adequate designing and pre-testing for an unambiguous wording and a clear indication of alternative responses.

(3) *Question order*. Directing respondents to intended answers means having the pollster go through a series of softening-up questions. This works well for political and market research polls. Researchers are also aware that if given three choices to answer a question, then most people will select the middle choice. The pollster need only structure the choices in the appropriate manner. The best overall structure includes interesting questions first, followed by the routine, with the thought-provoking in the middle and the controversial at the end.

(4) *Lying*. Studies show that between 10 and 15 per cent of respondents lie to pollsters. They keep extremist views to themselves, they are embarrassed to admit to ignorance, they give out socially acceptable and politically correct answers, or they are pathological liars. Some are even mischievous and want to distort results. Overall, though, people just don't want to sound stupid.

In making any evaluation/assessment of polls, researchers need to ask themselves the following questions.

- Who sponsored the poll? Polls are expensive, around $50,000 for any decent study. Who paid the bills, for what polling company, and why the poll was conducted are important evaluative points. The media seem to have lined up with their exclusive pollsters. For example, *Maclean's* uses Decima, the *Globe and Mail* uses Environics, the *Toronto Star* and Southam use Angus Reid, the Montreal papers use the Quebec firms CROP and SORECOM. When the media pay for a poll, they report it and treat its results seriously.
- When was the poll taken? Polls are static snapshots, never predictors or trends.

- How were the questions worded?
- How was the survey conducted? (telephone, in-home)
- Who was interviewed? Which groups dissent from the consensus?
- How large was the sample? This is important if selective poll results were leaked or privately obtained.
- What is the margin of error?
- What was the response rate? Who are the undecided?

Polls seem to have enormous credibility among the public. According to a poll, pollsters now rank just behind television reporters (31 per cent for the latter, 29 per cent for the former) as believable on matters concerning the public mood. These categories were followed by newspaper journalists at 25 per cent, with politicians lagging far behind with just 2 per cent. Canadians respond to polls today in much the same way as they react to advertising and television: they view polls as part of the consumer society, a usually reliable source of information as well as a way for ordinary citizens to have some impact on government. An astonishing figure (again, derived from a poll) is that one-third of Canadians polled had *already* taken part in a previous market research or public opinion poll. This figure is 58 per cent in the United States!

Researchers need to remember not to overinterpret poll results. They should also look at polls comparatively, checking previous poll findings (especially if there are conflicts). Other points of evaluation include comparing results from different regions and countries, different age groups, and different sexes. There might be significant differences that need to be commented on.

More details on polling can be found in Wilhoit and Weaver's *The Newsroom Guide to Polls and Surveys,* Hoy's *Margin of Error,* Nelson's *Sultans of Sleaze,* and Statistics Canada's *Market Research Handbook.* For monographs and individual studies, look through the news indexes (*CBCA, Reader's Guide to Periodical Literature, Social Science Index*) or information centre listings under the heading "Public Opinion Polls" or the name of a subject, subdivided by "Public Opinion." There are more than 200 polling organizations in Canada. Their work is available through *Surveys, Polls and Forecast Directory; a guide to sources of statistical studies in the areas of business, social science, education, and technology* (Gale Research Publications), which gives detailed descriptions of statistical compilations produced by government agencies, associations, organizations, unions, institutions, radio and television stations, newspapers and magazines, and survey and poll organizations.

There is also *Canadian Marketing Goldbook,* listing major marketing agencies. Researchers are aware of how expensive some publications can be. Monthly reports such as *The Reid Report* sell for $5,000 each. Information needs to be paid for, but most of it is dated and older studies can come cheaply. Other indexes include *Public Affairs Information Service Bulletin,* for articles dealing with public opinion polls and surveys; *FINDEX,* a directory of market research reports, studies, and surveys; *Gallup Poll Public Opinion,* which contains American opinions since 1935; and the *Index to International Public Opinion,* with data collected from many of the major American firms.

Regular periodicals that need to be scanned include the monthly *Canadian Gallup Report,* with detailed results of recent polls; *Gallup Report International,* a bimonthly report of surveys conducted in the United States and abroad by Gallup and its world-wide affiliates; *Public Opinion Quarterly,* a scholarly journal from the American Association for Public Opinion Research, with detailed articles on survey methodology as well as analyses of poll results and a selection of recent topics that have been polled; and *World Opinion Update,* a bimonthly with results of American and foreign polls.

Finding Specific Information

The next six chapters are concerned with search strategies for access to information in key subject areas. It is not possible to cover every single topic, for that would entail a book of about 100,000 pages. Such a project would also be fairly redundant since many resources would overlap in their coverage. However, there are six fairly controversial subject areas that seem to be of concern to many researchers and journalists. These chapters present material on:

- business and finance, including industry profiles;
- government and politics, including all federal levels and agencies, boards, and commissions;

- law and the courts, including legal research and court documents;
- society and the individual, including communications and social development;
- science and technology, including the environment;
- culture and the arts, including multiculturalism.

When people need to look up information, they usually think a library would be the best and most logical place to begin. Most, however, are overwhelmed by the mass of details to be found in the library. Those who know how to use the information structure properly can locate mounds of material on practically any subject with the least amount of effort. Indeed, the real problem becomes not how to find information but how to sort through it all in some logical, systematic, and comprehensive manner.

One of the biggest errors one can make when looking up information is to search for particular types of source material, such as "a book" or "an article." It is more important to realize that resources on any topic will fall into broad categories by subject matter and parameters than it is to memorize particular titles. Once the function of each subject or parameter is understood, then it is easy to decide which broad categories are appropriate to immediate needs. At that time, then, particular titles within the appropriate broad categories can be located and used as levers into the most pertinent available data on the subject.

In addition to the general search strategies discussed in this and the previous chapter, logical step-by-step specific search strategies can be developed for each particular subject area, and they may bear little relationship to the search strategies used in other subject areas. Each field is unique. The sections that follow are geared to specific subject situations. Researchers should remember that there are three highly useful types of subject literature materials.

(1) For each and every subject, there are *reference* books: subject encyclopedias, subject indexes, subject annual reviews, and subject directories, as well as subject information centres. These books define the limits of the subject area; they serve as springboards, suggesting names of institutes, associations, and experts for additional and unique materials.

(2) For each and every subject, there are *handbooks*: reliable

sources referring to established knowledge, such as formularies in the sciences, rules for court operations, and business ethics guidelines.

(3) For each and every subject, there are *guides*: maps to a subject field, presenting overall data and sources, suggesting which tools to use, with instructions on how and when to use them, and also why to use them. Guides suggest ways of carrying out research or search strategies in a subject area, including using specific information centres, contacting professional societies, reading those journals useful to the area, and suggesting hundreds of names of contacts and consultants.

To use all of this information efficiently, researchers need an adequate working knowledge of the applicable subject-oriented research tools. They also need to be aware of different database search techniques, and that as they move into entirely different subject fields, they also move to entirely different resource tools. Never count on one subject literature field looking like another. Here's a quick procedure to master any one subject area with minimum effort.

- Look for the subject *guides* and read them, making useful notes.
- Master the various *organizational structures*. Look at charts, the levels of responsibility and accountability, and check out the manner of appointments and hiring practices. One needs to know the territory and take note of record-keeping systems for documentation.
- Cultivate a reliable network of *sources and contacts*. Get to know subject librarians, other researchers, and public relations and information officers. Collect home telephone numbers and build a contact file for mid-level civil servants, clerks and custodians, janitors, taxi drivers, officials at various institutes. Figure out how much data one can get from each person, following up informal conversations and throwaway lines.
- Check the subject field *daily*. Log on to a computer database, look at the court docket, legislative agendas. Stay on top, read the fine print on documents, and verify whatever looks suspicious that day.

- Build a *clippings file*.
- Learn the *jargon*: how do you know what is happening if you don't know what its meaning is? It is absolutely essential that researchers have a good knowledge of definitions: get a specialized dictionary.
- See if the *practice* differs from the theory: ask questions, trade information, spend time being sceptical, look for motives and causes.

In the chapters ahead, we will see how researchers employ the search strategies and techniques in various fields. Resources will be introduced for finding answers on business, government, law, society, technology, and culture. Under specific subheadings within these six areas is practical advice on acquiring specific documents. Depending on the topic, the researcher can discover, among other things, how to search for bankruptcies, how to search for land titles, how the stock market works, how to trace company ownerships, how to read an annual report, how to find crime statistics, how to use a government budget, how to use lobbyists, how to find data about property development, and how to check into charities for abuses.

Summary

After a discussion of the reference collection needed for parameters (getting handles on names, places, dates, and forms of information packages), top reference works are listed as first places to go when looking for answers. Key parameters for access to information are categorized and discussed, with application to any subject area and situation. The standard approach is to use these resource tools first, although answers may ultimately be found in a variety of different tools. Thus, if researchers need subject background, they use encyclopedias. If they need definitions, they use dictionaries. If they need an address, they use a directory. If they need personal data, they use biographical sources. If they need a geographical fact, they use an atlas or gazetteer. If they need current data, they use a news database. If they need a review, they look at product evaluations. If they need multidisciplinary information, they use a computer database. If they need a figure, they use a statistical source. If they need opinions, they use a poll or survey. Specific titles for each kind of parameter are cited, showing their best and most productive usage and characteristics. As well, examples of searches are given, such as the basic steps in finding information about a living person or how to check quotations, and of specific strategies, such as uncovering a personal source by subject field or gathering specific statistics.

6

BUSINESS

The only difference between an optimist and a pessimist is that the pessimist is better informed. – old joke

It is better to know some of the questions than all of the answers.
   – James Thurber

This chapter presents material on:

- business profiles;
- industry profiles;
- business conditions;
- stock market;
- labour force;
- taxation;
- business indicators;
- public relations and lobbies.

Businesses try to inform people of their products, services, and activities. They do this through various devices that include advertising, favourable articles in the media, a reputation for reliability and service, and co-operation with the community. They try to create an image that will appear real to most people, usually through the public relations process. Corporate power does affect the quantity, the quality, and the method of dissemination for information.

Businesses are corporations under the law, and they operate for a profit or else they go out of business. Their goals are to produce profits for their owners and to stay in business so that they can keep producing profits. One way to stay in business is to know what the competitors are doing, to know what the weaknesses in government regulation are, and to exploit both their employees and the consumers as far as the law allows – and all this while maintaining a good image of being a decent, concerned firm. These salient conditions are mentioned here because it is precisely to achieve these goals that much business information is created and used. Businesses are generally willing to provide information from their own research, if doing so does not undermine their competitive advantage or their corporate image. Certainly, they will welcome the researcher with open arms if their edge and/or image could actually be enhanced.

The most easily accessible data come within the warehouse mode of library and computer. Many guides state the kinds of resources available (bibliographies, directories, indexes, statistics), the kinds of information to be found (management data, accounting, marketing, and production), plus research techniques that are unique to business on how to find financial facts. These guides include Barbara Brown's *Canadian Business and Economics; a guide to sources* and Lorna Daniell's *Business Information Sources* (which covers the United States). The regularly revised *Encyclopedia of Business Information Sources* (Gale Research Publications) is designed specifically for industry profiles.

The forms of printed/online sources in business include newspapers, trade magazines, business directories, conference proceedings, patents and standards, statistical sources, business services, market research reports, credit reports, advertising, government documents, individual company sources (i.e., insider reports and other studies filed with the regulation agency), industry profiles, and association studies. The search terms are usually limited to:

- corporate name;
- personal name, if appropriate for a directorship search;
- the name of the product (brand name, trade name) or its SIC (Standard Industrial Classification) number and industry name;
- various regional terms for area market research studies.

Some of the more important sources that will furnish quick background data on any business or industry include:

- *Financial Post Information Service,* which prints corporation cards annually, with quarterly updates; this will cover the larger Canadian companies;
- *CanCorp Canadian Corporations* (computer only);
- *D & B-Canadian Dun's Market Identifiers* (400,000 Canadian firms);
- *Canadian Key Business Directory*;
- *Directory of Public Companies in Canada* (Micromedia; lists 3,500 firms);
- *Guide to Canadian Manufacturers* (Dun & Bradstreet);
- *Canadian Trade Index* (Canadian Manufacturers' Association);
- *Fraser's Canadian Trade Directory*;
- *CNAM Database* (STM systems; lists all corporate names except for Quebec);
- *Scott's Industrial Directories* (for manufacturer listings in various provinces);
- *Standard & Poor's Register of Corporations, Directors, and Executives* (for North America);
- *Thomas' Register of American Manufacturers*;
- *Moody's Investor Service Manuals* (for North America).

Material will also be found through articles in the financial and trade press. To access these, researchers need to consult a number of indexes such as *Canadian Business and Current Affairs, Canadian Periodical Index, Business Periodicals Index, InfoGlobe, Infomart,* and the various services of Dow-Jones, McGraw-Hill, Prentice-Hall, Dun & Bradstreet, Standard & Poor, and Funk & Scott.

There is also a particularly timely information resource here: the business service letter. This is a periodical, usually in newsletter or loose-leaf format, addressed to a very specific business need. It may be issued daily, semi-weekly, or weekly via print or computer and is delivered by mail, courier, fax, or computer terminal. It may be intended to update previously available or issued information: up-to-the-minute legislation and regulations, court decisions, notices of contracts being let, new grant application procedures; tax, labour, commerce, credit rating, or investment information; personnel announcements; and economic and business forecasts. The "service" is supplemented by business directories that provide listings for such needs and allow the researcher to track down vital information, such as a trade name or a share capitalization. It is mainly a question of where to look, for all the information is there; in the interests of speed, however, more and more such information is becoming available only through an online computer, and it is being updated (and replaced) daily. There may be no paper trail for tracking, especially if the newsletters are accessed through such computer databases as *NEWSNET.*

The specialized trade press in Canada, probably employing about one-quarter of all journalists, provides data not found in the daily press, although newspapers are ranked highest of all sources in an American survey of financial investors (35 per cent listed newspapers as the "best" source to get information needed to invest wisely). The trade press is excessively laden with facts, with little attention to style of presentation and interpretation. Some of the leaders in the field include CCH Canadian and Butterworths Canada, with American sources including Commerce Clearing House and the Bureau of National Affairs (which publishes over fifty newsletters). Subscription prices are extremely high, for this is the selling of needed data, and these publications do a first-rate job of informing their business public.

Even more costly are reports that deal with information or investment analysis. Many fact-finding groups obtain and manipulate specialized data, turning them into marketing research studies, trade association publications, customized research on minute topics, and econometric data. These are immediate reports and often can be obtained later at a modest cost. Of value to the researcher is the fact that these "older" reports are always a less expensive source of needed data, particularly since most are cumulative and are missing only the really current data. They save a lot of research time if researchers need to dig out background material. And, as with the mosaic theory, these data can be re-used in ways for which they were not originally intended, especially if numeric tables are manipulated in spreadsheets and databanks.

To find the names of such market research firms, try the American *FINDEX; the directory of market research reports, studies and surveys,* which lists about 8,000 reports from more than 500 marketing publishers in fields such as health care, energy, transportation, travel and tourism, petrochemicals, and metals. Many of these firms deal with Canada, and some even have branches here. Also try the *International Directory of Published Market Research* (compiled by the British Overseas Trade Board), which lists over 7,000 studies from 125 nations. Other data may be available from the corporations that requested the market research; a useful guide to these publications is *Corporate Publications in Print* (Norback).

But there are specific differences between printed and online sources. For one thing, online searching is easier, since key terms are usually restricted to the name of the business, product, executive, or industry. Indeed, some databases are searchable by SIC code number; they can be searched daily by this number for an automatic updating. Specific topics can be keyed into general databases, such as specific market data (e.g., chemistry, health food), advertising campaigns for competitive products, government contracts allotted, trademarks and patents, and recent new product introductions. Current information on competitors' product lines and market share is obtainable from online databases maintained by Standard & Poor, *DISCLOSURE, PREDICAST,* the Moody manuals, and others. There are often financial details and thorough comparisons with the industry.

Even simple biographical data are useful. For instance, *ABI/INFORM* (which covers business and management worldwide through indexing 1,000 publications, most with summaries of their articles) uses an example for strategizing a search: a creative director at an advertising agency was considering using a client's CEO in commercials and needed to know whether that was an effective approach. He searched under the names of several prominent CEOs, such as Lee Iacocca at Chrysler, David Nichol of Loblaw International Merchants, and Victor Kiam of Remington, tagged with the SIC code for "advertising" (which is 7200). Thus, for material about Iacocca, the search looked for the occurrence of "Iacocca" and "CC=7200" in each database record. There was no need to look under "commercials," "advertising," "corporate image," "comparative advertising," "celebrities," "television advertising," "endorsements," or any similar topics. By reading and sifting through the summaries of articles that had appeared in *Business Week, Communicators Journal,* and *Advertising Age,* the creative director was able to note several points about similar advertising campaigns in under three minutes of search and ten minutes of overview reading –

without leaving the office, without looking through mounds of printed indexes and correlating cross-references, without tracking down and waiting for the periodical articles, and without even having to read all the articles. If he had had someone else do all the legwork, then he would also have had to take the time to explain what he was doing and then wait for the results. His total cost of using *ABI/INFORM*, at about $180 an hour plus communication charges, was approximately $35.

The next large mode of information after the warehouse is the generation of institutional documents, mostly from governments and the trade associations. Businesses must conform to the regulatory laws that require much disclosure. Remember that all businesses intersect with governments at all levels, from municipal licensing to federal taxation. The largest category of data is the voluminous public reports filed by publicly traded companies with regulatory agencies, government departments, and stock exchanges. These have details identifying stockholders and officers (salaries and bonuses), changes in ownership and finances, basic data on products, services, acquisitions, sales, divestitures, mergers, and a wide range of other indicators. All of these should alert investors and regulators to possibilities of takeovers, leveraged buyouts, challenged advertising claims, mergers, product safety, defect notices and recalls, and injury and illness data related to consumer products. Each regulator has varying requirements. For instance, salaries are difficult to obtain in Canada but are compulsory in U.S. Securities and Exchange Commission filings of American companies with Canadian branch plants and of Canadian companies doing business in the United States. These data are publicly available to foreigners; consequently, a Canadian citizen can look at Form 10K for a U.S. firm in Canada or at Form 6K for a Canadian firm in the United States to get some Canadian salary information. Parenthetically, it should be noted that some Canadian companies were unhappy about this, and the American law was changed slightly in July, 1991, to allow for the voluntary witholding of salary data for individuals (but the total of the salaries for the "management team" had to be filed). Some reports are not public, such as those to credit agencies, but they are routinely traded – and leaked – throughout the business world as documents privately obtained. Other public reports are from onsite visits, such as safety and health standards inspections, which cover eating facilities, restaurants, nursing homes, medical care, factory safety, elevators, and other facilities.

Government records are also collected, usually on a confidential, compulsory, but non-regulatory basis. These are mainly statistical data reported to Statistics Canada or to a provincial body, and are available to the public as aggregates or regional summary figures. Statistics Canada's *Census of Manufactures* is a good example of this. Other materials are collected on or for the industry by government, including Revenue Canada. Government auditors have some information about companies that do business with the government. The *Canada Gazette* lists tenders, contracts, and all sorts of miscellaneous notices that should be checked through its index under a company's name. There is also access to records dealing with patents and licences, and these, too, should be checked if appropriate. Many other things can be accessed through the Access to Information Act, provided that the company (known as "third party" in the legislation) allows the request to be filled (the company sometimes specifies that parts of the file must first be severed). Companies know the name of the requester and may become feisty, which is why some requesters use an intermediary firm of information brokers. Certainly, data about an industry can be accessed, and researchers can figure out some approximate information about a company within that industry, particularly if the company dominates the industry.

Trade associations have a wealth of documents that can be made available or leaked if it suits their purpose. Material is constantly being gathered and spewed out for their lobby posturing. Many documents can give a perspective on the industry for trends, and certainly a company's position can be figured out as an estimate. Citizen and consumer groups also have something to say about companies, usually with an opposite bias. Salaried researchers should be able to use their own company's lawyers, accountants, and human resource staff to pry loose data that they might have access to, for they are all working for and have loyalty to the same employer.

Notwithstanding the privacy of many reports filed with government, litigation creates court records that can be highly revealing of business. It has been estimated that up to two-thirds of companies are guilty of at least one illegal act over the corporate lifespan, such as evasion of taxes, unfair labour practices, dangerous working conditions, price-fixing, pollution, and kickbacks. If they are caught, then they go to court, which generates documents. Civil suits from breach of contract, estate probates, bankruptcies, and divorce claims also generate documents. What was previously private may be revealed as a public document if a point of law or claim is to be made (*duces tecum* is a court-ordered subpoena requiring the records custodian to bring the material to court). Exhibits can contain anything, even private tax records. Patent infringement suits will have materials on financial strategy and standing in the world of business, product design and manufacturing techniques, advertising and marketing tactics, franchise and dealership data, as well as tax records. Breach-of-contract suits are common, with former employees suing the company for salary settlements in wrongful dismissal actions. Judgements and claims awarded will form part of the case file, and this is usually accessible to anyone. It is precisely for this reason that many cases are settled "out of court." Companies are spared the expense of legal fees, the publicity of having a protracted case dragged through the media (if it is a sensational one), and the file of publicly accessible court records.

Another large mode of information, after the warehouse and the documents, is the expert. Almost everybody in the business world has something to gain by talking to outsiders. The best expert on a business is one of its top management, although information and opinion are bound to be biased. But not every researcher will have access to the chief executive officer or president. Many CEOs are excessively secretive, especially those in private companies, not wanting their competitors to have any knowledge. Others are simply shy. However, some are egocentric and love to talk and to manipulate. Another contact source is the company's public relations section or the firm that handles its PR, since these are the people who produce the annual report and smooth out any crises. And people who work at the governmental regulatory agencies have proved to be helpful, for they know the scuttlebutt. For smaller firms, the names of bankers, accountants, and auditors can be found through business directories. Business academics at the local university are usually keyed into the industry picture. Securities analysts, attached to brokerage houses and to banks, provide evaluations of companies; they are professional gatherers of business information. Some of them concentrate on specific industries, often with inside sources. It is their business to understand how political decisions impact or impinge on the industry, and they scrutinize trends to figure out future developments. Labour union officials often have a clear picture of a company's finances, where it stands within the industry, future policies, and personalities of the company's top management. Various associations can help out, not just the trade association and the chambers of commerce but also the citizen groups. Experts can also be found among the "little people": customers, neighbours, suppliers, employees, retired employees; whether satisfied or disgruntled, they will have many tips and stories to tell.

In numbers, private companies form the bulk of businesses (about 90 per cent of all companies), but they are small. They don't have to file many public reports to regulatory bodies, but they still can be taken over or merged, have advertising claims challenged, and be subject to occupational safety and health standards inspections. They must file requested statistics to the government, and they can belong to trade associations, be litigious, and be talked about by analysts and other experts. They also need incorporation records, licences, patents, and brand-name protection. Additional information about them can be leaked, stolen, or privately obtained. Estimates can then be made about a private company. Family-owned businesses might be part of other companies in a heavily regulated industry. They may buy a percentage of a publicly traded company or run an insurance company or a trust firm. This information about them will certainly be available. Researchers might also be able to find a comparable business run as a public company and begin making extrapolations. Whatever the circumstances, estimates can be made about any private company.

Profiling a Business

Finding a specific piece of information about a company depends on whether the company is public or private. Since private companies are not required to publish financial statements (although these must be submitted to Statistics Canada and other agencies), available information is usually limited to an address, phone number, the nature of the business, products or services, executives and key personnel, number of employees, and sometimes a gross sales figure. Any firm with more than fifty shareholders is classed as a public company in Canada. It must register with the securities commission in the region where it plans to sell stocks and bond securities. It must also report annually to its shareholders. Ownership may be further convoluted by the presence of wholly-owned subsidiaries, which are like private companies and hence issue no separate financial statements. Researchers can use Statistics Canada's *Intercorporate Ownership* to find out what company owns what subsidiary and vice versa. All companies doing business in Canada must incorporate either federally or provincially. There are advantages and disadvantages to both, but the provincial level requires fewer public filings. Most businesses operate only regionally, which apparently satisfies their needs. A company will not divulge any unasked-for information about itself for fear of competition. But it never hurts researchers to ask, and in a moment of forgetfulness a company might actually be forthcoming.

Who needs a business profile? In most cases, it is the competition trying to get an edge. Most users of the freedom of information acts (FOIAS), those who run afoul of the "third party" clause or who ask for restricted data, are in fact businesses trying to spy on other businesses. Nevertheless, the spinoff of information-seeking by business is a tremendous boon for the researcher, though there is much to be monitored and much that is irrelevant to the researcher's immediate needs. What most people look for can be categorized under *description* (product lines, history, current activity, addresses, people, experts, plant statistics, associations), *finances* (assets, liabilities, revenues, securities), *industrial status* (SIC, trends, forecasts), *research and new product development, government* (legislation, regulation, litigation), or *demographics* (market research).

Most descriptive data can be found through the various business directories. Additional biographical details may be necessary, but these can be located through such resources as *Who's Who in Finance and Industry, Financial Post Directory of Directors, Standard & Poor's Register of Corporations, Directors and Executives,* or the periodical databases. These will flesh out the bones of both top management and directors, such as how long they've been around, how many shares they own, their previous careers, ages, education, and salaries and bonuses from the U.S. SEC filings. Top management includes the heads of finance, marketing, sales, product development, planning, research and development, and human resources. Financial and legal information, including patents and trademarks, can be obtained from business directories and security commission filings, such as the *Financial Post Information Service, CanCorp Canadian Corporations,* and the Moody manuals (*Bank and Finance, Industrials, Municipal and Government, OTC Industrials, Public Utility, Transportation*). Court litigation can be monitored through various reporter series, as noted in Chapter 8, which deals with law and the courts.

Industrial status plus research and new product development can best be checked by profiling the industry (see below), which also involves using highly specialized resource tools, sophisticated online searching strategies, and magazine indexes. Researchers can also stay current about government legislation by checking an industry-specific business service newsletter. Demographics, which are difficult to find, involve sales and marketing information, distribution methods, public relations, trade associations, advertising, and market research. Material is scattered and hidden from competitors, but it might crop up in magazine articles. Generally, the higher the company's profile, the more demographic data will be available. Certainly these data are available on an industry-wide basis through trade associations.

An interesting overall source is the annual report. A public company that sells shares must issue an annual report that goes both to the regulatory agency and to its shareholders. The annual report serves many purposes. It can be useful for public relations, with lots of pictures and graphs; it reveals the financial health of the company; it speculates on the future of the company and the business, with industry-wide data about trends; and it provides biographic details. Some of these reports are difficult to read, some are obscure, some must be read between the lines. Among the numerous books and articles on "how to read an annual report" are *How to Read Financial Statements* (regularly revised by the Canadian Securities Institute) and *How to Read an Annual Report* (Merrill Lynch).

The *auditor's report* (usually at the back) presents an independent accounting firm's review of the company's books, and it tries to verify the accuracy of the financial statements. There will be large categories such as "balance sheet" (the company's financial position at a particular date), the "earnings statement" (showing money made or lost over the year, less expenses), the "retained earnings statement" (profits not paid out to stockholders as dividends but kept for reinvestment), and the "statement of changes in financial position" (cash flow). The footnotes, which are valuable for detailed information relating to the financial statements, cover such things as write-offs, windfalls, litigation, and changes in accounting procedures. There may be "five-year financial summaries," which would illustrate trends. The *report to the shareholders* is the main text, prepared by the public relations people, with insights into revealable future plans (acquisitions, marketing strategies, product lines). This tells how the company fared this year, and it needs to be read cautiously.

Annual reports can be obtained from the company itself, as can quarterly reports that have been issued since the latest annual report. The Ontario Securities Commission, through Micromedia, sells copies of those reports that must be filed in Ontario. Their file room is useful for looking at annual reports from smaller, out-of-the-way traded companies. Libraries will have some copies of annual reports, especially those public libraries that want to serve the business community. For instance, Metro Toronto Reference Library has reports from over 1,500 companies on file, and they retain previous reports for historical purposes. Academic libraries that support business programs also have files of annual reports. For raw data and quick facts, the *Financial Post Information Service* publishes corporation cards annually with quarterly updates. This information is taken from the annual report filing, and in many cases it may be all that is needed. Libraries have these cards as well. Annual reports are commented on in the press, and thus a search through an online database such as *CBCA*, *InfoGlobe*, or *Infomart* would certainly be useful. Use *DIALOG*, *Business Periodicals Index*, and *Wall Street Journal* for foreign countries. Other interpretations on the contents of reports can be had from investment brokers, relevant accounting firms, and the company itself.

Highly specific data that can be searched for profiling any type of company include the following.

(1) *Licences.* Files contain documentation on various municipally licensed professions such as electrical contractors, renovators, hairdressers, bakers, pawnbrokers, and taxi drivers. There are also licences for places (stationary businesses) such as bowling alleys, butcher shops, gas stations, and movie theatres. Provincial licences

are needed for such things as elevators and vendors (retail sales taxes). Federal licences and permits are needed, for example, for being customs house brokers, import-export firms, bonded warehouses, use of alcohol in the manufacturing process, and pharmaceuticals. The wide range of others includes television and radio station licences and vendor registration for the Goods and Services Tax.

(2) *Ownership registration*. This includes sole proprietorship, partnership, limited company, and co-operative. Researchers trace company ownerships through name searches, nominal and beneficial owners, corporate filings, merger and acquisition or amalgamation listings at securities commissions, intercorporate ownerships, and subsidiaries. Some of the common printed tools include Statistics Canada's *Intercorporate Ownership, Who Owns Whom: North America, Directory of Corporate Affiliation,* and *World Directory of Multinational Enterprises.* The more prominent and active the company, the more paper to be searched.

(3) *Brand names and trademarks*. Researchers can use *Brand Names: who owns what,* as well as such product directories as *Thomas'.*

(4) *Franchising*. Use *Franchise Handbook and Directory* for Canada, or the international *Directory of Franchising Organizations, Dow Jones Irwin Guide to Franchises,* and *Sourcebook of Franchise Opportunities.*

(5) *Geographic/region databases*. This includes directories specifically on a region, regardless of industry or company. Some prominent ones for Canada include *Scott's Industrial Directory for Ontario, Saskatchewan Manufacturer's Guide, Prince Edward Island Trade Directory, Northwest Territories Business Directory, Niagara Industrial Directory, Made in Quebec,* and *Alberta Manufacturer's Index.*

Profiling an Industry

Business Conditions

Additional data about a company, especially a private company, can be found by looking at the specific industry within which the business operates. Industrial information is easy to come by, since it is relatively non-competitive. Most data collection fields have been standardized, such as the preferred name for the industry, the SIC code number for the industry, trade associations to speak for the industry, size (number of players, significant companies, dollar volume), trade magazine coverage, newsletters, research studies, government regulation, and government databases. It would also be useful to know the names and addresses of securities analysts at stock exchanges and banks, for they have their fingers on the pulse of the industry.

A researcher can find almost everything available about an industry. One of the best places to begin looking would be in an online computer database, using either the name of the industry or the SIC number as an access point. Here are just a few:

- *Business Periodicals Index* provides international coverage of companies, industries, products, and services.
- *Canadian Business and Current Affairs* is the online version of the *Canadian News Index, Canadian Magazine Index,* and *Canadian Business Index.* It provides coverage of Canadian newspapers, magazines, and business or trade publications. Its indexing covers type of industry, product, service, and names for companies and top managers.
- *FP Online* indexes the full text of the *Financial Post.*
- *InfoGlobe* indexes the full text of the *Globe and Mail* and its "Report on Business."
- *Predicasts Funk & Scott Index International* indexes international articles for current product information, and corporate mergers and acquisitions.
- *PROMPT (Predicasts Overview of Markets and Technology)* abstracts articles in twenty-nine industries.
- *FINDEX* lists market research and industry reports.
- *Encyclopedia of Business Information Sources* (Gale Research Publications) is designed specifically for industry profiles and business-oriented topics. It has 1,300 of these, under such headings as nursing homes, profit-sharing, energy, public relations, and sweet potatoes. Each has a list of resources containing facts and figures, ranging from magazine articles and directories through handbooks, bibliographies, encyclopedias, dictionaries, and online databases.

Specific Canadian industry resources would include such examples as *Canadian Mines Handbook, Canadian Oil and Gas Handbook, Canadian Directory of Shopping Centres, Canadian Financial Institutions, Computer System Sources, Directory of Restaurants and Fast Food Chains in Canada, Financial Post Survey of Industrials, Franchise Handbook and Directory,* and *Microcomputer Market Place,* plus the various Moody manuals.

Some useful newsletters are "business information services," which are expressly geared to an industry. They can give the reader good information or market intelligence about consumer credit, market research, financial markets, regulatory affairs, accounting, and law. The point of these services is to allow business to maximize profits and minimize competition, and they are available only to those who can pay for business information. The services can be found at association headquarters and at relevant business libraries. Many newsletters are available online through *NEWSNET.* For a competitive edge, a business must keep up with its industry position.

For every kind of industry, then, there will be relevant trade and business publications, associations, services. and online databases that will present any or all of:

- a discussion of current developments;
- detailed reporting of developments in key areas;
- in-depth coverage of leading indicators;
- industrial statistics (national, regional, local);
- annual reviews of the industry;
- investment considerations of assets, liabilities, and financial conditions of specific or targeted companies;
- market analysis surveys and reports;
- implications of the industry's place in society;
- biographical profiles of the industry's leaders;
- advertising expenditures by product or brand name;
- general articles on the industry.

This information can be used to dig out data about smaller companies or even private companies. Other sources of information about an industry are linked to networks such as the stock market, the security commissions, the labour force, taxation, the business indicators, and the public relations-lobby function. These will now be examined.

The Stock Market

Information on how a stock exchange works is readily available from its own public relations: glossaries of terms, instructions on how to invest, what's inside an annual report, lists of member firms, and pertinent regulations. Information about the various stock markets in Canada is available directly from the Toronto, Vancouver, and Montreal stock exchanges and from the Winnipeg Commodity Exchange.

The Toronto Stock Exchange, for example, is regulated by the Ontario Securities Commission, which also oversees all the over-the-counter trading across the province. A computerized quotation and trade reporting system ensures that there is sufficient information about this trading. Almost all (95 per cent) of Canadian securities transactions are handled by members of the Investment Dealers Association of Canada. The IDA and the stock exchanges sponsor the Canadian Securities Institute, a national educational body with courses and publications about securities and investment for both the industry and the public.

Although the stock market is heavily regulated to prevent scams and unscrupulous behaviour, the buying and selling of public company shares is still a case of *caveat emptor*. Consequently, a large amount of data is available on businesses and their respective industries (see above). Directories are of some help in gaining data on business stocks and bonds. *Canadian Key Business Directory* is useful for companies most likely to be listed on the Toronto Stock Exchange because it profiles the top 3 per cent (size, sales, or net worth) of all Canadian businesses. *Directory of Business and Financial Services* is useful because it lists about 100 Canadian publications, divided into different fields such as insurance, investment, government regulation, and commodities. *Business Periodicals Index* and *CBCA* have many articles written about the stock market and about specific exchanges. With knowledge of the jargon used in the securities business, these tools are probably the most helpful to keep abreast of stock market activity. *InfoGlobe,* through its "Market Search Plus," lists the highs and lows in volume trading – going back five years on a weekly basis and one year for daily quotations.

InfoGlobe has the *Globe and Mail*'s "Report on Business," while *FP Online* has the *Financial Post*. Both newspapers are essential for market reports and interpretations. Investment strategies seem to be part of "personal finance," but can be accessed as regularly recurring articles in *Report on Business Magazine*, *The Financial Post Magazine*, and *Canadian Business*. Also, there are hundreds of business newsletters with tips and advice. For a listing of these, consult the *Newsletter Directory*.

The regulation of the marketplace is dominated by the various securities commissions set up to monitor trading. A commission's board and staff are made up of lawyers, accountants, securities analysts, investigators, dealers, and investors. Its board formulates policy, sits as an administrative tribunal in hearings, acts as an appeal body from decisions of the various exchanges, and makes recommendations to the government for changes in legislation. Its staff has the power to investigate, suspend, cancel, or impose terms on registration; grant or deny exemptions from regulations; order funds frozen or put into receivership; and regulate insider trading. Since the American stock market crash in 1929, which preceded the founding of securities commissions, they have been the watchdogs of the financial community.

This activity tends to generate a lot of data, most of which is open to researchers. Every company trading shares must file a prospectus, which gives such details as the purpose for which the securities are being issued, the business and properties of the company, its financial statements, and information about the company's managers and promoters. For example, section 137 of the Securities Act (Ontario) requires certain information to be made available for public inspection, such as the prospectus and related documents on insider trading or reports by nominee holders. Private and confidential information will be collected but not released to the public, especially if it affects the competitive edge. Public material is available for retention for a fee, but at the Metro Toronto Reference Library it can be seen for free.

The Ontario Securities Commission publishes a weekly *Bulletin* containing information such as notices and press releases; decisions, orders, and rulings (with reasons); cease trading orders; insider trading reports; policies; and public filings. It is usually very detailed and accurate, for the legislation makes it mandatory that the companies keep the investing public up to date on important changes in its affairs. Whenever an event occurs that could significantly affect the value or market price of its securities, then the company must inform the public by press release and file a report with the OSC. This system ensures that everyone has equal access to information ("timely disclosure") upon which to base investment decisions. "Insiders" who work for companies, and anyone else associated with the firm (such as lawyers, accountants, and brokers) and having privileged information, are expressly forbidden to take advantage of what they know. The OSC also has an information centre.

Some securities commissions have tighter filing rules than the OSC, such as the U.S. Securities and Exchange Commission, which demands salary data not called for in Ontario, while other commissions in Canada have less stringent regulations and hence appeal to more shady operators.

The Labour Force
Information about labour has always been difficult to obtain, primarily because the unions are suspicious of the purpose to which the data will be put. Labour has always been burned by management, occasionally by the media, and sometimes by the government. Only about one-third of Canadian workers are unionized (contrasted to Europe, which has between 45 and 75 per cent unionization), and only 16 per cent of American workers belong to a union.

A "labour union" is a generic term describing employees who have formed an independent organization for the purpose of regulating employee-employer relations. Different kinds go under different names: trade, guild, and craft. Most occupational groupings are covered by provincial legislation. Thus, members of the police force (but not security guards) come under the Police Act, public school teachers under the Education Act, full-time firefighters under the Fire Departments Act, hospital employees under the Hospital Labour Disputes Arbitration Act, provincial government employees under the Crown Employees Collective Bargaining Act, and most of the other groups under the Labour Relations Acts. Those groups covered directly by federal legislation are excluded, as are domestic workers, farmers, professionals (architects, dentists, land surveyors, lawyers, doctors, engineers: these have their own acts), and anyone involved in a managerial function.

The system of labour-management relations is adversarial, and any deviation from that point of view (such as management helping a union or its employees) is definitely strange, including the various "sweetheart" deals in which unions come to terms with management rather quickly on salary levels and clawbacks. Also, some managements have "yellowdog" contracts with their employees, prohibiting unions.

For an understanding of and successful research on labour issues, a number of particular approaches and entry points must be considered.

(1) Researchers need to be familiar with the labour-management history of businesses within the industry. For instance, it is not enough to know about the Canadian Auto Workers at General Motors. They also need to know about the CAW at Ford and the other automobile manufacturing businesses, not to mention having some familiarity with relations between the CAW and the UAW in the States and with labour-management relations in the U.S. Some useful resources include John Anderson and Marty Gunderson's *Union-Management Relations in Canada* (Addison-Wesley) and, for Ontario, Dan Koen's *Union Organizing Activity in Ontario, 1970-1986* (School of Industrial Relations and Research at Queen's University, Kingston). A good book for dealing with the "system" is Leo McGrady's *A Guide to Organizing Unions* (Butterworths).

(2) Researchers need to obtain the relevant collective bargaining contracts through, for example, the Ontario Ministry of Labour's Collective Agreements Library. These show which jobs are covered by the agreement, the pay ranges, the issues subject to grievance procedures, and the trends in negotiations. Arrangement is by Standard Industrial Classification (SIC) code number.

(3) Researchers need to get on the mailing lists of relevant labour unions and management groups, for their newsletters and press releases. In this way they will know agendas. Check the *Directory of Labour Unions in Canada,* which also contains a handy glossary and descriptions of union structures.

(4) Researchers need to become familiar with, for example, the Ontario Labour Relations Board (a regulatory agency), its work, and its publications. It has an information centre with collections of arbitration cases, employment standards decisions, accreditation decisions, case law digests, and all the similar decisions from across the

country. By knowing which Ontario act governs which particular occupation, researchers will have a considerably easier time locating precise sources of official documentation. The Ontario Labour Relations Act states that information must be disclosed and filed at the ministry; this is useful because it is all centralized. Thus, occupational health and safety decisions resulting from inspections and safety violations have their own collection here. Unions are closely regulated, and each union must file an annual audit and all its financial plans with the ministry.

(5) Researchers need to look into the political activity of unions. They form "political action committees" or they may affiliate with the New Democratic Party. Remember, though, that unions are private institutions. They don't have to give researchers any data, not even that which is on file with the Ministry of Labour. The majority of unions are "affiliated" to various councils and labour federations, such as the Metro Toronto Labour Council or the Ontario Federation of Labour.

(6) Researchers need to familiarize themselves with the jargon of labour-management disputes, such negotiable things as: the fringe benefit package (including retirement/pension plans, extended health care, long-term disability plans, dental/vision plans), cost-of-living increases and cost-of-living allowance (COLA) clauses, vacation leave, staffing levels, worker safety measures, grievance rights, strike rights, employment equity, pay equity, discrimination in hiring and promotion, flextime in work scheduling, occupational safety, wage negotiations, and many more. All of these are connected to a myriad of government legislation. Researchers need to also get their "numbers" right, for labour and management will have different sets of figures.

Taxation

Taxes are normally thought to be confidential. But one can calculate property taxes from the assessment rolls, tax statements do turn up as public records in court cases dealing with divorce or probate or litigation, and businesses declare most taxes as part of their annual reports. Tax aggregates by location and by industry are available from Revenue Canada and Statistics Canada. And, of course, businesses and people can simply tell researchers what they pay out in taxes (but then, this should be verified).

Knowledge of how the tax system works can be gleaned through the following works. *Income Tax Research; a practical guide,* by David M. Sherman (Richard De Boo) contains an outline of income tax systems in Canada, an overview of the sources of data, and information on how to read the Income Tax Act. J. Harvey Perry's *Taxation in Canada* (regularly revised by the Canadian Tax Foundation) is a readable historical overview and explanation of Canadian tax and budgetary systems. *Sales Tax Guide* (regularly revised by CCH Canadian and the Canadian Manufacturers' Association) explains the federal law, departmental memoranda, and rulings, and includes samples of forms. For the provinces, *Ontario Retail Sales Tax* (CCH Canadian) includes copies of tax guidance notes issued by the government, bibliographies of books and articles, tax law cases, a government directory, and a list of publications by the government. There is also the *Provincial Sales Tax Handbook* (Canadian Institute of Chartered Accountants), a three-volume loose-leaf service that includes a glossary and comparisons of provincial taxation methods.

Other loose-leaf services include *Canadian Tax Reporter* (CCH Canadian), *Canadian Tax Service* (Richard De Boo), *Ontario Taxation Service* (Richard De Boo), and *Income Taxation in Canada* (Prentice-Hall of Canada), all of which contain tax cases, news releases, and forms. They are updated and revised constantly since they are meant for accountants; consequently, they are very demanding to read. For tax law, consult *Dominion Tax Cases* (CCH Canadian), which is published annually, reporting the full text of judgements on federal tax questions. For tax shelters, there is the *Canadian Tax Shelter Directory* (Insight Press). Finally, *The National Finances* and *The Provincial Finances* (Canadian Tax Foundation) analyse revenue and expenditures of these two levels of government.

The best information centres are the Canadian Tax Foundation and Revenue Canada libraries. The Canadian Tax Foundation, in Toronto, is an independent research organization. It publishes *Canadian Tax Journal* and research papers, holds conferences, and has the largest tax library in Canada. This contains all tax-related government publications, provincial and federal budgets, data on the Canadian income tax system since its inception in 1917, and tax information from other countries. Each issue of its journal has a "checklist" section that summarizes legislative debates and news releases, and that has references to appropriate committee hearings and government records.

The Revenue Canada Library in Ottawa and at various regional offices throughout Canada has reading rooms with versions of their Taxation Operations Manual. This tells how Revenue Canada does audits, and one can read it under the supervision of an employee. It can also be photocopied for nominal cost. Staff are available to help explain the various forms, circulars, and bulletins.

Most of the major accounting firms have tax libraries that researchers might use, and they can even talk to tax experts there. These firms often publish their own booklets on taxation and investing for their clients, and usually they'll just give researchers a set upon request.

Other organizations with information centres include Canadian Institute of Chartered Accountants (CICA), Institute of Chartered Accountants of Ontario, Canadian Federation for Independent Business, Canadian Manufacturers' Association, and the library of any university with a business degree program. Generally, these facilities are not open to the public, but they will answer some questions, they may publish reports that are available elsewhere, and the expert officials or teachers could provide an accounting or business perspective about taxation.

For specific tax information about a business or government agency, it is relatively easy to use a printed or online database. Just search under the name along with the type of tax, and existing data will turn up. For information about taxes in a global context, *Canadian Tax Online* (CICA) has news releases, court decisions, Revenue Canada's interpretation bulletins and information circulars, status of tax bills in the legislature, recently enacted regulations, drafted regulations, telephone directories for Revenue Canada and the federal Finance Department, schedules of tax court sittings, lists of cases under appeal, and upcoming seminars and conferences. *QL Systems* is a vendor that offers tax court reports and an annotated version of the Income Tax Act. In addition to selling the online version of the *Globe and Mail, InfoGlobe* is also a vendor with government press releases and some of the same material as *Canadian Tax Online*. The *Accountants Index* (published since 1912) is a subject arrangement of books and periodical articles about accounting and taxes in North America. *Business Periodicals Index* and *CBCA* also cover the presentation of taxes in well over 1,000 industry-specific trade magazines, scholarly journals, and newspapers.

Business Indicators

Business conditions are indicators of the relative health of an industry or a region. They are primarily statistical and can be tabulated with a spreadsheet, compared in a time series, put on a graph, seasonalized, and manipulated. But many figures can be scattered over a wide range of sources. For example, all of the following can indicate the state of the economy.

(1) Railroad carloadings (which may not always be broken down by region) by volume and dollars can be obtained from Statistics Canada, CN Rail, and CP Rail. Higher figures mean lots of activity, hence, prosperity.

(2) Data on public utilities consumption can be gotten from the local hydroelectric commission and from gas companies, as well as business and market guides for a region. Also, water and sewage treatment is susceptible to both activity and climate factors.

(3) Department store sales, as aggregate totals, measure spending patterns of consumers. Statistics Canada reports on "major" and "junior" sales (the latter being a euphemism for "discount stores"), breaking them down by numbers of stores and sales by urban centres. Lately, for example, sales are up about 10 per cent in the discount stores and down about 10 per cent in the major stores. More data are available through *Financial Post Canadian Markets*.

(4) Real estate conditions include office space vacancy rate for both the city downtown core and the suburbs, residential rental vacancy rate, property prices, and transfers of sales by region. Data can be accessed from a local real estate board or board of trade, from Statistics Canada, and from *Financial Post Canadian Markets*.

(5) Commodity prices produce the consumer price index at Statistics Canada. Additional data can be found in *Financial Post Canadian Markets*.

(6) Building permits issued for commercial and industrial real estate and for residential homes are another indicator of economic activity. Information is gathered locally by the construction associations and by Statistics Canada.

(7) Employment trends are to be found through the employ-ment rate, hourly earnings, strikes and lockouts, and employment opportunities, and these data can be collected from local trade boards, *Financial Post Canadian Markets,* and Statistics Canada.

(8) Corporate earnings can be obtained from Statistics Canada, and are collected from industrial corporations with assets exceeding $10 million. Statistics Canada also has commercial corporation financial statistics.

(9) Information on mortgage foreclosures comes mostly from banks, with a reporting service conducted by Dun & Bradstreet. Other information can be obtained from local real estate boards.

(10) Insurance data are collected by the Insurance Bureau of Canada, Statistics Canada, and (in Ontario) the Superintendent of Insurance. Categories include life, health, automobile, home, busi-ness, accident, marine, casualty, surety, and pension.

(11) Tourism is a good indication of the quality of life, with categories here for arrival and departure data (by air, train, car, bus), accommodation (hotels and motels), meals (restaurants), attrac-tions, and conferences. Researchers need to check with local and provincial governments that get together to sponsor tourism advertising, as well as travellers' aid groups, visitors' associations, convention centres, and hospitality groups of restaurants and hotels.

Facts and figures from these diverse sources may lead to inconsis-tency in the tabulation of data. Thus, references should be very care-fully checked and verified.

International Business

Global business sources include, of course, all the materials already mentioned for Canadian businesses that export or have branch offices outside this country. Indeed, every country has some sort of counterpart to Canadian business information resource tools. And there are new, and different, tools to present data about the flow of trade between countries and continents. Here are some suggestions on discovering what has already been written and where to go for background.

(1) Many world trade centres exist around the globe: they have commercial agents analysing trade and libraries full of data on the economic health and wealth of a nation (see below, on public

relations). These are good places to begin for basic information. As a courtesy, these centres probably would not charge for small services. Also of value are the branches of the svp chain of information brokers, which developed in France after World War Two to furnish business data. But as a business, svp must charge for its services. If information is immediately required, then certainly – for a fee – svp would be happy to fax material.

(2) Financial newspapers from around the world are available, in English, online: Asahi News Service (covers the Far East, through *NEXIS*); El Pais (covers Spain and Spanish-speaking countries, through Reuters *Textline*); *Financial Times* (London) (through *DIA-LOG, NEXIS,* or *Textline*); *Frankfurter Allemagne Zeitung* (covers Germany and Europe, through *Textline*); *Globe and Mail* (Canada and the world); *Japan Economic Daily* (good for stock exchanges, through *DIALOG*); *Le Monde* (France and Europe, through *Textline*); *Los Angeles Times* (good for Asian business, through *NEXIS*); *The Economist* (good for Africa, Asia, and the Middle East, as well as Europe, through *Textline* and *NEXIS*); *Wall Street Journal* (through Dow-Jones News Retrieval).

(3) Online databases provide access to records maintained by governments or by business directory services. These include *Disclosure Online,* with data about 12,000 American companies traded on stock exchanges and about 5,000 non-U.S. companies that do business in North America (including Canada). Information here is about institutional ownership and insider trading. There are also copies of forms filed with the sec, such as the 10K (annual reports) and 8K (material change notice). *Disclosure Online* can be used to find out if a company is in legal or environmental difficulty. Another source is *EKOL* (European Kompass Online), available through Micromedia in Canada. This is a database of 300,000 companies in twelve Western European countries. It is essentially a business directory, with standard information about the company names, addresses, telephone numbers, languages used, number of employees, names of officers, products manufactured, and whether exported or imported. *NEEDS-Company* is a database of 15,000 public and private Japanese firms.

(4) Every country has incorporation records for its companies, similar to those in Canada. Data include names, addresses, officers

or those who founded the corporation, directors, and lawyers. Some countries have regulatory bodies that work similar to the Ontario Securities Commission. Public companies that trade shares on a stock exchange are required to disclose figures about their operations. The amount of disclosure will vary from country to country. If the company for which you are seeking data operates on a global basis, then try the country that requires the most corporate disclosure. For Canadian companies, this will mean the U.S. Securities and Exchange Commission.

Public Relations and Lobbies

Every industry or product has a trade association designed to promote its positive benefits, as well as to lobby the government at all levels for a better break in the commercial marketplace. The edge of competition is keen here, and most researchers and media people are welcomed with opened arms – so long as the resulting report or story is not damaging to the industry's image. And even then, most associations might just shrug it off, for that is how the game is played. A researcher unable to get further information from an association or public relations firm that he has burned in the past can always use a third party.

The basic source of PR data is the *media kit*. Its contents are useful but only in the context of public relations slants or biases. Everything must be verified. The kit usually contains:

- cover letters, with contact names and numbers;
- news releases, written up for immediate typesetting;
- full texts of speeches;
- fact sheets or backgrounders to provide a context;
- documents: briefs, reports, submissions, presentations;
- description of firm or association: annual report, brochure;
- biographical profiles of upper management;
- illustrations: graphs, charts, photographs (people, places, events);
- pre-packaged audio-visual tapes for sound bites and clips.

Overall, it is easier to get data from an association or a public relations firm than from a company. Their staffs are used to dealing with requests: they are goal-directed toward researchers. And it is possible to get company information through an association or a public relations firm, or at least the name of a source at the company. Many small companies contract out the PR function to firms that handle many clients.

Often, in the urban centres, a chamber of commerce seeks to be a voice for the business community. It takes a stand on a wide range of issues (such as transportation, education, pensions, labour) through its lobbying capacity. It provides both a business and a social atmosphere for its members to exchange business cards, make contacts, and do networking. It can also be known as a board of trade, and it can be extremely useful for researchers. Usually a board of trade has an information centre for members only, but it is accessible for data about the local community. Salaried researchers should be able to use it by virtue of their own company's membership. Chambers of commerce publish newsletters, magazines, market guides, and annual reports covering business trends and issues within the region, (such as *Directory of Trade and Professional Associations in Metropolitan Toronto*).

Some of the larger urban centres such as Toronto will also have a world trade centre, which encourages international trade through the activities of member centres world-wide. These provide members with market research information, trade knowledge, and global computer networks that allow members to advertise products or services and to reach other trade centre members easily, at reduced costs. They hold educational seminars and lectures for members. Their information centres supply data, some privately gathered, on products, industries, and the nature of the import-export business, as well as trade legislation from around the world. A world trade centre has a publishing program of data sheets and newsletters, and often a magazine. Like the board of trade, it can provide networking facilities and a social club. Internationally, they are linked by the World Trade Center Association, which promotes the *WTC Network* database of trade opportunities, leads, and statistics.

Yet another source of local commerce activity can be a convention and visitors' association, the purpose of which is "to bring dollars to the city" and promote local business and tourism. It is hooked up with hotels, restaurants, and auditoriums for conferences, corporate meetings, "international congresses," and trade shows. Sometimes it operates a convention centre, either free-standing or in conjunction with a local hotel. It thus has much information about upcoming events and conferences and names of sources with appropriate phone numbers, as well as statistics about the hospitality industry within the region.

Finally, a better business bureau is a non-profit public service that monitors the business community and aims to increase consumer confidence in business. There are seventeen bureaus in Canada and 175 in the United States. The BBB attempts to identify businesses that fail to meet certain standards and seeks to communicate these data to consumers. There are public service announcements and tips to consumers through its publications: its *Directory and Consumer Guide* lists businesses that meet bureau standards; its annual report is invaluable, with statistical data about complaints and charts on comparisons in consumer attitudes and concerns; *Canadian Business Life*, its magazine, includes interviews and articles on businesses and scams. Usually there is an information centre at each bureau office, with data about businesses, corporate frauds, and the like. For consumer advocacy groups, the bureau does not seem to go far enough (it can only police its own members), but it is a beginning point for research.

7

GOVERNMENT AND POLITICS

There is something addicting about a secret. – J. Edgar Hoover

This chapter presents material on national governments, provincial governments, agencies, boards and commissions, and municipal governments. Next to business, government and politics are the richest areas to mine for information. Public accountability brings with it an enormous amount of paper baggage, and hence, paper trails. As with any system, researchers must learn how governments operate, how they produce information, and what portion of the information is available in publicly accessible documents. Specific organization charts are crucial, for these will show the shape of federal, provincial, and municipal government structures, listing the services and programs available, the personnel, and the ensuing documents. These charts show that many functions also take place in regional offices, such as those of Revenue Canada, Statistics Canada, and environment assessment panels. These local branches can be approached directly without having to go through the head offices in Ottawa.

Governments are not as secretive as they are made out to be. The researcher who understands how the system works should eventually, and often easily, find what he or she is looking for. "Secret" information can be gleaned by simply perusing public records (and this involves knowing how to get them, how to digest and use them, and how to link them) and by observing the system's accessibility and talking to both highly placed bureaucrats and the little people, to exploit that one big grapevine called "government." Indeed, the hardest aspect about government secrecy is the verification of what is found.

National Government

The Canadian Parliament has a bicameral structure: the House of Commons and the Senate. This leads to a parallel series of documents, for everything appears to be done twice. In both places, there are the three readings of a bill, the debate on the bill, the committee hearings, and the question periods. A good explanation of the process is contained in Olga Bishop's *Canadian Official Publications* (Pergamon). Understanding the legislative process will allow researchers to access directly the type of data they need if it was generated by that process.

Daily agendas are issued in pamphlet form each day that Parliament is in session. These include routine proceedings such as written questions, petitions, reports, motions, statements by the government, private members' motions, and introduction of bills in first reading. As well, it has the orders of the day and committee activities, all with summaries and indexes. The official minutes of the previous meeting are also available, and here are listed the actions that occurred. At the end of each session, these votes and proceedings are collated as the journals of either house, which have general subject indexes, indexes to bills (government bills, private members' bills, and private bills), plus an index to those sessional papers that were tabled.

The debates are verbatim accounts of speeches and actions; they are issued daily, with a bit of a time lag, and are indexed separately at the end of each session. This indexing also includes references to the proceedings of committees considering the budget estimates. Debates are colloquially known as Hansard, named after Luke Hansard, who commenced printing the journals in Great Britain in 1774. Committee publications result from deliberations in hearings. Select and special committees are set up to consider a topic of special concern. Standing committees review bills, estimates, and annual reports. Verbatim accounts are issued as part of the debates series, with subject and witness indexes.

Bills are proposed pieces of legislation. They are printed after first reading and are numbered sequentially in two series, one for government and private members' bills, and one for private bills (which deal with private companies that require changes to their incorporation). When royal assent has been given, bills become acts and are assigned individual chapter numbers, along with the name of the reigning sovereign and the regnal year (thus, an act from 1991 would begin 40 Eliz. II, 1991, c. #). Both the public and private acts passed each session are gathered together as statutes. Each volume of the statutes contains indexes, such as an alphabetical listing of acts by their short titles, tables of public statutes that include amendments, proclamations for the acts and the dates on which they come into force, tables of regulations, and a listing of acts and parts of acts not yet proclaimed in force. The passing of an act does not mean that it comes into force right away. Some have operational dates months or even years ahead. From time to time, "office consolidations" of acts and regulations are published, for the convenience of the office of a department. These are unofficial compilations prepared by the respective departments responsible for the administration of certain statutes and scores of regulations. This makes it easier for the researcher to see what a department is supposed to be doing and its legislated scope. Also, about once a decade, statutes as amended are brought up to date. These are cited as revised statutes, abbreviated as RSC for Canada. These multi-volume works are the current law of the land, being supplemented only by the current sessions. Thus, the 1990 RSC would be augmented by the 1991 statutes, and by any other acts passed since 1991.

Regulations are changes to law thought to be too inconsequential to be brought forward to Parliament. These are instructions on the application of the law and the penalties imposed for failure to comply with the law. Many changes to the law are buried here. Most are minor, but cumulatively they can effect a major shift in emphasis of the legislation's intent. Hardly anyone really questions these regulations until after they have been passed and found to be ineffective. They are published as part of *Canada Gazette,* parts I, II, and III. Part I is the official news medium of government for a variety of notices and announcements, ranging from the Order of Canada awards and divorce notices to postal rates, bankruptcies, and regulations affecting private business. Regulatory Impact

Analysis statements in this weekly give advance notice for the changes to business. Part II contains new government regulations and new statutes. Part III contains the new statutes in chapter order as "acts." All parts of the *Canada Gazette* are indexed from time to time, but not cumulatively. The regulations are cited as Statutory Orders and Regulations (SOR), and they are consolidated from time to time.

The budget process (how governments appropriate funds and how they spend them) is always of great interest to researchers looking into government production. All levels of government have budgets with essentially the same process; only the names are different. Most budgets go through a process of proposals, presentations, review, and then approval. At some point the budget has to be voted on by politicians, but every step of the process needs to be scrutinized so that researchers know where the money is coming from, what changes there are, how the budget is balanced, the audit, and the government's political goals in spending the money. New budget items and substantial changes in existing ones should be noted. All these changes need extensive documentation to justify their existence.

The budget system needs to be learned so that researchers can spot curious discrepancies. Budgetary materials are usually very helpful, but they can be awesome. Overviews and summaries, economic performance, charts, and key indicators are always present. "Highlights" should be noted. The complete set of budget papers (which are not released simultaneously) comprises:

- the budget statement and estimates and forecasts (what the government says is going to happen);
- the public accounts (what happened last year, according to the government);
- the public auditor's report (what actually happened last year, and whether it was worthwhile).

Financial reports are distributed throughout the budget papers and contain valuable information on policy issues such as housing, tax laws, public transportation, cutbacks in federal spending, universities, and health care. The auditor's report often will contain "horror stories" of government incompetency in spending and other problems with the budget agencies. The jargon needs to be explained, for people seem to have problems understanding the difference between "debt" and "deficit" or knowing what "medium-term fiscal outlook" or "transitional costs" means. Many accounting firms produce a booklet of analyses of the current budgets, and these are free for the asking. Government officials are always happy to explain things their way, and do so with alacrity. For outside opinions, read the annual *How Ottawa Spends,* by G.B. Doern and A.M. Maslove. Online databases for the current federal budget are available through *QL Systems* and *InfoGlobe.* These have the budget speeches, the papers, and many of the tables plus their analyses.

Irregularities in the system are mostly concerned with timeliness. Budget estimates are often finally voted on almost at the end of the fiscal year to which they apply, long after they have been tabled. However, they have been looked at extensively during that period. Planned reviews seem to bear no relationship to the huge sums or policy implications. Quite often, debate will be held up by members dickering over little things. Cursory reviews occur when the government must have quick approval. Non-approval of any part of the budget can be taken as a vote of non-confidence in the government, and some legislators would vote for the budget as a whole rather than hold up or decline individual sections. Generally, too, the auditor's reports are ignored. Yet, a wealth of detail about government, such as costs of programs, salary ranges, travel allowances, and irregularities, is noted through the auditor's report. The budget-making process normally begins as a closed procedure, but once it has been tabled it is open for public debate and approval.

Executive materials come from the departments. If these have been published, then they are generally available in most public and academic libraries through the government's depository system. Most libraries select what they want, but the larger libraries (such as the legislative libraries in each province, leading academic libraries, and the prominent public libraries) have "full" status. They get everything publicly available, unsolicited, provided that they allow public access to the materials. Current items are also available for purchase from government-appointed agents, usually associated with book stores. Free items must be requested from the relevant department. Older items are generally only at the libraries or available on microfiche through Micromedia. Whatever has been released has also been listed in *Canadian Government Publications*

Catalogue, which is produced monthly and cumulated quarterly and annually. Many special reports are listed and indexed in *Microlog* (Micromedia, the publishers who also supply microfiche copies of the documents), while all government items are catalogued by the National Library of Canada's *Canadiana* bibliography. Much information is also available online from *QL Systems* and *InfoGlobe.* An unpublished item can be obtained through the Access to Information Act, so long as it is not exempted from release (see Chapter 3). Material can also be privately obtained through a contact.

The third branch of government is the judiciary, and court materials from this system will be considered in Chapter 8.

The sources of government information and policies are numerous. An understanding of the political process will show where the bottlenecks are, where the potential leaks can be, where the local nodes of data may reside. For example, members of the cabinet (either individually or in cabinet committees such as that on Priorities and Policies) can easily leak or cause to leak material that is good for their careers, their departments, or the country (in their opinion), or damaging to other departments or to individuals (again, in their opinion). Scuttlebutt flies around the capitals of the world, and motives are always suspect. Thus, although information can be obtained, it has to be verified. That, of course, is the tough part.

Department sources include branches common to all line departments and agencies. They go under names such as the Evaluation and Planning Branch and Environment Assessment Panel. The senior officials here put together special study teams that do cost-benefit analyses, create scenario packages, and speculate with five-year plans. Most of these reports are readily available. In fact, a lot of government information is readily available if it is asked for. But government officials will not usually offer to say that they have the stuff. They prefer to "confirm or deny" only or to provide "records for inspection." This passive role can be frustrating, which is precisely why researchers need to know what is in the file and what is available. They should not count on bureaucrats to help in this regard.

Central agencies also have bottlenecks. All studies and policy reports must pass through the Prime Minister's Office, the Privy Council Office, the Finance Ministry and Treasury Board, the appropriate Ministries of State, and the Office of the Comptroller General.

The parliamentary system and political parties generate useful information beyond the official legislative materials noted above. The legislative members in Question Period, which is an oral encounter, use such tactics as surprise and showmanship, designed to attract a national television audience. But some parliamentary questions are answered in writing only, and these are tabled and then reproduced by Micromedia as part of the sessional papers. The originals are filed in the Library of Parliament, another excellent information centre source for unique copies of reports and memoranda. Committees of Parliament receive briefs in support of or in opposition to legislation or policy. Sometimes these are not published, but they are available through Micromedia and the Library of Parliament and are a good source for obtaining the names of experts and additional data. The Auditor General has much documentation backing up his annual report, which details the misspending of government programs; contacts named in his report are extremely useful. Senate committees, unlike House committees, are just a bit quirky and are not well attended. Here, the potential for slips in data is enormous. Each political party also has a research section, which would be happy to promote its own party and to damage the reputation of the other parties.

Lobbyists are not a new development, but the 1989 Lobbyists Registration Act required full- and part-time lobbyists to register their names, clients, and subject matter in an online registry. This allows everyone to know who the players are in the process of policy-making. These lobbyists and lobby groups are useful as contacts and for reports. The top firms include former politicians, who are massaging their former colleagues as they trade their political favours and obligations. Some of the top subject matters, according to the registry, include matters of international trade, regional economies, government procurement, consumer issues, investment, and the environment. The registry can give a name, previous career, and what clients are represented. Insider newsletters that cater to lobbyists include the *Lobby Monitor* (biweekly) and the *Lobby Digest* (monthly). For more details, consult Nick Schultz's *Lobbyists Registration Act* (CCH Canadian, 1991).

Policy institutes are not bodies of government, but they interact as consultants or lobbyists. They are funded by associations, foundations, and individuals. Some people call them "think tanks," but they also have different political persuasions. Their active publications programs (newsletters, seminars, reports, studies, books) help pay some of the bills. They are an excellent source for contacts and data. Some of the more important ones in Canada include the C.D. Howe Research Institute, the Conference Board of Canada, the Institute for Research on Public Policy, the Canadian Institute for Economic Policy, the Fraser Institute, the Centre for Policy Alternatives, the National Foundation for Public Policy Development, the Canadian Council on Social Development, the Canadian Tax Foundation, and the Canada West Foundation. They all have information centres that contain the data upon which their reports are based.

Royal commissions, task forces, and judicial inquiries are investigatory bodies appointed under Order-in-Council to inquire into a specific public concern. They report back to a cabinet minister, but before doing so they collect and generate much data. Not all of this information is made public, but most of it is publicly accessible. Materials and back files are deposited in academic research libraries or government archives. All these investigatory bodies had research officers and information centres. They investigated sudden or catastrophic events, examined the conduct of public service employees, and assisted the government in determining policy. Royal commissions are the weakest in getting an adequate response out of the government, while judicial inquiries are the strongest because they examine special legal circumstances and pass judgements based on government policy or law. Resulting policy or changes become green papers (proposals) and white papers (policy) tabled in the legislature, and these, too, generate discussion and more paper. Listings and indexes of these investigations are in *Federal Royal Commissions in Canada; a checklist* and in various finding aids for commissions of inquiry at the National Archives in Ottawa.

Further afield are policy institute and royal commission research contracts at universities, and sometimes their archives end up in these academic libraries. Universities also have research grants for studies, accessed through the *Directory of Federally-Supported Research in Universities*. *Microlog* often will index the resulting reports. Media coverage of policy fields, political happenings, and government edicts can be accessed through the online systems of

CBCA, InfoGlobe, and *FP Online.* These will mention dates, names of sources, and background details for obscure actions or policies.

Private newsletters are a useful source of federal government information. There are *Ottawa Letter* (CCH Canadian), *The Public Sector* (Corpus Information Services), and *Ottawa Weekly Update* (Informetrica). Monthlies published by lobbyists include *Capital Briefing* (Government Consultants International Inc.) and *Parliamentary Alert* (Henry and Gray Inc.). All these newsletters cover the activities of Parliament and the federal departments, with information about new legislation, new departmental policies, statistics, appointments, summaries of reports, and announcements of both past and upcoming events. They provide concise, easy-to-scan data at a reliable level of credibility. Some are available as part of an online computer database, through *QL Systems* or *InfoGlobe.* Their subscription lists include associations, embassies, federally regulated companies, provincial governments, and even the legislators themselves, who are looking for analysis of the impact of legislation on the health of the country.

Specific government departments seem to be oriented to researchers, and they are forthcoming in furnishing names and data. These include:

- the Department of Consumer and Corporate Affairs: for business registration, estate planning, trademark registration, amalgamations, bankruptcies, combines and competition, financial statements;
- Agriculture Canada: for farming, the environment, federal-provincial relations, farm subsidies;
- Labour Canada: for industrial relations, collective bargaining;
- Department of Finance: for bank loan information, federal budget;
- Statistics Canada: mandated to collect and disseminate a wide variety of statistics about Canada;
- National Library of Canada: access to just about everything that has been published by and about Canadians or in Canada, as well as manuscripts (if they don't have it, they will find it);

- National Archives of Canada: original materials from the past (maps, letters, telegrams, reports, registers, architectural plans, photographs, manuscripts, illustrations, engravings, drawings, computer tapes, sound recordings, films, videos, materials for genealogical tracing);
- Library of Parliament: useful for tabled reports and unique material such as written answers to oral questions, along with background material on all the subjects that Parliament debates.

Recorded or published listings of government sources include the following, which are available at most libraries.

Guide to Federal Programs and Services (Supply and Services Canada) is published about yearly, providing brief information on 1,500 departments and programs, along with 4,600 names of contacts, addresses, and phone numbers.

InfoSource (Sources of Federal Government Information), available both in print and as online, tells how to use the Access to Information Act and the Privacy Act. It has over 100 chapters on the federal agencies covered by these acts, describing their background, responsibilities, legislation, organization, and information holdings, along with phone numbers of people who are access contacts. Also included are public inquiry units, departmental libraries, and other federal information offices.

Canadian News Facts (Marpep Publishing) is a semi-monthly news digest service that covers Canada. It also lists changes in the federal government (new deputy ministers, new cabinet ministers) with excerpts from speeches or texts, all of it well indexed.

Legal Materials Letter (Canadian Law Information Council) is a non-jargon monthly newsletter commenting on new sources of legal information for Canada and the provinces.

Canadian Parliamentary Guide (*InfoGlobe*) contains annual biographical information on Canada's members of Parliament and the provincial and territorial legislatures. Other data here include results of federal and provincial general elections and by-elections, information on current members of the Supreme Court, Federal Court, and Tax Court of Canada, members of the Press Gallery, the Library of Parliament, and agencies, boards, and commissions (ABCs), plus a list of all the ministries since Confederation, governors general and staff, Canadian representatives abroad, and diplomatic representatives in Canada.

Corpus Administrative Index (Southam Communications) is a listing of senior government officials: 20,000 in the 1,400 federal and provincial departments, agencies, boards, commissions, and Crown corporations. Given are the names, titles, addresses, and phone numbers (plus telex and fax numbers), arranged by jurisdiction and then by operating branch. Included are departmental and executive assistants who frequently control access to upper management. This is revised quarterly, with about 2,000 changes in each issue.

Canadian Federal Government Handbook (*Globe and Mail*) provides data about government and public officials: names, biographies, addresses, phone numbers, functions of 100 major departments and ABCs. It is meant for businesses that want to sell to government.

Microlog (Micromedia) is a combination monthly listing and catalogue service to thousands of special reports and briefs submitted by, to, or on behalf of government agencies. The reports are identified by authors and subject fields and then indexed. Some of these studies are from consultants and academics; others are from government agencies at all levels, right down to municipal agencies (such as social planning councils) for cities across Canada. In their original print form, these reports were limited in quantity. But Micromedia stocks microfiche copies. This is an extremely valuable service for obtaining a rare, minor report from more than a decade ago.

Canadian Almanac and Directory (Copp Clark Pitman) and *Corpus Almanac and Canadian Sourcebook* (Southam Communications) are annuals with background data about governments, along with names and numbers for all levels.

The "blue pages" (Bell Canada) in the back of the telephone directory provide a list of government offices and services identified by level of government and for the calling area of the directory. Frequently called numbers are highlighted, and there is always a central inquiry or referral service. For instance, the Reference Canada service (which is strictly a referral to other names and numbers) for Toronto is 973-1993. This service, available across Canada, has a different number in each province or region, and is useful for tracking down a federal government service or program.

These kinds of sources of government data – legislative, executive, judicial, general – are duplicated more or less for other countries such as Great Britain and the United States and for the Canadian provinces and the fifty American states.

For example, current U.S. federal documents can be obtained from consulates and embassies, as well as from Washington, D.C., sources. There is a *Monthly Catalog of U.S. Government Publications*, which lists the published data. The FOIA can be used for unpublished materials. Guides to American records include Joe Morehead's *Introduction to United States Public Documents* (Libraries Unlimited) and Jerrold Zwim's *Congressional Publications; a research guide to legislation, budgets and treaties* (Libraries Unlimited), as well as the annual *U.S. Government Organization Manual* for a look at policy programs and organization charts. Congressional Quarterly, a publisher, produces the online *Washington Information Directory*, also available as an annual. The important legislative publications include *Congressional Record* (the debates), *Federal Register* (the gazette), *Code of Federal Regulations, United States Statutes at Large, CISUS Index of Congressional Committee Hearings, Declassified Documents Retrospective Collection*, and *Official Congressional Directory*. Older and out-of-print items can be located at larger academic libraries. The National Library of Canada, the University of Toronto Library, and the Legislative Library of Ontario have the most extensive holdings in Canada.

For other countries, researchers should begin with the relevant embassy or consulate. These have access to most current publications and statistics and are in constant fax contact with their home countries. Older items are probably available in or through the larger academic libraries, although the embassy might know of different holdings in different locations within Canada. Certainly, the strongest holdings of any national government will be that country's national archives, national library, and/or legislative library. With fax machines and international flights, there should be no problem in obtaining a known document or statistical figure.

The real difficulties remain: trying to know if it exists, trying to figure out where it might be, trying to pry it loose, and then trying to verify it. Materials are readily identifiable, and three beginning points will be: (1) a government documents librarian at a university or legislative library; (2) printed guides such as John Pemberton's

British Official Publications (Pergamon) or Peter Hajnal's *Guide to United Nations Organization, Documentation, and Publishing*; (3) catalogues such as *HMSO Publications Catalogue* for Great Britain and *UNDEX* (United Nations Document Index).

Other documents are issued by treaty NGOs (non-governmental organizations) such as OECD (Organization for Economic Co-Operation and Development), GATT (General Agreement on Tariffs and Trade), the World Bank, and NATO, and sections of the United Nations such as Unesco. These meet regularly to deliberate on such subjects as nutrition, disarmament, and money supply. They all have information officers, libraries, publications, statistics, and indexes, producing information about their decisions and the reasons for their actions. Some could be suspect, falling into the category of "non-authoritative" sources. For example, the Organization of Petroleum Exporting Countries (OPEC) maintains the OPEC News Agency, whose mission is to "provide information on OPEC to about 77 countries and counteract inaccurate reporting by some other sources." In Canada, many of the currently published materials from the NGOs are available through the federal government or from an authorized bookstore.

Provincial Government

Most of the preceding notes on the Canadian federal government apply to the provinces as well. Needs for specific information will change because of the different responsibilities under the Constitution Act, 1867 (formerly called the British North America Act). Documents can be found at the larger public and university libraries within a province, but not so readily outside that province. It is all a function of size, importance, and geography. But all of the provincial legislative libraries exchange materials, so they become good places to begin a search for out-of-province data. Otherwise, current items can be purchased by mail.

Important legislative items include the gazette (with provincial topics such as corporation notices, dissolution of partnerships, changes of name, sheriff's sales of land), the debates, the bills and statutes, the revised statutes, and the regulations. For knowledge about provinces there are catalogues of publications such as the monthly *Publications of the Ontario Government* and the annual *KWIC Index to the Government of Ontario,* which covers a wide assortment of topics, including car pooling, mushrooms, and welfare, with the appropriate names and numbers. The Archives of Ontario has historical materials such as records and documents of royal commissions. *Corpus Administrative Index* also shows organization and names of government areas for all the provinces. And the blue pages in the telephone book have handy referral numbers such as Ontario's 965-3535 in Toronto.

Other resources for finding provincial data include:

- FOIA: some kind of register will be available for the eight provinces with this type of legislation, and this listing will show government organization and the location of files. The FOIA is useful when applying for reports with limited distribution.
- *Canadian News Facts* for news of government changes.
- *Legal Materials Letter* for updates on legal changes.
- *Canadian Parliamentary Guide* for annual biographical information.
- *Microlog* for special studies from agencies and consultants.
- *Canadian Almanac and Directory* and *Corpus Almanac and Canadian Sourcebook* for annual lists of names and numbers.
- *Provincial Legislative Record* (CCH Canadian), published monthly, for news and views of government bills progressing through the legislative assemblies, notices, commentaries on tax changes.

Agencies, Boards, and Commissions (ABCs)

Agencies, boards, and commissions are created under specific acts administered by an appropriate department at any of the levels in a federal system. Some are unfunded, while others are directly funded or have access to the Consolidated Revenue Fund. The ABCs perform one or more of three basic functions: (1) *advisory* (such as Ontario's Advisory Council on Senior Citizens); (2) *regulatory* (such as a liquor licensing board); (3) *operational* (such as GO Transit, the commuter service at the western end of Lake Ontario).

ABCs vary in size and activities and are structured accordingly, depending on whether program delivery requires operational flexibility or particular publicity (such as a lottery corporation), or whether program delivery should not be subject to undue influence from a department (such as the quasi-judicial provincial labour relations boards). Ontario, for instance, has about 550 ABCs at the provincial government level.

The type of ABC that plays the biggest role in anyone's life is the regulatory ABC. There are more than 1,500 of these throughout Canada at the provincial and national level, and more at the municipal level. (These latter are mostly known as "special-purpose bodies.") Some regulatory bodies are administrative tribunals because of their quasi-legal structure. These range from the Ontario Labour Relations Board (only the courts can review its decisions) to the Canadian Radio-television and Telecommunications Commission (only the federal cabinet can review its decisions). A high profile is maintained by the Unemployment Insurance Commission, which regularly hears over 30,000 appeals annually from claimants, while a low profile is kept by the Wolf Damages Assessment Board, which at one point had not even met for about thirteen years.

Other actions: the Ontario Securities Commission told the Canadian Tire Corporation dealers that they could not take over the company; the CRTC told the CTV network to produce more Canadian television programming; the Canadian Human Rights Commission found a member of Parliament to have sexually harassed a woman employee; and the Assessment Review Board of Ontario turned down my appeal concerning a high property assessment (and I lost a subsequent appeal to the Ontario Municipal Board; I could have appealed *that* decision to the Ontario cabinet).

A wealth of material is now available on various ABCs. They can be accessed through the various FOIAs that operate at all levels of government. Most files, unless they concern privacy, are open. Here is the kind of detail that should be available:

- *Appointments* are undeniably political, but the terms do not go on forever. Most are for one to three years. The law relative to the appointments should indicate qualifications for the role.
- *Legislation* establishing the ABC will list several specific areas

of responsibility, along with regulatory authority, acts administered, and appeal procedures.

- *Identification* will include address, numbers, names of officers, reporting structures, name changes, staffing, salary ranges, budgets.
- *Funding sources and expenses* should be explained, including budget proposals, accounts, audited figures, advertising.
- *Review* of the ABC is conducted by a responsible department or senior official.
- *Public records* exist of decisions, annual reports, newsletters, staff bulletins, forms.
- *Information centre/archives* will contain unique materials.

Effectiveness can be judged by inquiring among suppliers, customers, and those regulated.

Municipal Governments

Municipal documents are useful for digging up material about local government and also for the verification of information about a person or a business. Normally, documents with financial data or private information about a person are closed. But that should not stop researchers from requesting verbal information or even a verbal confirmation. So long as researchers have not seen the document they are in compliance with the law. In the case of closed documents, only the person whose name is on the document has access to it. But in some cases an agent may be authorized (such as a lawyer or real estate broker for a property transaction), or the document is introduced as evidence in a court case (voluntarily or as a subpoenaed *duces tecum*). Sometimes records custodians are slack in their job and won't be strict about proof of identification, especially over the telephone. Acting like a student can be effective in some cases, and acting authoritarian can be effective in others. Each situation must be sized up separately, especially since some clerks are extremely generous in giving information while others are tight-fisted – even when they are both behind the same counter!

The political arena at the top of city politics is the council, which acts like a legislature. It generates minutes of proceedings, which are kept on file before being transferred to archives. What's important about the minutes is that they include committee reports and all by-laws passed. Usually, these are noted as appendices and must be watched for. The minutes often have indexes to the by-laws and to council actions, which speed retrieval of specific motions or policies. The quantity of minutes will vary enormously, but generally the larger the urban structure the fuller and more widely recorded will be the minutes (including videotapings). The smaller towns keep a record of just the motions and activities, and not of the debate itself.

The city clerk is the most powerful municipal mandarin. This office is responsible for all administrative services of a city council, and it is the place with the original copies of by-laws, minutes, resolutions, reports, and files. Employees are knowledgeable about what currently goes on in all the departmental sections and local special-purpose bodies. Information available includes lists of senior staff, organization charts, and salary ranges for employees and management. For data more than a year old, it might be better to begin searching with a municipal archivist or a records management officer. In Ontario, the Municipal Freedom of Information Act opens many files previously not regulated as either closed or open (most clerks had a "policy" about accessibility).

Unlike provincial and federal governments, which deal with people mainly through letters or toll-free telephone numbers, the city clerk's office has the reputation of being a drop-in referral centre. Unless researchers are inquiring about a faraway locality, they are close enough to their local city hall to be able to get counter service and to see a variety of custodians. This is especially useful if researchers get shunted from area to area, for virtually no travel time is expended. Because so many documents are available, counter staff do not usually supply answers to queries. Instead, they supply documents: they may give researchers the whole thing or just part of it, read from it, or only confirm or deny. Documents are said to be available for inspection, and answers can be found in an inspected document. This is one of the major principles behind FOIA legislation: answers are not produced but rather documents are; materials are not interpreted for the researcher but are supplied for his or her inspection. Once this is understood, then a whole range of document procurement activities is possible. Some offices allow photocopying and tape recording, while others allow only handwritten reproduction. Some counter clerks don't even allow this: researchers must inspect and then memorize.

Most municipal documents are at city hall, the public library, and the civic archives. Important publications include: city council minutes, minutes of subcommittees of council, by-laws, the official plan and an assortment of planning reports to support the main plan, annual reports of civic departments and of ABCs, financial and audit reports of the municipality, reports from outside consultants on special problems, maps, and departmental newsletters. The public library does a good job of maintaining vertical files about issues and departments. It retains clippings, news bulletins, and pamphlets, along with briefs, hearings, and reports from associations concerned with local government. For faraway cities, newspapers are invaluable, providing information on local issues and reports, which is useful for gauging reactions following a report's release. Online computer databases furnish articles with the names of the key players, including the by-lines of reporters who then become additional sources.

Numerous types of municipal or municipally related documents can be accessed. These are discussed below.

(1) *Licences and permits.* At the municipal level, licensing covers a variety of trades, businesses, and occupations. These are usually set up by local by-law for the purpose of generating revenue, controlling who operates what in the region, consumer protection, and public health and safety. Licences are issued for one year, except in certain large urban areas where such categories as "adult entertainment" parlours must be renewed every six months. The fee structure is publicly available. In the transportation category for Toronto, for example, fees range from $50 for operating a driving school to $4,500 for a taxicab owner permit. There can be over 200 different types of licences.

Provincial municipal licensing acts allow municipal councils to make licensing decisions based on local needs. Smaller towns usually give the licensing function to the police, while the larger cities have a separate commission. Such bodies can also be tribunals since they have discretion to grant, refuse, suspend, or revoke licences. By handling complaints from consumers, they can keep an eye on improper conduct by tradesmen or services, and they can suspend licences. Complaints also allow the commission to pinpoint unlicensed tradesmen or services.

Licensing seeks to regulate competency and product quality. The licence file application may contain details about a person's character, certification from a trade school (with records of verbal and written exams), driving records, and criminal records if any. Denial of a licence can be appealed as far as the Supreme Court of Canada.

Statistics are kept and files are maintained, but rarely is the material accessible to the public. Municipal Freedom of Information Act applications can pry loose certain features, such as aggregate statistics. Commissions often read out certain information such as names and addresses for confirmation, but researchers are not allowed to see the documents. In some cases, custodians also state whether there have been any complaints against a company. Occasionally, researchers have been told that if they require a name or an address, or anything else, then they must send a letter to the commission, stating a reason. The commission's discretion to give it out or not can be arbitrary, and this seems to be a factor of whether the request is considered to be serious and whether the clerks have the time to dig out the file. Further information on licensing can be found in J. Bossons *et al., Regulation by Municipal Licensing* (University of Toronto Press).

(2) *Water and sewage bills.* Sometimes water bill information is available, although such bills are relatively uninteresting when there is a flat charge in effect. Metered bills can tell researchers how many occupants there are in a house, by dividing the bill by the rate for a "normal" consumption. Owners can, of course, access their own previous water and sewage history, as can real estate brokers or lawyers acting as authorized agents.

(3) *Special-purpose bodies.* Agencies, boards, and commissions have many documents and policies that can from time to time (and under differing circumstances) be made available. They have promotional material such as annual reports, descriptive pamphlets, and organizational charts. While they might explain their policy (or even have written policy statements), they will not give out privately held data, such as circulation records from a public library or the character of residents in a housing project. Documents and minutes of board meetings are the minimum that can be inspected, but some

ABCs do allow public attendance at regularly scheduled or special meetings.

(4) *Voters' lists.* The list of voters eligible to vote in a municipal election is put together for two reasons: first, to see who is eligible to vote, and second, to offer the opportunity for other voters to contest the inclusion of certain names. This last function is rarely used, except occasionally by a political machine that might question what looks like list-padding. Usually, the voting lists are compiled from the assessment rolls, but this does not always determine citizenship. Some property owners and tenants who were not Canadian citizens have been allowed to vote because their names have appeared on the list. Voters' lists are often prepared about a year in advance of a municipal election (with updating to a month before the election) because the election dates are known, unlike the federal and provincial elections. Most voters' lists from the past can be obtained for a small fee. Information on current lists includes: name (first and last), address, whether public or separate school supporter, ward, language preference, and whether the person is an owner, a spouse (that is, a non-owning spouse), or a tenant (that is, a renter or any offspring of voting age). The arrangement is by street, in ascending order, much like a city directory.

(5) *Assessment records.* These are compiled for taxation of land (they are a provincial-level responsibility in Ontario). Information contained in the assessment roll includes name and address, year of birth, occupancy status (owner, tenant, or spouse), marital status, school system supported, residential address if different, property dimensions, amount of cleared and non-cleared land (if applicable), "assessed" value of property (which may be its market value), and total number of residents. If researchers know the mill rate, then the realty tax can be calculated. In the past there used to be an indication of occupation, number of children, and animals that had to be licensed. Older rolls can be accessed, showing history of an area or of a person's family. Because neighbourhoods are homogeneous, if a particular assessment seems to be too low or too high in terms of the surrounding assessment, then there might be a good reason, and this needs to be checked out.

(6) *Committee of adjustment records.* COA records can usually be found in the building or planning department of a municipality. Applications are made to the COA by the building owners, requesting

the municipality to allow the subdivision of a property or a minor variance to a zoning by-law, such as building a third floor (or a deck) or increasing occupancy in a licensed residential care facility. Hearings are open, to allow local residents to support or protest the change. Files are open, and these contain the application, any drawings or plans submitted, evidence that the local neighbourhood was informed, correspondence from the neighbourhood, and the committee's decision. Files date back (to 1939 for Toronto) and are accessible, but generally, only the current year is kept active. Some parts of the submitted application may not be viewed by the public in the interest of privacy, but usually names, addresses, phone numbers, and mortgages are listed.

(7) *Work orders*. Violations of city by-laws as they pertain to residential and commercial properties can be accessed discreetly from city departments, particularly if leaking the information might get the work performed (through the owner's fear of media exposure). Often, a lawyer who is an authorized agent for a potential buyer can have access to outstanding work orders.

(8) *Back tax records*. Delinquent taxes are essentially private records not open for public inspection. Both unpaid taxes and taxes from previous years are accessible by the individual concerned or by a lawyer who is an authorized agent for a potential buyer. Back tax records are made available when properties are auctioned off to pay these taxes and, of course, when produced as court documents.

(9) *Building codes*. These sets of building requirements minimize the risk of injury and property damage from structural failure, fire, and health hazards. Building codes are specified by provincial acts, but municipalities have been delegated to enforce them. Copies of the act are available in public libraries, or the act can be purchased. It covers use and occupancy, health and safety requirements, structural design methods, requirements for wind and water and vapour protection, requirements for the installation of heating and ventilating and air conditioning, the requirements for the building of houses and small buildings, plus residential renovations.

(10) *Building permits*. These permits allow homeowners and contractors to make changes to buildings and to build new houses. They are official certificates that are accessible, as are the applications: construction permit (which many people refer to as a "building permit") for building, adding to, or making changes; demolition

permit for removing a building or part of it; and permits for installation and alteration, heating, plumbing, and signs. Drawings, surveys, names of owners and contractors, addresses, telephone numbers, and estimated cost of the structure must be included, and they are generally accessible. But if researchers need copies of the contents of the permit, then they need to produce an original letter from the architect or builder giving authorization. A proper search through the building code, the building permits, assessment rolls, and COA files can reveal all manner of discrepancies in the building of residential and commercial structures.

(11) *School support lists.* This is one way to define the supporters of the public and the separate school boards. It is a spinoff of the voters' list and the assessment rolls, with the same information (owner or tenant, citizenship, residency), but because the school support lists are arranged alphabetically by name, researchers can see a list of all the local properties that each person owns.

(12) *Land titles.* Although land records are a provincial function in Canada, land titles and land registration systems mesh well with municipal documents. Assessment rolls and voter registration are also done by the Ontario provincial government on behalf of the municipalities. It is important to note that there are two types of land records. In the land titles system, the province guarantees that the title is good and clear of encumbrances such as outstanding mortgages, liens, or easements. In the land registry system, nothing is guaranteed on the title and searches must be made, usually as far back as forty years, to show no outstanding claims on the deed.

To search the land registry, the researcher must have the lot and plan number. This can be obtained by searching the assessment rolls under the address. The rolls show researchers the legal description of the lands and the addresses of all property owners. They also show when the last reassessment was done. Doing a title search can reveal some or all of the following documents or facts:

- mortgage instruments (and subsequent discharge)
- transfer/deed
- leases
- vendors ("grantors")
- buyers ("grantees")
- amount of mortgage ("consideration")

- land transfer tax forms (used to find the selling price)
- tax payments
- description of land
- improvements built
- liens
- bail bonds
- surveys and maps.

To be completely up to date, researchers need to view the day book. This lists any current registrations against the title that have not yet been recorded. Other materials and strategies can be found and explained in such texts as *Title Searching*, a loose-leaf manual from the Law Society of Upper Canada. Legal publishing companies such as Carswell, Butterworths, and CCH Canadian also have data. Professional title searchers can be employed, for they have experience in tracking down elusive or quirky items that an unexperienced researcher might miss.

(13) *Lobbyist disclosure.* Some urban areas now have a lobbyist disclosure by-law. In the City of Toronto, lobbyists must complete a publicly accessible form if they deal with politicians or bureaucrats regarding applications about: official plans, zoning by-laws, rental housing, vending location, boulevard cafés, grants or loans above $15,000, leases from the city, lottery licences, consulting services, and tenders on contracts. On the form, paid representation to politicians and bureaucrats has to be indicated, and forms must be filled out for every activity, whether or not the lobbying actually occurs. The researcher will soon be able to discover the quantity of representation in heavily trafficked areas. The repetition of certain names would certainly suggest a further look.

(14) *Contract tenders.* Because there are no legislative provisions in the provinces requiring municipalities to tender in a specific manner, all kinds of inconsistencies and variables have turned up. What may be true in one city is not true in another. *Municipal Tendering, Common Practices* is a book based on a review of 100 Canadian municipalities with different procedures in 1984. It provides good basic information about tendering to those who wish to know more about the process.

Every tender needs to have clear and concise directions to bidders, and every tender must maintain the integrity of the actual selection process. Some jurisdictions, such as the City of Toronto, have used these principles to their advantage. Bidders in Toronto are required to meet standards of a fair wage policy, code of ethics, employment equity, lobbyist disclosure, and Canadian content. As well, there are legislated conditions such as workers' compensation, insurance, and bonding. Potential bidders can complete a Bidder's Application and go on a Bidder's List. Toronto has about 1,000 companies on its list, which is not generally available to the public. Regular information seminars are held for potential suppliers. In Toronto, contracts for over $25,000 worth of goods or services must be advertised. If under $25,000, then formal quotations in writing are made from those on the Bidder's List only. Tenders are received and opened in public, reviewed and accessed by the user department, and then decided upon. Contracts for a large amount usually get debated in council.

Policies on tendering are generally available from a municipality's purchasing department, and they serve quite well as an additional piece of paper to add to paper trails. Hawley Black's *How to Sell to the Government* (Macmillan of Canada) is an excellent source for doing business with Canadian federal departments, Crown agencies, provincial governments, and even the United States government, and provides the where, why, and who in the contract business, with strategies and forms. Much of it is also applicable at the local level. In any searching for the pork barrel in politics, it is crucial that the system of contract awarding be understood and that project prioritizing, quality control, and review measures be understood. Publicly financed projects need to be monitored, and by examining the documents and the sources of funding, researchers are able to get a clear picture of the effects of the project.

(15) *Records management and archives.* Many urban areas maintain an archival collection, with historical data about the community, photographs, maps, files, clippings, official documents that are not deemed current, and personal files of local politicians and bureaucrats. Sometimes these archives are held by the public library system and have been augmented by donations and church records. Often, too, there will be a records management section related to or attached to the archives. This section preserves documents of a more mundane character. Generally, whatever is in the archives is publicly accessible and whatever is in the records is not, unless the researcher

has special dispensation. In some towns this is unfortunate, because some mundane records such as city directories, voters' lists, zonings, permits, and so forth might be more useful if they were accessible through the archives instead of through the records. Statutory requirements and the municipal FOIA will also affect record retention.

Here is an example of the use of municipal documents in finding information about property development.

"When the railroad comes through, we'll be sitting pretty – so long as we're the only ones who know about it!" That sums up the main issues in property development: the enhancement of land values and the secrecy to deny others a chance to cash in. One of the best pieces of advice for researchers embarking on the paper trail has always been to "follow the dollar" – monetary transactions, profiteering, conflict-of-interest disclosures, regulatory filings, court cases dealing with fraud. Perhaps the richest lode to mine for information about politicians, bureaucrats, businessmen, and organized crime is the laundering of money through real estate development. Property always increases in value. The action of improving it or turning it over to a different use increases its value faster. It is no wonder that shady deals can create a rise in real estate values, for it is very easy to hide the property's appreciated worth. For instance, an assessor could be persuaded to reduce the market value of a property so the owner can avoid higher tax payments or can pursue its re-use in a different form. A Committee of Adjustment member could be persuaded to allow a minor variance that would enhance the resale value of a particular property. Land could be subdivided, or severed, assembled, and recast again to allow for a different mix of commercial and residential usage.

Nevertheless, while land development is one of the quickest routes to power and wealth, the whole process is detailed in many public documents. The secret for developers lies in possessing inside information, buying cheaply, improving for little cost, obtaining tax concessions or tax holidays, unloading at maximum land use, or selling high to government – not to mention using someone else's money for the down payment and mortgage at the beginning but getting all the inflated dollars back at the end in real cash. The rate of return is phenomenal, usually over 1,000 per cent. For government officials, the payoff comes whenever the government sells public land, or controls its use, or changes its value, taxes it, and discloses privileged information. Nepotism, patronage, and favours are part of this system.

The official plan of a city will give researchers virtually all the significant data needed to find out how development is proceeding in that municipality. The plan gives amendment information, zoning information, and various provincial approvals. The larger cities, such as Toronto, have a *Directory of Development Control Information* containing addresses, phone numbers, and names of people working in the building inspection department, public works department, and planning and development department, and it has a map showing office locations throughout the city. The provincial ministry responsible for municipal affairs has booklets on such topics as the Planning Act, official plans and amendments, zoning by-laws, minor variances, subdivisions, land severances, building permits, and (for Ontario) the Ontario Municipal Board. A proper understanding of how the system works, the basic process of community planning or land use planning, will show researchers what documents must be filed when and where, and how to get at them to check up on the property in question.

In the example of property development, zoning by-laws regulate the use of land and the erection, use, size, height, and location of structures. Zoning can be manipulated (such as rezoning, or switching air rights) by a land use committee. An unusual request to the Committee of Adjustment allowing for a minor variance in any of these regulations could be viewed suspiciously and checked out. Land title searches may reveal multiple ownerships, dummy corporations, mortgages, liens, sales, and sales that never went through (as in the case of former B.C. Premier William Vander Zalm). A look at the various types of building permits (construction, demolition, heating, plumbing, and signs) and their inspection records may show that tax money was spent to improve someone else's private property. But researchers must be aware of what is available and where the documents are. Only then can they exploit the system and find some answers, such as locating data about property enhancement due to non-conforming land use. Some developers are strong enough that they don't have to jiggle the assessment or sever land; they simply change the system by getting council to pass or repeal by-laws.

Computers are now heavily used by cities to keep track of property assemblies, money involved, staff reports, various drawings and plans, recommendations for zoning amendments, proposals for landscaping, garbage removal, and so forth. Development projects are usually indexed by both address and subject headings, which allows for easy retrieval no matter where the project is within the region. For instance, for Toronto, this would include "Dome Stadium," "Don River Clean Up," "Day Care," and "Port of Toronto Economic Impact Study." By means of the address, an extremely thorough search can be made on a property: history, past zoning amendments, number of bedrooms and bathrooms, square footage, water consumption, and plans and surveys.

Most decisions concerning municipal development in Ontario that are variations from existing by-laws can be appealed to the Ontario Municipal Board, an administrative tribunal. Appeals to the OMB's decisions are heard by the Ontario cabinet. All of its reports, cases, and decisions are publicly available for monitoring.

8

LAW AND THE COURTS

You know my methods. Apply them. – Sherlock Holmes, by A. Conan Doyle

One of the great tragedies of life is the murder of a beautiful theory by a brutal gang of facts. – La Rochefoucauld

This chapter presents material on: legal research, criminal court documents, civil court documents (divorce, probate, bankruptcy, inquest), and public inquiries and administrative tribunals. The field of law and the courts also includes the administration of justice, legal research, and court documents. The last two are relatively easy to learn about, although data retrieval might be hampered by the form of legal administration, which sometimes makes it difficult to get information. Yet this is the area that researchers have to go through to get information from court documents.

In the legal process (whether civil or criminal), someone files a complaint before the court. The person charged responds to the complaint. The case is heard before a judge, a panel of judges, or a jury. A decision on the case is made. The award is announced or the sentence is passed. All of these are subject to motions, counter-motions, rulings, judgements, and appeals, which can tie up a case for several years. A lower court may find itself rehearing a case because an appeals court ruled that an error in law was made during the trial, but both the appeal and the rehearing can be subsequently appealed and either or both can be stayed. Throughout all this, the real power lies with the police, the officers of the court, and the records custodians. They form part of the administration of justice: law enforcement agencies (police), adjudicatory agencies (courts), corrections (jails, forensic psychiatry), and crime prevention (rehabilitation, halfway houses).

Reporters have found themselves in contempt of court, a charge that relates more to justice administration than to legal procedures. They have unknowingly reported on something that they should not have because they didn't attend all of the hearings or see all the documents, or they did know what happened but went ahead anyway, hoping that no one would notice. The best way to avoid contempt is to be aware of the procedures of law when recording courtroom events. Researchers need to examine the daily police occurrence sheets to see who has been charged with what offence, but these have been known to be inaccurate and must be checked later against the informations (i.e., the charges against the accused). Researchers need to make inquiries regularly of the various police divisions.

Probably here more than in most areas, contacts are needed to assist any deep probing into a law enforcement agency. Material that is privately obtained cannot, of course, be publicly used, but it can be used to confirm suspicions or verify other existing data. Contacts can alert the researcher to problems within the police force, point her or him in the right direction, or even smuggle out documents for a viewing. Police divisions trade data within their own system and with other law enforcement agencies at provincial, national, and international levels. Materials that are difficult but not impossible to obtain include crime statistics, subpoenas, coroners' reports, reports of internal investigations, police arrest records, jail books, complaint records, monthly summaries, and annual budgets. Occasionally researchers might have to use something like Ontario's Municipal Freedom of Information Act, but they need to be aware that this process is slow.

Dealing with the courts is like dealing with the police. Here, too, there are lots of close-mouthed officials, commonly called "officers of the court." They include the clerk of the court, the Crown attorneys, the defence attorneys, various deputies and bailiffs, police in attendance, judges, and probation officers; sometimes even jurors and witnesses are placed in this category. Overloaded courthouses tend to encourage overreaction, lost or misplaced files, sharp tempers, potential for bribery, contempt of court citations, and general shambles. It is up to researchers to guide themselves through the maze by scrutinizing court lists, sounding out defence lawyers and prosecutors, interviewing judges (but not about current cases), and getting along with the judge in court. For back-up, the well-positioned researcher could seek out private investigators for information, try to obtain useful data from coroners and forensic scientists, interview inmates, and check with rehabilitation officers.

As in any subject field, once researchers know how this system is supposed to work, then they can check the ideal against the local norm: ask the right questions in evaluating the system, look at the speed of the system in the context of other systems (too fast? too slow?), and use computers to see the larger picture (what is happening elsewhere? what has happened over the past twenty years?). Diligence will pay off if the databases are checked, as well as the documents and the experts.

Legal Research

Legal research is fairly well codified. Law schools offer courses that students must take to qualify for bar admission programs, and legal researchers are attached to all law firms, including those of just one lawyer. For Canadian law and the court system, useful guides to legal research include legal indexes, law report series, dictionaries, encyclopedias, legal periodicals (for commentaries), statute citators and digests to court decisions, and online computer databases.

All of these will be found in law libraries, such as those maintained by the law schools or universities with law courses and by legal firms (whose libraries may double as meeting rooms), as well as in courthouse, city hall, and government libraries. People are always available to help, although less so in the private practices.

Some of the experts for each case include the lawyers, the judge, the clerk of the court, even the jury (once discharged), although disobedience to gag orders can be grounds for mistrial. Researchers need to tread carefully here. But certainly it does not hurt to approach the lawyers for both sides, various court officials, the records custodians, and other knowledgeable legal researchers.

Typical printed materials include the following.

(1) Some provinces, as well as the national government, have set up various law reform commissions to make recommendations on the modernization, improvement, and communication of the law in Canada. They publish working papers, research notes, and final reports on various laws. Of course, governments still have to act on these studies, but nevertheless, problems and inconsistencies are pointed out and can be accessed.

(2) The *Canadian Encyclopedic Digest* gives overviews, with references to both statute and case law. This is published in different editions for parts of Canada and in loose-leaf form for ease of updating.

(3) Indexes are used for tracking down commentaries written about laws and legal opinions. They are also useful for determining the intent of legislation (also known as "legislative histories"). The *Index to Canadian Legal Periodical Literature,* which began in 1961, covers about 100 periodical titles published in Canada. Indexes to non-Canadian law journals include *Index to Legal Periodicals* (with 500 titles indexed) and *Legal Resources Index* (with 750 titles). In 1987, the *Index to Canadian Legal Literature* began to be separately published by Carswell. It covers periodicals, monographs, and government publications, with a table of cases, table of statutes, and a book review index. *Canadian Current Law* (issued biweekly) acts as an update to the *Index to Canadian Legal Literature.* The law journals, along with the record of the legislative debates and the committee hearings (as well as newspaper accounts), serve as useful forums to understand why a particular statute was passed and how it might be interpreted or subsequently amended. In addition to legal indexes, then, a researcher might also want to consult the *CBCA* database and the index to the legislature *Debates.*

(4) Case law reports are an essential part of the common-law system, and they consist of judges' written opinions (decisions, judgements) in court cases. The burgeoning law report series are too many and too varied to explain in detail. By 1991, there were over seventy such reporter series, with cases appearing in duplicated form. Almost all are commercially published for profit, so researchers would find it far more efficient and less expensive to download applicable cases from a computer database. Types of case law reports include national, regional, jurisdictional, and subject reporter series; all of these give the full text. *Canada Supreme Court*

Reports and *Canada Federal Court Reports* are both available as government publications. *Dominion Law Reports* (CCH Canadian) selectively covers the nation, with regional matters appearing in *Ontario Reports, Quebec Appeal Cases, Atlantic Provinces Reports,* and the *Western Weekly Reports.* In criminal cases, there are *Martin's Annual Criminal Code,* the *Canadian Criminal Cases,* and *Criminal Reports.* The Canadian Charter of Rights and Freedoms is selectively covered by the *Canadian Rights Reporter.* Some other case law reports include *Labour Arbitration Cases, Municipal and Planning Law Reports,* and *Reports of Family Law.*

Reference to a cited law report should include enough information to identify the report and to indicate its location with a court abbreviation. Retrieval is a simple matter of looking it up, for all law reports publish cases in chronological order. Sometimes case digests can be used as an index, especially if the case was prominent. (For example, *Butterworths Ontario Digest* might refer to a case dealing with municipal planning, and its full text can be found in the *Ontario Municipal Board Reports.*) A law report's index can be used when the researcher knows the specific subject, since the index is made up of alphabetical listings of subject headings, sub-headings, and cross-references.

A third access to case law (after the digest and the report) is by the tables of statutes, rules, and regulations. This is efficient when the title of the legislation is about the same as its subject matter.

The profusion of case report series leads to many digests and summaries. Some of the original cases would go unreported if they were not first digested. Thus, if a digest exists but no copy of the case, then a copy is usually available from the commercial publisher for a fee. The largest digest is the *Canadian Abridgement (2d),* which covers every reported case in Canada except for a few from Quebec. Topics are arranged alphabetically, but there are more than fifty volumes, many already revised. Some volumes are permanent, others are loose-leaf. It is extremely complicated to use.

(5) The basic elements of statutes have been detailed in Chapter 7. To identify those court cases that relate to sections of statutes or to find those cases that have resulted in a change in acts, statute citators must be consulted. Statutes, their amendments, and repealed sections are listed alphabetically by short title. Cases are listed and

digested under the appropriate section of the statute. If there are no cases or amendments to a section, then the section is not listed; on the other hand, if there are no cases or amendments to an act, the act is listed with an appropriate note. The *Canada Statute Citator* and the *Ontario Statute Citator* are leading examples, and there are also citators for the regulations.

(6) Associations such as the Canadian Association of Law Libraries and the Canadian Law Information Council feel responsible for interpreting legal jargon to the public. Members can be a source of information, acting as intermediaries within the legal system. The *Canadian Law List* and the *Canadian Legal Directory,* both annuals, list addresses and phone numbers of law firms, as well as of individuals, and they also contain information on court and administrative offices. Both annuals are arranged by place, across Canada.

(7) Guides and textbooks, especially monographs for first-year law students or for legal research courses, include such titles as *Introduction to the Study of Law, Using a Law Library, Legal Research Handbook,* and E. Swartz's *Procedures for the Legal Secretary,* a text that details Canadian legal administrative procedures, as well as presenting over 200 samples of documents, certificates, and forms.

(8) Online computer databases are tailor-made for the legal profession. For one thing, all costs are passed on to clients as an itemized necessity. For another, the scope of near completeness and currency is breathtaking. There are three main legal database vendors in Canada. They now provide the full texts of the majority of court decisions, as well as the texts of services digesting recent cases. One database is *SOQUIJ* (Société québécoise d'information juridique), which began in 1976 and covers the legislation and case law of Quebec.

Another is *QL Systems,* which from 1972 has had a broad range of full-text databases such as the *Revised Statutes of Canada,* the statutes of six provinces (Alberta, British Columbia, Manitoba, New Brunswick, Ontario, and Saskatchewan), the federal statutory orders and regulations, the regulations of Ontario, *Supreme Court Reports, Ontario Reports, Trade Marks Opposition Board Judgments, Excise Ruling Information System, Ontario Securities Commission Bulletin,* and *Dominion Tax Cases.* In abbreviated form as digests or headnotes, *QL Systems* has *Canadian Regulatory Reporter* (summaries of

decisions of the Canadian Transport Commission, National Energy
Board, Canadian Radio-television and Telecommunications Commission, and other regulatory boards), *Dominion Reports Services,*
and the *National Reporter System* (court decisions from across Canada). All of these judgements are fully searchable and each case or
digest can be downloaded to a personal computer for further study.
Within a week of a judgement being made, the material is available
online.

A third system is *CAN/LAW,* which started in 1987 when Canada
Law Book, a publisher, withdrew its materials from *QL Systems* and
set up its own competing online databases. *CAN/LAW* has *Dominion
Law Reports, Canadian Labour Arbitration Summaries, Canadian Patent Reporter* (court decisions in patent cases and in trademark and
industrial design cases), *All-Canada Weekly Summaries, Canadian
Criminal Cases,* and other versions of its published series.

Unfortunately, there are still different protocols in computer
searching. For example, *QL Systems* permits the user to combine
databases to be searched prior to beginning the search; *CAN/LAW*
does not, but it has already merged some databases so that some
things do not need to be combined before searching. But the search
may turn up unwanted duplicates. Ranking of cases is, on *QL Systems,* automatically given out as a "relevancy ranking" (this can be
changed to ranking by date), while *CAN/LAW* automatically ranks
in reverse chronological order. *QL Systems* is easier to use, while
CAN/LAW is more flexible. A skilled researcher needs a thorough
understanding of each database vendor's retrieval policies.

Other specific systems include *CT Online* (the Canadian Institute
of Chartered Accountants), which lists the federal Income Tax Act,
regulations, applications, interpretation bulletins, tax treaties, as
well as tax information circulars and advance rulings, along with
commentary on tax matters and the full texts of tax-related judgements from the Supreme Court, the Federal Court, and the Tax
Court of Canada. A similar service is offered by CCH Canadian in its
ITA Series, but instead of being online, it is available as a CD-ROM
product for networking. American products include *WestLaw* with
the Bureau of National Affairs' *International Trade Daily* (U.S.
federal judicial, legislative, and regulatory activity affecting U.S. foreign trade) and *Antitrust and Trade Regulations Report* (restrictive
trade practices), and Mead's *LEXIS,* which has the full range of

Commerce Clearing House reporters as well as *Securities Law Daily* (full-text legal and regulatory material). Through *WestLaw* and *LEXIS,* a researcher can also get access to the *Index to Legal Periodicals* and the *Legal Resource Index,* although these indexes are also available on *Wilsonline* and *DIALOG* respectively.

Court Documents

Researchers use court records chiefly because these could contain verifiable confidential information on people or companies, information that might not be available from any other source except as rumours, leaks, or brown envelopes.

In theory, everything in a judicial proceeding is available; in practice, what is available is at the whim of each court. This can range from open hearings and document examinations to closed proceedings and only fifteen seconds to look at a document in its entirety. Some courts only allow for a "yes" or "no" answer to verify facts, while other courts will deny total access to the document. Each court has a policy that needs to be consulted, in much the same manner as a preface to a book can help the researcher to know how to proceed. Yet, court policy is not always rigidly adhered to. If a clerk does not like the way a researcher acts, then that researcher might be denied access. If the researcher pleads ignorance or is, for example, a student working on a project, then she or he might be shown the odd item or two. Circumstances such as time of day and blood sugar levels can be determining factors in access to court records. A legal researcher who is well known or a polite investigative reporter might have quick and easy access. In other words, the system is quirky; but if researchers know the rules, they can play the game.

To begin finding court records, researchers need to know the alignment of courts within the province or region, including all of the jurisdictions. They can pay a visit to the public library to inquire about the set up of the local courts, finding the names of judges, law clerks (who maintain the trial records), bailiffs (who keep order), and court reporters (who do the official transcript). On arrival at the courthouse, they should be polite and deferential.

There are two immediate steps for researchers to take if they are continually denied access to court documents. Many courts let the involved parties look at court files, so it might be possible to get one of the parties' lawyers involved. The other step is to go to court to force the court to open its files. Remember, all judicial proceedings are open to the public unless specified by statute, by regulation, or by powers granted to the parties involved. It all depends on the weight of competing interests. Certain restrictive statutes include the Charter of Rights and Freedoms, the Official Secrets Act, the Privacy Act, and the Criminal Code of Canada. These balance the right to information against such competing interests as the right to a fair trial, the right to privacy, and the need to protect trade and state secrets. There is no blanket rule regarding public access to court documents.

This section will concentrate on what types of cases there are, what courts have jurisdiction, and what types of documents will be in the case file. Researchers need to know all three (case, court, and document) before even making requests of legal staff. If they need to know what is coming up in the schedule of future cases, then they should consult the docket for the next month, and prepare themselves adequately.

Any Canadian law textbook gives a good overview of the structure of the court system. In the Canadian federal system, the national level is responsible for taxation, immigration, banking, certain aspects of citizenship, and agriculture. The provinces have most of the rest, including most law enforcement. Names of provincial courts vary across Canada, and the fact that there is an appeal process necessitates checking through the appeals divisions. In addition, researchers need to remember that there is a difference in access between cases currently being tried and cases disposed of. For current cases, the court is concerned about prejudicing a fair trial or interfering with the course of justice. For disposed cases, the researcher must be sure that appeals have not been filed, or, if they have, that they have been followed through the system to resolution.

There are two proceedings: criminal and civil. Criminal cases involve crimes against individuals and/or societies, as spelled out by the Criminal Code of Canada. There are serious crimes (indictable offences) and less serious crimes (summary convictions), and the person charged will be heard in an appropriate court. Information about the persons involved is very difficult to obtain because of the need for privacy. Law clerks almost always demand reasons for information requests, and they alone determine the validity of these reasons. It may be more fruitful to work through the lawyer involved in the case. Names of the accused, dates of court proceedings, and location of the court can be found through the local newspaper (if reported) or, if the case has been completed, through *Weekly Criminal Bulletin* (online through *CAN/LAW*). Ongoing cases are extremely difficult to monitor because of the potential for mistrial.

Court documents that might be found in criminal cases include:

- The *information* is the charge against the accused. It will have the name, address, age, date of committal to trial, specific offence charged, location where alleged crime was committed, name of victim, name of investigating officer, complete history of court appearances, Crown attorney involved in the case, name of defence counsel or duty counsel, sentence, terms of probation, and the names of judges presiding over the various hearings. A record of court appearances will give the history of remands, trial dates, and various motions; multiple charges will result in multiple informations. Terms of probation may be unusual.
- A *search warrant* is the legal document giving the police a right to search a specified premise to seize specified objects. For each search warrant, the police must file an "information to obtain" that explains why they believe a crime is being committed and how the warrant will help to solve the crime.
- Bail hearings may be held in order for the accused to be released from custody, and such hearings produce *bail documents*. These transcripts, as well as "Bail Order Release Papers," may give indications of the accused's friends, family, employer, and background. Conditions placed on the accused might include bail guarantees, avoiding association with specified individuals, surrendering a passport, or residing at a psychiatric hospital. If the accused is released into the custody of other people, then their names and addresses are recorded here.
- *Pre-sentence reports* are prepared by an officer of the probation service or by someone from the John Howard Society or Elizabeth Fry Society. These reports serve as background

for the judge and help to determine an appropriate sentence.

- *Psychiatric reports* are ordered by the judge, but not always introduced into evidence. Sometimes they are sealed and kept apart from the court documents made publicly available.
- *Exhibits* – physical evidence and documents – may or may not be returned to their owners after the case has been closed. Some exhibits may be kept in storage, others destroyed. Some, if they are documents, may be attached to the file.
- *Jury panel lists* contain the name, age, address, and occupation of each potential juror; the names of jurors selected for a case can be matched against this list.
- *Criminal records* are referred to in evidence in open court, at bail hearings, and after rendering a verdict.
- *Transcripts* of preliminary hearings (which determine whether there is enough evidence to proceed to trial), or of the trial, will include testimonies of witnesses. Transcripts are usually ordered through the court reporters.
- Complex cases have a series of *judgements, rulings, voir dire, orders,* and *appeals on judgements.* These may or may not be kept in the case file. There may be background notes on subpoenas and memoranda by the judge.

Details on how the criminal justice system works can be found in Harold Levy's *A Reporter's Guide to Canada's Criminal Justice System* (Canadian Bar Foundation). The most common offences seem to be possession of drugs, shoplifting, impaired driving, driving while licence suspended, traffic tickets, young offenders, and complaints against the police. The most serious (and usually reported on) include robberies, burglaries, sexual assault and abuse, and murder.

Civil cases include litigation involving personal or business relationships that have been breached. Once a case has been completed, the documents and records are stored in files at the relevant courthouses. They may be immediately accessible, or there might be a few hours delay if they are stored off-site. Older records are kept in less-expensive storage areas, quite possibly miles away. These may not be available for a week or more, or may require a special visit.

Often, microforms are available, but these vary from courthouse to courthouse. Until researchers are familiar with a court's policy, they need to keep asking the law custodians in charge of records.

Many cases are settled out of court, after both sides have determined what evidence is available and what kind of settlement can be satisfactorily accepted by each side. Usually, an individual or corporation files a lawsuit that seeks relief (in the form of money as compensation) for certain allegations that it must prove in court. At the "examination for discovery" stage (a pre-trial meeting), both sides can try to settle their dispute by looking at what each has lined up for evidence. A number of documents have already been generated by this time. But at any point along the way, either party may have applied for (and been granted) an order restraining publication. Researchers need to check to see if such an order was made, if it was subsequently lifted, and what conditions the ban had. For example, it may be possible to use "facts" from documents and not reproduce all or part of the document, or researchers may need the facts or document only to verify information obtained from other contacts or sources.

The major entry point for civil suits is the name of one of the parties ("style of cause"). With this name, one can search through the various indexes at the courthouse where the records are stored. A search by surname of the plaintiff (or applicant or petitioner) will produce a reference number (known also as a writ number, or an action number, or a statement of claim number); a search by surname of the defendant (or respondent) will also produce this number, but it is more difficult since the indexes are usually arranged alphabetically by plaintiff. The files, then, are requested by using the reference number. Depending on the court system and its location, some or all of the file may (or may not) be available for perusal for as long as researchers need it, with (or without) photocopying being available.

The two types of courts include those for dealing with monetary claims (such as a small claims court with its relatively informal rules, or the county and district courts, or other provincial courts for such matters as libel), and the unique courts that vary from province to province, such as family courts, probate courts (wills), and special administrative tribunals.

Some types of documents (each with its reference number at the top right corner) include the *pleadings* (statements prepared by each party in a civil action setting forth the facts of the case from each side's point of view):

- "statement of claim" – the complaint by the plaintiff and the damages being sought, often accompanied by an "affidavit of service" and location sought.
- "statement of defence and counterclaim" – the answer or denial by the defendant, with his or her side of the issue stated.
- "reply" or "statement of defence to counterclaim" – by the plaintiff to this countercharge.
- "writ of summons" – issued to the defendant, including monetary claim, with the name and address of the defendant.

The pleadings must be filed with the court, and as soon as this is done, researchers can obtain copies from the court clerk's office. The clerk has an index card for each file with a checklist for the various pleadings, noting whether they have been filed or not. There are time limits for the filing of these documents with the court.

Once the pleadings have been filed, each party is entitled to discover what evidence and documents (letters, invoices, contracts, agreements) the other party plans to use at the trial. For example, for a fired employee in a wrongful dismissal suit, such documents would include attendance records, medical records showing absences, letter of dismissal, evaluations of employee being dismissed, correspondence from plaintiff to the company advising that the plaintiff will sue, and more. The "examination for discovery" often leads to an out-of-court settlement. At the examination (which is itself done by the parties' lawyers, not in court before a judge) both parties cross-examine each other and present more evidence to determine if the case should proceed to trial. A "court report" is made, and a transcript of the proceeding is available to either party upon request. This transcript is not filed with the court unless one of the lawyers decides to introduce it during the trial to show that contradictory evidence was given. Once the transcript is introduced, the information is available in the file. Alternatively, the transcript can be obtained from one of the lawyers involved, whether it has been introduced or not.

A "pretrial" is held after the examination. This is one last chance for a settlement before the trial. If the settlement occurs, then the "minutes of settlement" will be filed with the court. Other documents will include "motions" (with arguments of fact and law) that may amend the pleadings and the subsequent "motion record," "orders" by judges pursuant to motions, "interim orders," "injunctions," "endorsements," "affidavits," and "rulings." When the judge reaches a final conclusion on the action, he will issue a "judgement" in a document filed as "reasons" with the court. This states why a decision was reached, but a judge is under no formal obligation to release these reasons. Occasionally, courts keep judgements separately on microfilm and not in the general file. "Minutes" of the trial are also available, but only 10 per cent of these civil cases go to trial.

Many documents are available in the court file. In most cases, the clerk brings out the entire file for researchers to wade through. Some actions contain several boxes of information, exhibits, affidavits, and motions. Researchers should know precisely what they are looking for in order to obtain the data quickly. But they need to be aware of any restrictions on the file by looking closely for notices of appeal, rulings, gag rules, limitations on access, and restrictions on publishing. Any contravention of a court policy will result in a contempt of court conviction, in addition to possible defamation suits. There is no privilege in law for those disseminating court documents. Several books point out that the laws guaranteeing public access to the courts are far clearer than the laws that provide for public access to those court documents (*Journalists and the Law,* by Bert Bruser and Brian Rogers, Canadian Bar Foundation, and the Law Reform Commission of Canada's *Public and Media Access to the Criminal Process*).

Some specific documents result from court cases. One leading example, used especially by real estate lawyers employed in guaranteeing land titles, is the "writ of seizure and sale" (in Ontario). A court judgement empowers the sheriff to seize and sell assets of a debtor who has defaulted on payments. This indicates to a buyer that a lien has been registered against a property. The sheriff's office has the document, as well as the court judgement (from which researchers can determine the location of the original case and access the whole file at that courthouse).

Many other files can be obtained from specialized courts dealing with divorce, wills, bankruptcies, inquests, public inquiries, and administrative tribunals.

Divorce

A divorce action can be started in any province or territory if either spouse has been "ordinarily resident" there for the past year. A divorce becomes effective thirty-one days after a court order granting the divorce, unless one spouse appeals. Divorce records are kept in the county courthouse where the divorce was granted, and all records are open to the public. Access is by last name of the spouses. Older records may be in storage and researchers may have to wait for them. There is no charge to look at a file, but certified copies of the judgement cost money. Statements and documents include:

- grounds for divorce;
- general background and outline of facts;
- custody orders;
- support orders;
- property settlements;
- financial statements;
- settlement conference memoranda;
- registration of divorce proceedings form;
- marriage certificate;
- exhibits;
- court transcripts;
- judgement.

The exhibits are a rich vein. The more convoluted and contested the divorce, the more information and documents that will be presented, including confidential-but-now-accessible income tax statements, pension earnings, property values, and insurance records. Court transcripts are notable for recording acrimonious testimonies.

Wills

A will is a document that gives instructions on how assets should be disposed of and obligations met upon death. If an estate is small or simple, then the provincial governments have provision for people who die intestate (that is, without a will). Handwritten, simple wills are also legal. It is only when a person wants to provide for a wide range of dispersal of assets, or cut someone out from the will, that a formal will needs to be created, signed and witnessed, and then filed in a probate or surrogate court. *The Permanent's Surrogate Guide,* published by Canada Permanent Trust, provides phone numbers and addresses for all surrogate courts in Ontario; in addition, it explains intestacy, probating (establishing the validity of) and contesting a will, as well as presenting samples of the various forms. (Most of the people who examine probated wills are simply looking for information on their family trees.)

Everything in the probated will is public information, although researchers have to wait until its completion. This may take years if the will is complicated or contested. Surrogate courts maintain files as space allows, although some of these files might be in microform. Other wills are available from some centralized storage space usually maintained by the provincial archives. As with divorces, researchers need to know the original location of the action. But researchers can phone specific surrogate courts to locate a will.

With a name and the year of death, researchers get access to the file. Everything can be photocopied. In the file one might find:

- application for probate: this shows personal data of the deceased (name, address, marital status, last occupation, place and date of death, date of last will, and other materials);
- application for administration: this shows data about the deceased, location of assets (homes, automobiles, investments, bank accounts, personal assets of significant value, real estate and businesses owned), names and addresses of those persons entitled to share the estate, details of any previous marriages/divorces/annulments, the value of the estate;
- caveats, contestations, and affidavits filed.

Documents otherwise kept confidential are freely available if they are needed for probating wills. These include income tax returns, assessment reports, and bank statements. Wills are a good source from which to learn about heirs and living associates of the deceased.

It is also interesting to see what was not owned or who was left out of a will. Contested wills show rivalry in families and reveal figures about the deceased's standard of living.

Bankruptcy

A bankrupt person or company is one who has surrendered assets for the benefit of creditors ("assignment") or one who has been forced by a court order to surrender assets ("receiving order"). In either case, the bankrupt has more liabilities than assets. The *Canada Gazette,* pt. I, has the names of individuals and companies (along with a reference number), listed by province, with occupations, dates of bankruptcy, dates of first meeting of the creditors, and the involved trustee (usually a chartered accountant). These are administered by the Bankruptcy Division of the Department of Consumer and Corporate Affairs, which also has on microfiche the lists and statistical figures on bankruptcy dating back through 1975. Previous years are in storage. These files have:

- the assignment;
- the receiving order;
- the statement of affairs;
- the trustee's questionnaire (to the debtor, about forty questions);
- the official receiver's report;
- the minutes and attendance of the first meeting of creditors.

The trustee controls and discharges whatever assets there are, under the federal Bankruptcy Act. Documents are available only through the trustee. At some point there is a "discharge of bankrupt," which is where the Bankruptcy Court gets involved. All creditors must be notified, and upon application the court may grant an "absolute discharge," a "suspended discharge," a "conditional discharge," or disallow the bankruptcy. The debtor needs to supply financial statements of income and expenses to the judge. Most individuals need a discharge if they are ever to deal with money again.

Details of bankruptcy litigation, then, are available from Bankruptcy Court, from which one can also obtain certified copies of the discharge. The acts of "declaring bankruptcy" and "discharging bankruptcy" are straightforward, and they follow a specified checklist as outlined in the Bankruptcy Act.

Inquests

A coroner's inquest is a judicial investigation to establish the facts about a death that may not be the result of natural causes. These include death by foul play, suicide, accident, negligence, and malpractice, and any nursing home death. Police collect information, witnesses are called, exhibits and documents are presented. The coroner, a medical doctor, directs a constable to select a jury of five persons; their role is to make recommendations directed to the avoidance of death in similar circumstances. About 75 per cent of all recommendations are complied with, mostly through public responsibility or moral force.

In Ontario, about 210 inquests are held each year. The Annual Report of the Ministry of the Solicitor General gives a broad description plus a range of statistics. Both Ontario's Coroners Act and the *Coroner's Inquest Manual* describe procedures. The documentation and recommendations from any inquest in Ontario are available through the Office of the Chief Coroner. A look at inquests is a good way to check out compliance with occupational and safety health features of the working environment.

Public Inquiries and Administrative Tribunals

Public inquiries and administrative tribunals allow the public no real right to inspect documents, exhibits, or other evidence derived from their proceedings. The presiding official or judge will determine whether or not there is to be access. Examples of public inquiries include royal commissions and special task forces, and any government investigation beginning with the words "Public Inquiry into ..." Administrative tribunals have been established by a legislative act to determine claims and decide disputes arising in connection with the administration of legislative schemes. These are often of a regulatory nature, and they form part of the ABC structure. They exist outside of the ordinary courts of law, but their decisions are subject to judicial control by the doctrine of *ultra vires* and by errors of law. Some examples of these tribunals, all drawn from Ontario, include:

- The Ontario Municipal Board hears appeals on municipal and planning matters such as zoning by-laws, subdivision plans, and matters falling under the Planning Act, Assessment Act, Expropriations Act, Municipal Act, and Rental

Housing Protection Act. Decisions are binding, but appeals can be made to the Ontario cabinet. Documents are fully accessible.

- The Office of the Public Complaints Commissioner hears complaints against the police force, with the power to impose direct penalties.
- The Assessment Review Board hears complaints against real property assessment and business assessment. Hearings are open, but previous documentation is available through the Freedom of Information Act.
- The Criminal Injuries Compensation Board looks into compensating eligible applicants when death or injury results from an unprovoked act of criminal violence. Some cases, usually sexual assault, are closed to the public. Appeals can be made on a point of law.
- The Board of Negotiation mediates in negotiating a settlement when real property is expropriated by government and no agreement can be reached on compensation. Either side can request denial of access by the public.

Other tribunals in Ontario include:

- Consumer Relations Appeal Tribunal
- Environmental Assessment Board
- Information and Privacy Commissioner
- Ontario Racing Commission
- Pension Commission of Ontario
- Rent Review Hearings Board
- Residential Tenancy Commission
- Social Assistance Review Board
- Workers' Compensation Appeals Tribunal.

Many documents are available either directly or through the Ontario FOIA. The older the case, the more likely it is that the tribunal will surrender its documents. Of course, many materials can also be obtained privately.

Other aspects of the law and courts, for which varying amounts of information are available, include: (1) the prison system (paroles, halfway houses, probation); and (2) the morality squad operated by law enforcement agencies (obscenity, pornography, border patrols).

Easy legal information can be gotten in the form of "dial-a-law" programs that cover a wide variety of topics using pre-recorded taped messages in everyday language, or through the local Crown Law Office, which will attempt to find the current law about anything (look in the local blue pages for the telephone number). Specialized law firms deal with legal aid, family law, juveniles, employment, real estate, medical law, native peoples, immigration, and the environment. Lawyers with these firms can be used as experts when explanations are needed.

9

SOCIETY AND THE INDIVIDUAL

It seems that in our world of television and radio, everywhere that man sets his foot, he puts his mouth in it! This even applies to the first steps on the moon, which were immediately televised around the world, including the astronaut's first words which proved to be inaccurately transcribed. – Harley Parker, media consultant

The natural skill humans have is that we are pattern-recognizing machines. We recognize similarities and differences in patterns rather quickly. – Marshall McLuhan

This chapter presents material on media communications and social development. The state intersects with the individual at so many junctures that it is impossible to spell out all the many sources of information open to the researcher. Thus far we have examined business, government, and law. Other major areas include education systems, religion, work and employment, ethnic studies, family and home, genealogy, aging and death, and scholarly topics such as philosophy and languages. Two topics of interest to researchers are media communications and social development.

Media Communications

Communications embraces a wide range of materials, including communication theory and methodology, advertising and market research, public relations, public opinion, broadcasting (which itself includes radio, television, satellite, and cable), communication technology and policy, media law, photography and film documentary, book publishing, magazines, newspapers, media management and economics, and mass communication and society. The orientation of communications is toward business, government, research, and journalism.

Some of the important background materials include both *Webster's New World Dictionary of Media and Communications* and *Communication Handbook*. These carefully define terms. For a range of introductory essays, see *Encyclopedia of American Journalism*, *International Encyclopedia of Communications* (four volumes), *World Communications* (a 200-country survey of press, radio, television, and film), *World Press Encyclopedia* (which profiles the press and electronic media in over 170 countries in articles describing censorship, laws, ownership, press-state relations, basic statistics, and bibliographies), and *Handbook of News Agencies in the World*.

Information controllers are represented by numerous bibliographies and indexes. For bibliographies, there are Eleanor Blum and Frances Wilhoit's *Mass Media Bibliography; an annotated guide to books and journals for research and reference*, *Communications Booknotes* (a bibliography published bimonthly since 1969), Jo Cates's *Journalism; a guide to the reference literature*, Fred and Nancy Paine's *Magazines* (Scarecrow), Minko Sotiron's *An Annotated Bibliography of Works on Daily Newspapers in Canada, 1914-1983*, and *Canadian Telecommunications Regulation Bibliography*. For indexes specific to mass media and communications, there are *Communication Abstracts* (which is international), *Journalism Abstracts* (which also covers theses and dissertations), and *Topicator* (a classified article guide for advertising and market research, covering audience measurement, cable television, and pay television). For actual locations of materials, see Donald Godfrey's *Directory of Broadcast Archives, Newspaper Indexes*, and *Union List of Canadian Newspapers*.

Among yearbooks and annuals, there are *Communication Yearbook* (reviewing the year's highlights), *Annual Review of Communication Research, Broadcasting/Cablecasting Yearbook*, and *Editor and Publisher International Yearbook*. Some government reports fall into this category, especially those from Statistics Canada on figures and studies done by comparable bodies in the United States and in Great Britain. Annual reports from businesses are also a good source of data.

For areas such as media law, there are Stuart Robertson's *Courts and the Media,* Michael Crawford's *The Journalist's Legal Guide* (a guide for Canadian journalists, broadcasters, photographers, and writers), *A Sourcebook of Canadian Media Law,* and *Media and Communications Law Review,* a quarterly published by Carswell. For photography, some key resources include *Guide to Canadian Photographic Archives, Stock Photo and Assignment Source Book, The Picture Researcher's Handbook,* and *Picture Sources 4.*

Directories include:

- *Gale Directory of Publications and Broadcast Media,* which lists all radio TV, newspapers, and magazines in North America, providing facts and figures for each;
- *Bowden's Media Directory,* which also includes Canadian radio and television stations, as well as daily and weekly newspapers and magazines;
- *Matthews Media Directory,* which lists Canadian daily papers and broadcasting stations and supplies detailed information about ownership, publishers, editorial staff names, circulation, news services, and the Press Gallery;
- *Sources,* a directory of contacts for editors, reporters, and researchers in Canada, covering about 500 groups;
- *National Media List,* published by the Canada Council and listing various media outlets, with subject classifications;
- *Creative Source,* which concerns Canadian photography;
- *National Directory of Newsletters and Reporting Services,* which has North America as its scope;
- *O'Dwyer's Directory of Public Relations Executives;*
- *The Knowledge Industry 200,* which profiles the top businesses in North America that control communications;
- *The Working Press of the Nation,* an American tool;
- *Willing's Press Guide,* a directory covering Great Britain, the Commonwealth, and some of Europe;
- *Benn's Media Directory,* a similar tool for Great Britain and Europe.

Statistics are important for determining the worth of circulation, audience, market research, public relations, and the like.

- *B.B.M. Bureau of Broadcast Measurement* provides detailed audience profiles and demographic data for major Canadian cities;
- *C.A.R.D. Canadian Advertising Rates and Data* is a monthly magazine covering Canadian newspapers, the ethnic press, and business, farm, and religious publications;
- *C.D.N.A. Selected Data on Canadian Daily Newspapers,* published by the Canadian Daily Newspaper Association, lists circulation and line rate advertising figures;
- *Community Markets Canada* is an annual listing statistics for the weekly and community newspapers in Canada;
- *N.A.D. Bank Audience Profiles,* from the Newspaper Audience Databank, details newspaper readership by age, occupation, education, employment status, and income;
- *P.M.B. Print Measurement Bureau* gives magazine readership by age, occupation, and education, with separate volumes for major Canadian cities.

Market tools suggest names and addresses of publications and broadcasting units for communicating, as well as statistics about the relevant industry. These include *Canadian Writer's Market, Magazine Industry Market Place, Literary Market Place, Information Industry Market Place, Photographer's Market Place, Writer's Market, Writer's Handbook,* and for Great Britain, *Writers and Artists Yearbook.*

Useful magazines and scholarly journals in this field include (from among the thousands world-wide): *Broadcaster* (Canada), *Broadcasting* (United States), *Cable Communications Magazine, Canadian Journal of Communication, Columbia Journalism Review, Content, Editor and Publisher, Folio, Gannett Center Journal, International Press Institute Report, Journal of Broadcasting, Journal of Communication, Journalism Quarterly, Masthead* (Canadian magazines), *The Masthead* (U.S.), *Media, Culture & Society, Media and Communications Law Review, Nieman Reports, Public Opinion Quarterly, The Quill,* and *Washington Journalism Magazine.*

Associations, networks of contacts, and information centres can be located through the various general resources such as

Encyclopedia of Associations, Directory of Associations in Canada, and *Directory of Special Libraries and Information Centers.* For instance, the Canadian Journalism Database is supported by the Centre for Mass Media Studies at the University of Western Ontario. The database provides updated online information about mass media in Canada, and includes bibliographic references, original research, conference papers, and notices and abstracts of current research.

Social Development

Social development covers a wide range of topics, such as social work, social welfare, and social services. This has become a mushrooming resource area, with several types of groups to cover. For example, local governments have many special-purpose boards, ranging from school, recreation, library, and transit districts to special education and water districts. Each provides social services but many are reluctant to divulge information concerning their own private inner workings. Ontario's Municipal Freedom of Information Act encourages access to previously "policy closed" files, but of course, not every province has such legislation. At the national level, there are many direct regional programs, such as Canada Manpower, while the provinces have their own direct regional programs dealing with public assistance, rehabilitation, employment security, and mental health services. There are regional governments, a sort of provincial umbrella embracing local and county-wide services, and regional quasi-governments of special-purpose planning agencies, such as area agencies on aging, health planning, employment and training, regional housing, and regional development.

In the private sector, there are the voluntary service delivery agencies such as charities, family service associations, the United Appeal, the Salvation Army, Goodwill Industries, mental health associations, homes for the aged, nutrition programs, seniors centres, and many others. All of these can issue tax receipts for donations, and therein lies a potential for scams (see below). The Metro Toronto Community Information Centre publishes the excellent *Metro Toronto Community Services Directory,* updated monthly, with many names and addresses for anything in the Metro Toronto area concerned with social development, such as financial programming, family problem-solving, counselling, recreation, education, addiction, employment, health services, legal services, and housing. For places outside Toronto, this tool also serves as a guide to the kinds of things available in other locations.

To complete the picture on social development groups, there are also the private or proprietary agencies such as nursing homes, group homes, and homecare agencies. These exist to make a profit, and sometimes they hire out or contract out for non-profit agencies to do the work. For example, nurses and doctors can be paid through hospitalization plans even if they work for a private-sector agency. A for-profit group home can accept clients who are paid for on a per diem basis. Social workers can be privately hired or publicly hired – it all depends on who their employer is. The larger the urban area, the more social problems it is going to have and the more infrastructures will have to be erected. Knowing the system will help in extracting needed data quickly. A network of contacts can be useful for information privately obtained.

The Canadian Council on Social Development has been creating databases for social development use. First, it opened an Information/Resource Centre in Ottawa, with displays, reference and resource materials, and computer terminal access to *SocioNet, ERN* (Employability Resources Network, which collects information about job-readiness programs in Canada), and *Social Services Information Exchange*. Second, it developed (both for off-site use and for sale) *SocioNet Interaction,* billed as "Canada's online social development network and database." Its major subject areas include employment, income security, health, justice, education, housing, social services, and citizenship. The Council emphasizes new social policies, legislation, programs or projects, media releases, bibliographies, directories, social statistics, advance notices of conferences, newsletters, and material on new trends. Other networks in Canada, accessible through *SocioNet,* include the Community Health Network, the Social Planning Network, the Governmental Network, the Information and Referral Network, the Social Work Network, the United Way Network, and the Associations Network. As well, there is access to non-profit organizations in more than sixty countries via APC networks.

A good way to understand the social services system is to investigate the series of synonyms in that system. This will reveal the scope of the system and will also generate further references. For example, under "family relations" researchers might find terms such as divorce, teenage pregnancy, child abuse, single parenting, working mothers, adoption, foster home care, battered spouses, alcohol/drug abuse effect on families, elders, elder abuse, abortion, same sex marriages, sibling rivalries, and extended family.

To find information on the "extended family" in Canada, for example, any researcher should be able to dig out quickly and easily all of the following:

- a concise, sociologically relevant definition of "extended family" plus any international variations;
- lists of books and articles written on the subject;
- discussions of different theories of the impact the extended family is having on the Canadian economy and Canadian society;
- contact names of people to interview and to use as verifiers of data, along with specific examples of real extended family members (perhaps drawn from the media) and relevant attributable quotations;
- reviews of books and other materials to help select balanced coverage, context, classification, and analogies;
- government reports containing government-collected statistics about extended families, according to age, geographic region, ethnicity, and social background.

As a non-profit association that also keeps tabs on legislation in Ottawa, the Canadian Council on Social Development (CCSD) acts as a lobby group. It files briefs, appears at committees, and informs people of the "social development" issues behind such recent legislation as changes to the Unemployment Insurance Act, the clawback of family allowances and Old Age Security, the Goods and Services Tax, the capping of the Canada Assistance Plan (freezing federal funds for health care and post-secondary education), and the prepaying of the child tax credit to more families.

As another example of information available in the area of social development, the researcher could track charities and foundations. To begin with, the researcher should step back and review the triad of databases, documents, and experts. For databases, there are the *SocioNet Interaction* described above, the Information/Resource

Centre of the CCSD, and the Canadian Centre for Philanthropy (CCP). Both centres have the usual journals, directories, annual reports, and biographical and statistical information.

Selected, useful resource books include the *Canadian Directory to Foundations* (published by the CCP) with data on names, addresses, histories, purpose, interests, limitations of grants, geographic scope, source of grants, and financial data on receipted gifts and total assets. *Canadian Donor's Guide to Fundraising Organizations in Canada* (also CCP) has provincial listings of charities, with their registration numbers and head officers, as well as a subject listing. *Taft Directory of Non-Profit Organizations* and *The Foundation Centre: sourcebook profiles* both contain information about American charities. Indexed magazines that provide specific data include *The Chronicle of Philanthropy, Foundation News, The Grantsmanship Centre News, Grants Magazine, Journal of Volunteer Administration, Nonprofit World Report, Nonprofit and Voluntary Sector Quarterly, The Philanthropist*, and *Voluntary Management News*. There are also several newsletters, such as *Canadian Taxpayer* and those of the Canadian Council on Christian Charities. Articles from general magazines are indexed under the name of the group or under "charities" in the *CBCA* database. Arthur Drache's *Canadian Taxation of Charities and Donations* (De Boo) is also useful.

For documents and institutes, the provincial public trustee offices (charities division) have information concerning the status of a charity: whether it is legitimate and registered properly and whether any discrepancies have been reported. These offices contain audited financial statements, annual reports, and incorporation information. The provincial companies branch of a consumer affairs department can provide names and addresses of the executives, registration numbers, annual reports, and a list of the services the foundation provides. The Ontario Companies Branch publishes *Not-for-Profit Incorporator's Handbook*, which is very thorough. Most investigations originate with the Public Trustee Office.

Revenue Canada has information circulars such as *Registering Your Charity*, which defines charities, amateur athletic associations, and foundations with respect to the law and taxation. This circular tells what kind of information must be filed under the Income Tax Act: identification, executive members' names, calculations of receipts of disbursements, assets and liabilities, remuneration, description of the charity's purposes and activities, volunteer information, and the sum of gifts to qualified donors for the year. All but the financial statements are available from the Charities Division toll-free number (1-800-267-1871). On written request, a copy of each charity's annual T 3010 form (finances) can be provided. In addition, even the Ontario Law Reform Commission has an angle since it is studying the law of charities. For instance, the current disbursement quota (80 per cent of receipted donations must be spent in the following year) could be changed.

For a quick check on fraudulent fund-raising, the Ontario Ministry of Consumer and Commercial Relations has the pamphlet *Phoney Charities – Scams for All Seasons,* describing questionable telephone solicitations and phoney chocolate bar sales, and giving guidelines for donations. The Better Business Bureau has a Philanthropic Advisory Service that keeps files on charities. The toughest overseer against abuse is the Public Trustee Office. It actively investigates to see that charities do not carry on unrelated business activities, do not pay their directors a salary, do not misappropriate funds, do not occupy land for non-charitable purposes, do not abuse trust funds donated through a will, and do not direct funds to personal or non-charitable uses.

Resources that can give a good overview or background to the area of society and the individual include *Encyclopedia of Philosophy* (eight volumes), *Encyclopedia of the Social Sciences* (eight volumes), *International Encyclopedia of the Social Sciences* (seventeen volumes), *Encyclopedia of Religion* (sixteen volumes), *Encyclopedia of Education* (ten volumes), *Encyclopedia of Educational Research* (four volumes), *Encyclopedia of Social Work* (two volumes), and *International Encyclopedia of Psychiatry, Psychology, Psychoanalysis and Neurology* (twelve volumes). The *National Faculty Directory* and the *Directory of American Scholars* will lead the researcher to names of important academics in the social field. Magazine indexes, both print and online, include *Social Sciences Index, Religion Index One and Two, Philosopher's Index, Education Index, Canadian Education Index, International Bibliography of the Social Sciences,* and (for Canada) the *CBCA* database. More details and guides for almost any other matter dealing with society can be found through William Webb's *Sources of Information in the Social Sciences.*

10

SCIENCE AND TECHNOLOGY

It is a very sad thing that nowadays, there is so little useless information. – Oscar Wilde

I don't care if I'm understood. I just don't want to be misunderstood.
– Barbara Frum

This chapter presents material on the environment and waste management. The area of science is one of both constants and rapid change. Ching-Chih Chen's *Scientific and Technical Information Sources* is a good beginning guide. Encyclopedias are useful for broad overviews and summaries of material that is not really part of the change mechanism, for topics that have already been discovered and verified according to the scientific method. *McGraw-Hill Encyclopedia of Science and Technology* (fifteen volumes) is a leading example; so is *Van Nostrand's Scientific Encyclopedia* (two volumes) for shorter articles that identify terms and concepts. The *Encyclopedia of Bioethics* (four volumes) does a good job in presenting the different sides of moral issues within medicine, and other similarly useful, specific scientific encyclopedias are available. Dictionaries are needed for nomenclature and terminology (e.g., *McGraw-Hill Dictionary of Scientific and Technical Terms*), as are handbooks with their tables of constants, values, and formulas. A guide to all of these is the *Handbooks and Tables in Science and Technology* (Oryx Press), while the best handbook of considerable breadth remains the Chemical Rubber Company's *CRC Handbook of Chemistry and Physics*.

The rapid advances in science, however, also necessitate shifts in use of resource materials. Books are far too slow for the dissemination of information, since a book may take anywhere from nine months to two years to create and publish. Yearbooks are useful for changes, since they give summaries of important events and can serve as updates. *Science Almanac* is one example, while *McGraw-Hill Yearbook of Science and Technology* is another. Most annuals are quite specific, and their titles usually begin with the words "Annual Review of," "Progress in," "Advances in," as in *Annual Review of Microbiology, Progress in Thermodynamics, Yearbook of Nutrition.*

Indexes and abstracts are important because they index and summarize the numerous periodicals that report on new discoveries and new methods, and they also provide English-language abstracts of foreign research reports. All of these tools are available online; in fact, *Index Medicus* (from the U.S. National Library of Medicine) pioneered the computerized retrieval of journal articles back in 1960. General indexes include *Applied Science and Technology Index, General Science Index,* and *British Technology Index.* Specialized ones include *Biological and Agricultural Index, Index Medicus, Biology Abstracts, Chemical Abstracts, Engineering Index, GEO Abstracts, Nutrition Abstracts and Reviews,* and scores more. There are also two special-format indexes, at opposite ends of the scientific time tunnel. One is *Science Citation Index* (from the Institute for Scientific Information), which indexes the footnotes that appear in an article. The more times an authority is quoted, the more prominent or "expert" he is seen to be. This is a good source for finding the top people in any science field. (There is also a *Social Science Citation Index.*) The other special format index is *Current Contents on Diskette,* which is a listing of tables of contents pages (and hence, titles of articles) from thousands of scientific journals published within the previous week. One can search under title words, key words (author-assigned), and subject descriptors. There are eight multi-disc editions: Agriculture, Biology and Environmental Sciences, Clinical Medicine, Engineering, Life Sciences, Physical, Chemical, and Earth Sciences, Technology and Applied Sciences, and Social and Behavioural Sciences. Scientific researchers browse through these to review developments in a particular area of interest.

Perhaps even more important than the journal article (which could take months to publish) is the conference paper. These may (or may not) get published in a periodical, but they are usually available either from the presenter or from the conference organizers. To find out where the conferences are, try the publications *Scientific Meetings* or *World Meetings* (or, if there is an association involved, try *Encyclopedia of Associations* to get a fix on conference dates and cities). Most conferences even issue author abstracts of the papers in advance, so that researchers have a short summary of the contents. For the proceedings and conference papers, check the monthly *Conference Papers Index, Index to Scientific and Technical Proceedings,* and *Proceedings in Print.* For research generated by dissertations, look at *Dissertation Abstracts International* and *Comprehensive Dissertations Index.* Translations are available through *World Transindex,* although many abstracting services offer English-language summary translations in their abstracts to foreign-language scientific papers. For research-in-progress, try the *Canadian Register* CD-ROM, which contains data on over 4,200 academics currently working on projects.

For association publications, try *Scientific, Engineering, and Medical Societies Publications in Print.* For patents and trademarks, check Canada's *Patent Office Record,* Great Britain's *Official Journal (Patents),* the U.S.'s *Official Gazette of the U.S. Patent Office,* and the weekly *World Patents Index.* There are also useful guides and indexes associated with these patent listings. For standards, look at the Canadian Standards Association's *Standards Catalogue* and the Standards Council of Canada's *Directory and Index of Standards.* Researchers could also look at the various handbooks mentioned above. *Government Reports Announcements and Index,* from the United States, does excellent work in alerting researchers to new reports. To find names of people involved in conducting research, look at *American Men and Women of Science* and *Who's Who in Technology.*

The yearbooks and annual reviews keep researchers abreast of details, while the reference book mechanism of dictionaries/handbooks/manuals frees them of the need to memorize countless bits of data. Books and encyclopedias are useful for explanations and background confirmations.

By and large, most scientists avoid controversies. They report their research under carefully guarded controls so that their research can be replicated elsewhere. To a scientist, research is an evolving pattern of minute steps forward. But very little appears in the media about the actual nature of the research; instead, summaries and metaphors dominate, and reporters seem preoccupied with words such as "cure for," "race against," "breakthrough in." The media cover scientific research as a series of dramatic events, concentrating on theories of behaviour (sociobiology, genes, racism), health issues (cholesterol, AIDS, artificial sweeteners), and environment (ozone, acid rain, dioxin, PCBs, nuclear materials, extremely low frequency [ELF]). They press for solutions that are not forthcoming. Thus, in doing research work in the sciences the researcher should avoid the general newspaper or popular magazine article, unless one is able to confirm its contents or is just looking for new leads. These articles are biased toward a news peg or an angle based on a "breakthrough."

An example of a large issue that has many subdivisions is the environment. Related to this topic are health issues, government regulations, businesses, organized crime, and energy. Researchers must be familiar with environmental concerns and protections within their own geographical areas and need to be knowledgeable about the agencies that monitor toxic waste, pesticides and herbicides, animal abuse, overpopulation, endangered species, and energy abuse. The number of sources is immense: politicians seem concerned about the issues; business people want cost-benefit analyses before they'll do anything; bureaucrats at different levels are anxious to enforce the law and regulations; citizen groups lobby for environmental protection. All levels of government, but particularly the local level, must contend with toxic wastes, radiation leaks, air pollution, noise pollution, water pollution, solid waste disposal of sewage, and bacterial contamination. A good place to begin looking for the players is the *Canadian Environmental Directory*, listing government departments, organizations, lawyers, and information services.

Researching energy-related environmental issues calls for use of specialized subject databases dealing with the atmospheric and climatological sciences, business and industry, electric and nuclear power, water resources, toxicology and health, and legislation and government policy; for each of these subjects the researcher must also check ongoing research, procurement and contracts, and even patents. Specific topics to investigate include acid rain, deforestation, forest fires, occupational health and safety, global warming and ozone damage, oil spills, and ocean dumping. For instance, after a train derailment spills some chemicals, a quick look at *TOXLINE* (devoted to explaining the toxic nature of chemicals, alone or in conjunction with other chemicals) will provide the known hazards of the substances to human health. A search through *MEDLINE* under the name of a disease such as herpes or cystic fibrosis, or a drug such as Lysine, will turn up scores of articles. A search under the name of a company suspected of dumping hazardous waste will provide articles that confirm or deny. The *ASBESTOS* database, from the University of Sherbrooke, can provide the latest data about asbestos, production figures, medical research into occupational diseases, and consumption figures. Researchers using the *Compendium of Pharmaceuticals and Specialties* (from the Canadian Pharmaceutical Association) can solve queries related to prescriptive drugs and their reaction to each other. Hazardous materials in the work environment can be checked out through the Canadian Centre for Occupational Health and Safety database, *CCINFOdisc*. By shooting the words "toxic waste" and "dump" through numerous databases, researchers will find scores of articles that may be useful. The law reporter series *Canada Energy Law Service* (De Boo) comments on and describes statutory administrative tribunals, case law, board decisions, the National Energy Board, rate and traffic regulation, pipeline accidents, export and import of resources, oil and gas pricing, and trade.

In the more narrow area of waste management and pollution control, the emphasis is on local government, which collects and disperses garbage, but industrial waste is hauled away by private contractors at the industry's own expense. Sometimes business and commercial waste is also privately contracted out. It is here that organized crime has seen a way to launder money, by buying up probable landfill sites and contracting for pickup and removal. Sub-issues within waste and pollution are landfill sites, recycling programs, hazardous waste, and water quality (drinking and beaches). These can all be checked through *Pollution Abstracts* and *Energy Abstracts,* both in print and online. To make the public aware of waste and pollution, some municipalities, such as Toronto, have set up solid waste management resource centres, usually at public library branches.

Provincial bodies determine planning, policy, public education, research, and grants (at about 50 per cent of cost) to municipalities, and likewise they can initiate waste reduction and waste transfer projects (recycling, composting, consulting fees). They usually monitor water and air pollution with their extensive lab facilities and do some enforcement while working with industry. Some programs in Ontario include Municipal/Industrial Strategy for Abatement (MISA), which tries to reduce water pollution from industry and the municipalities, Drinking Water Surveillance Program (DWSP), Clear Air Program (CAP), Air Quality Index (AQI), Countdown Acid Rain (CAR), Municipal Recycling Support Program (MRSP), and Industrial Waste Diversion Program (IWDP), all with their own reports, statistics, experts, and enforcement mechanisms.

Environment Canada, at the national level, focuses on international issues such as acid rain, oil spills, and the ozone layer. It publishes many studies and background reports on just about every type of environmental issue, from global warming to the destruction of PCBs. Also, through the Canadian Council of Ministers of the Environment (environment is essentially a provincial responsibility), it provides financial and research support for waste management programs. Environment Canada meets regularly with the United States on such issues as transboundary air pollution and acid rain. It also operates the World Ozone Data Centre and is involved with various United Nations environment programs. And, of course, it has responsibility for all aspects of waste and pollution on Crown lands and the territories.

One huge problem in the area of environment research is to prevent issues from slipping through the cracks. This is where citizen groups come in, such political watchdogs as Citizens for a Safe Environment, Ontario Recycling Information Service, Toronto Reduction and Reuse Action Committee (TRAC), Greenpeace, and Pollution Probe. They are extremely useful for getting names and numbers of experts and authorities. With a little time and some phoning around, the environment researcher can understand the system and tap the right resources. For another look at issues, re-read the end of the section on multidisciplinary topics (Chapter 5), which deals with logging in Temagami.

CULTURE AND THE ARTS

I find that a great deal of the information I have was acquired by looking up something and finding something else on the way.
 – FPA (Franklin P. Adams)

More than half the information I find while looking for something else. – S.K. Wolf, author of thrillers

This chapter presents material on literature, the arts, sports, and multiculturalism. Changes in the arts and culture are not as dramatic as in science. They are evolutionary and cumulative. Systems in place are the ones most researchers are comfortable with. Literature (and folklore and mythology) is such a vast subject area, covering time, place, and language, that it is difficult for researchers to limit themselves to just a few sources. The information needed can be so general or so specific that many resources need to be searched. It is obvious that the *Oxford Companion to American Literature* is of little value when dealing with the literary history of Canada, except for how the U.S. could affect Canada. We have our own series of literary history handbooks (see below), as do other countries.

Literature as a type of information is more academic than other subject areas, and specific academic resources have been developed to meet common information needs, such as author biographies, book reviews, quotations, location and explanation of poems, plays, and short stories, essays, character identification (from novels and plays), plot summaries, and histories and explanations of national literature movements. What follows here is a concise presentation for English-language materials; there are similar resources in other languages and for other countries.

The best place to start is with a guide such as Richard Altick's *The Art of Literary Research* or Frederick Bateson's *A Guide to English and American Literature.* These books have been designed to locate, describe, and evaluate literature, covering all time periods and suggesting several different search strategies for literary research. The annual Modern Language Association's *MLA International Bibliography of Books and Articles on the Modern Languages and Literatures* locates current materials (criticisms and texts) published in books, journals, dissertations, and miscellaneous collections. About 20,000 items are listed each year, one-quarter of them abstracted. It also covers the subject field of linguistics. It is not complicated to use, but its online version is both cumulative and easier, since the computer can pick out terms hard to look for manually in the printed version. Researchers can retrieve in less than five minutes items that would have taken them hours in the print version. Unfortunately, while material written in 1921 (when the bibliography began) is just as valid as materials written last year, these older items are not mounted on computer and hence are not searchable online. Only since the mid-1970s can the MLA material be accessed online. Searching through the past volumes of many resources can be tedious.

Quotations on a subject or by somebody are useful; the access points are a person's surname or the topic. Common sources for finding quotations or confirming wording and dates include *Bartlett's Familiar Quotations, Oxford Dictionary of Quotations, Home Book of Quotations, Colombo's Canadian Quotations* (and its sequels), *Dictionary of Canadian Quotations and Phrases,* and J.B. Simpson's *Contemporary Quotations. Granger's Index to Poetry* also subject-arranges both titles and first lines. A look at the Oxford *New English Dictionary on Historical Principles* reveals about three million quotations that illustrate usage (access is by word being defined), and even more quotations if researchers use its online system *OWLS.* In looking for acceptable quotations, researchers must cast a wide net, for these books and others have many different sets of quotations.

Explanations of literary allusions, words, and quirky meanings from the past can be found through *Brewer's Dictionary of Phrase and Fable,* Benet's *Reader's Encyclopedia, Funk & Wagnall's Standard Dictionary of Folklore, Mythology, and Legend,* and *New Golden*

Bough. For character and name identification, try *Everyman's Dictionary of Fictional Characters* or *New Century Cyclopedia of Names.* The "Oxford Companion" series explains a limited topic through a dictionary-arranged handbook; some titles include *Oxford Companion to Music, Oxford Companion to Art, Oxford Companion to Theatre,* and *Oxford Companion to Sports,* as well as the "literature" series. All of the Oxford books help to explain literary allusions. *The Literary History of Canada* (four volumes) explains our own language and literature development, while larger works such as *McGraw-Hill Encyclopedia of World Drama* (five volumes) or *New Cambridge Bibliography of English Literature* (four volumes) point out their respective paths.

Journal indexes include *Essay and General Literature Index, Short Story Index, Speech Index, Granger's Index to Poetry, Canadian Literature Index, Play Index,* and others that also cover a wider scope, such as *Humanities Index* and *British Humanities Index.*

Sources of biographical data include *Contemporary Authors,* but for deceased and important writers, researchers need to consult the H.W. Wilson "Authors" series or Gale Research's *Author Biographies Master Index,* which lists over five million names. In Canada, there is *Who's Who in Canadian Literature,* 1982-.

Another part of culture is fine and applied arts. Fine art usually means painting and sculpture, while applied arts embraces graphic arts, photography, fashion, design, architecture, popular culture, crafts, hobbies, and recreation. Another "applied" area is the performing arts (music, drama, theatre, film, sports). Because of its sprawling nature and the proliferation of resources, the subject area of the arts has a number of excellent guides. A. Robert Rogers's *The Humanities* is a selective source handbook. Lois Swan Jones's *Art Information: Research Methods and Resources* is a guide to finding fine art information. Donald Ehresmann's *Fine Arts* and his *Applied and Decorative Arts* both suggest basic search strategies in finding reference works, histories, and handbooks. Eleanor Lambert's *World of Fashion* gives books, periodicals, names of designers, and groups of merchandisers for North America. The *Handbook of American Popular Culture* (three volumes) is a massive guide to resources in about sixty areas such as animation, automobiles, comics, popular music, radio, stage entertainment, and television. Each has a short history of the topic, along with an indication of sources of information, where those sources are physically located, and the scholars/

collectors working in the field. This is useful for contacts and offbeat topics. Vincent Duckles's *Music Research and Reference Materials*, David Cheshire's *Theatre: history, criticism, reference*, and Peter Bukalski's *Film Research* all outline, survey, and suggest search strategies. Barbara Pruett's *Popular Entertainment Research* is designed to assist researchers in film, television, theatre, popular music, and recorded sounds.

For encyclopedias, there are *McGraw-Hill Encyclopedia of World Art* (fifteen volumes), *New Grove Dictionary of Music and Musicians* (twenty volumes), *Encyclopedia of Music in Canada*, and *Complete Encyclopedia of Popular Music and Jazz* (five volumes). For handbooks, there are *International Cyclopedia of Music and Musicians*, *Larousse Encyclopedia of Modern Art*, *Focal Encyclopedia of Photography*, *International Dictionary of Films and Filmmakers* (five volumes), and *Encyclopedia of Painting*.

Some annual reviews include *International Motion Picture Almanac* and *International Television Almanac*. Biographical data can be found in these specific sources: *Performing Arts Biographies Master Index*, *Who's Who in the Theatre*, *Baker's Biographical Dictionary of Musicians*, *Who's Who in Music*, *Biographical Dictionary of Dance*, *Who's Who in Art*, *Who's Who in American Art*, and *Artists in Canada*.

Indexes to people, activities, objects, and places include *Film Literature Index*, *Music Index*, *Art Index*, *Sculpture Index*, *Costume Index*, *Illustration Index*, *World Painting Index*, and *Photography Books Index*. Films, paintings, records, concerts, and books can be reviewed, and these were looked at in Chapter 5 as "product evaluations." Just about everything in the area of the arts is a product, and it is a collectible. Thus, there are series of price guides for established collectibles, and these define the field of collecting for the hobbyist. These guides tell what is out there and the range of "bid" and "ask" prices. Common guides include Scott's for postal stamps and Charlton's for coins. Price guides also exist for phonodiscs, clocks, glass, furniture, guns, lamps, moulds, pottery, quilts, costumes, wines, comic books, antiques, and automobiles. Through the price guides researchers can find names and addresses of collectors who can serve as sources or experts. For example, *Art Sales Index*, a computerized database with monthly microfiches, has current information on art sales at auctions in Great Britain, North America, Western Europe, and Japan. Full descriptions, dates, and prices are the main accessible fields. *Canadian Art Auction Record* lists sales for Canadian artists and their works sold in Canada; *Art Prices Current* covers non-auctions in North America, and *International Auction Record* deals with major pieces.

Another area worthy of looking at is sports. For updated information and records, use the *New York Times Index*, *Infomart* for Canada, and various almanacs. Otherwise, for identification or rules, try Nunn's *Sports*, a guide book. Both *Webster's Sports Dictionary* and *Oxford Companion to World Sports and Games* trace the development of specific sports and explain the way that each game is played. Both books have many drawings, diagrams, and photographs, as well as explanations of playing field specifications, sports equipment, officials' signals, and scoring. *The Big Book of Halls of Fame in the United States and Canada: Sports* lists specific fields arranged alphabetically with applicable halls grouped under each type of sport. It also has histories, memberships, brief biographies, and an index by year. Ferguson's *Who's Who in Canadian Sport* describes 1,300 professional and amateur athletes and coaches. The annual *Sports Directory* covers Canadian associations, government bodies, clubs, agencies, and sports awards, with an annual calendar of events. The *Sports and Recreation Index* covers 800 international journals; its online version is known as *SPORT DATABASE*. For information on a specific sport, researchers need only to look up its name in the library catalogue, index, online system, or the subject analysis of any tool that suggests associations or experts.

Within the arts and culture area, there is also the subject matter of multiculturalism, which is unique to Canada. Unfortunately, information is very political (read, is needed for re-election) and this results in multiple layers of dense information choices to fit the Canadian mosaic. All three levels of government have data, as do community groups within the private sector. For example, in the Metro Toronto area alone, more than 120 libraries contain information on multiculturalism. Some have comprehensive collections of government documents, studies, and scholarly theses. Others have materials that relate to only a handful of ethnic or cultural groups. Some of these centres are described below.

The Mayor's Committee on Community and Race Relations works to strengthen federal and provincial human rights legislation in areas of multiculturalism relating to the City of Toronto and its agencies. It has released many studies through its Multicultural Access Program, and it also operates an information hotline.

Metropolitan Toronto's Multicultural and Race Relations Division complements the Mayor's group. Its key areas of responsibility are policy and program development, design and implementation of training programs, a translation bureau, grants in support of multicultural and race relations activities, community relations, and conflict resolution. It recently began promoting ethno-racial access to Metropolitan Toronto services, developed a Council Action Committee to combat racism, and did a race relations audit in the Metropolitan Toronto Police Department. It sponsors English as a second language (ESL) programs for new immigrants. Recent studies have been titled "Improvements in the Race and Ethnic Relations Climate in Metro Toronto" and "Enabling Access and Participation of Racial and Ethnic Minorities at the Government Level," both containing legislative initiative, key facts and figures, changing demographics, and emerging identifiable issues.

The Cross-Cultural Communication Centre has an extensive collection of newsletters and newspapers, books, government documents, and studies. The main focus is on immigrant women and racism at all levels. It has online computer capability, with material (and subject descriptors) from the ERIC system.

The Toronto Board of Education Centre Reference Library and the North York Board of Education Minkler Library have materials on multicultural education issues, race relations, and ethnocultural groups.

The Toronto Public Library has extensive file holdings at most branches, under the heading "Minorities," and it has a special administrative office titled Multicultural Services as part of its public relations section. There are also a native peoples collection at the Spadina branch and specialized ethnic collections throughout the city. Other public library boards in the Metro Toronto area have similar materials. The Metro Toronto Reference Library operates the Municipal Library at City Hall, with its extensive holdings of cultural materials and the regional Multilanguage Department with books, magazines, and newspapers. It also features a strong collection of audio-visual resources and has published *Guide to the Multilanguage Collections of the Public Library Systems of Metro Toronto*.

The Urban Alliance on Race Relations contains books, documents, and research studies focusing on race relations in Canada, the United States, and Great Britain. The Alliance has extensive clipping files from most of the local ethnic press and daily newspapers. The Third World Resource Centre, Ryerson Polytechnical Institute, has one of the city's best collections of ethnocultural information, while the Native-Canadian Relations Theme Resource Centre at York University, with extensive holdings about native peoples, publishes a newsletter and a bibliography.

The Refugee Documentation Project at York University has materials in refugee policy, crisis research, refugee settlement, legal research, and the creation of research tools. It also contains over 8,000 documents, journals, newsletters, and bulletins, plus audio-visual materials, photographs, and clippings. It is complemented by the national agency Immigration and Refugee Board Documentation Centre. In a similar vein, the Community Information Centre of Metropolitan Toronto maintains a collection of current, up-to-date materials and publishes *Directory of Community Services in Metropolitan Toronto,* which lists 7,000 groups.

A third political layer (after "City" and "Metro") is the Ontario government, which has a wider mandate. The provincial Ministry of Citizenship, charged with the responsibility for multiculturalism, operates a Resource Centre with books, documents, journals, and studies, concentrating on immigrant adjustment, race and inter-group relations, immigrant newcomer services, cross-cultural training, and special ethnic data. It also promotes the *Ethnocultural Database,* which offers statistical printouts of demographic information relating to mother tongue, ethnic origin, place of birth, religion, and the number of people entering Canada during any given year. The Ministry of Culture and Communications promotes cultural expression and development and encourages heritage preservation. These two ministries co-ordinate and assist other provincial ministries and various community groups dependent on provincial funding to implement multicultural policy. Typical publications include *Multicultural Audio-Visual Resources* and *Multicultural Printed Resources,* and newsletters such as *News Directions,* an interministerial bulletin on multicultural issues. Political statements include *Multiculturalism: a new strategy for Ontario* (with implementation guidelines, interpretations, and applications) and *Canadian Scene,* a biweekly that contains news and information for the Canadian ethnic press.

Several provincial ABCs operate in the multicultural sphere. First and foremost is the Ontario Human Rights Commission, which has a long history of combatting discrimination. It has an information centre with the usual database back-up and publishes *Guide to Race Relations Organizations.* The Ontario Advisory Council on Multiculturalism and Citizenship is made up of sixty members who advise the government on policy formation and program development and delivery; the Council examines and comments on the effectiveness of policies, programs, and delivery mechanisms. The Multicultural History Society of Ontario, with its Resource Centre, receives funding from the provincial government. It has data on more than fifty ethnic/language groups in the province, with an oral history collection of about 7,000 hours, immigration records from the National Archives in Ottawa (with point-of-entry records), and other archival material on church and association records, original manuscripts, older ethnic newspapers, passports, tickets, photos, and other memorabilia. It also publishes *Polyphony,* a biweekly magazine. Other older materials can be located through the Toronto Area Archivists Group or through TAAG's directory.

As multiculturalism is an extremely politicized area, it should come as no surprise to learn that all political parties in Ontario maintain extensive contacts with the communities. Each party has a listing of all the ethnic newspapers and magazines in Ontario (which includes names of editors and writers, and something about the philosophy or scope of each publication), and also a listing of community groups, associations, and contact persons. These are arranged either by the language or by the name of the group, and they can be privately obtained. As a last stop for additional data, a researcher might want to try her or his local member of the legislative assembly or an MLA in a relevant ethnic group's area.

At the federal level, multiculturalism is more hazy. Federal politicians, who are as concerned with re-election as other politicians, maintain, to that end, lists of names of ethnic leaders and the ethnic press; the researcher can sometimes obtain the needed names privately through the offices of the federal politicians. The Department of the Secretary of State of Canada has the Multiculturalism and Citizenship Canada division, with its local offices across Canada. It has been charged with the responsibility for strengthening "the solidarity of the Canadian people by enabling each person to participate fully and without discrimination in our society." To this end, it tries to separate itself totally from immigration, which is another government department. Two of its major publications are *Multiculturalizing*, a four-volume resource guide for educators, and *Ethnic Publications in Canada*, a directory. Like its provincial counterpart, it co-ordinates and assists other federal ministries and other levels of governments. It is actively moving on cross-government commitment, race relations, heritage cultures and languages, and community support and participation. At the national level, there is also the Immigration and Refugee Board Documentation Centre in Ottawa. It has background information on ethnic groups or countries of origin. The Centre searches international databases and global wire services for data and then stores it. A recent search on Afghanistan turned up twenty-three articles on the activities of the Hezbe Islami during the 1989-91 period.

Federal government cutbacks in other areas are affecting support for multiculturalism. ESL programs and integration programs for new immigrants are suffering from the capping of federal funds. These multicultural programs are on other political levels, but they do have some federal funding. Redressing previous grievances is a thorny issue not really part of federal multiculturalism policy, but the groups involved have to be dealt with and they do represent votes. Grievances include the Chinese head tax, the Japanese internment, the handling of Italians and Ukrainians during war years, and the native peoples issue of rights, reserves, and treaties. Also complicating these issues are employment equity and pay equity. Two Ottawa-based groups attempting to act as lobbyists (and from whom additional information can be obtained) are the Ethnocultural Council and the Canadian Council for Multiculturalism and Intercultural Education.

PULLING IT ALL TOGETHER

Good newspaper people wear both belt and braces: check and doublecheck, for they are not going to be caught with their pants down.
– journalism saying

Why is there never enough time to do it right but always enough time to do it over? – unknown

This chapter seeks to pull it all together, with material on the researcher mode, with tips and advice; some shortcuts; some failures; some successes.

The Researcher Mode

Seasoned researchers always have a bountiful collection of tips that modify approaches to finding answers; they generally offer such advice with alacrity. Let me share some of my more successful "secrets." These are in random order and should be read piecemeal, not gulped all in one reading.

(1) Researchers organize their *library research time.* Many researchers do not like working in certain libraries because of the physical environment or atmosphere. Thus, they take full advantage of every library visit so as to avoid numerous trips. They use their own home resources, and they phone reference libraries for quick factual data, addresses, specific statistics. When they do visit

libraries, they work on a number of projects at the same time. A research log to record data keeps everything straight and helps the researcher to avoid repeat searches in the same sources. This means they only "touch" a particular index once, doing all the searches together, or they bunch their computer requests to minimize expenses. By copying down all the bibliographic data at this time they don't have to retrace any steps later for footnoting, for giving data to a fact checker, or for authenticating evidence.

(2) Researchers watch out for the *embedded fact.* This is the information that researchers need, but it is buried in an article or a book or a computer database. It can be the name of someone (possibly with different spellings), a source for additional contact, a statistic within a table. It might be a photograph, a map, or an illustration; it might be embedded within the caption to the illustrative material. It might be an attributable opinion. This embedded fact has not been indexed anywhere, and it occurs only as part of the source document. Indexed entries might not tell researchers that the material they require exists in this shape. They have to read the whole article and maybe others, and footnotes and bibliographies need to be checked as well. The only embedded fact that can be retrieved by a computer is a name. Since, to a computer, every word in an article is equal, then shooting a name through the system will reveal the articles in which that name appears, sometimes highlighted so researchers cannot miss it. But it is important to remember that both computers and indexes only locate articles – they do not locate the required information. Researchers still have to read all or most of the material to glean the quality data needed.

(3) In addition to focusing on a subject, researchers also look for *angles* that may reveal more information. The easiest way to do this is to examine the subject from a regional perspective, getting a "local angle." This could mean looking around for local experts, contacts, institutes, and documents. A broad national issue such as cutbacks in federal transfers of education funds could be localized. News databases such as *Infomart* could be searched to see what other provinces have done in response to cutbacks. Or the subject could be examined from a national or international angle. For this, researchers consult our own national experts and institutes and those from other countries. All of this is simply sliding around the research matrix, probing at the angles, leaving no stone unturned.

(4) Researchers need *special skills* to abstract or select information from non-print sources. These skills include: computer searching literacy, interpreting visual information (stills, drawings, film, realia, i.e., artifacts), knowledge of symbols and keys, listening, ability to read handwriting or shorthand, transcribing from tapes, interviewing techniques, adroit "people" skills (such as bluffing, good manners, pleasant persuasion, "whipsawing"), and private investigative skills (surveillance, impersonation, infiltration, squeezing, undercover, and cozying).

(5) Researchers *understand* what they uncover before they go on with their work. They compare information drawn from more than one source, and they relate information to what is already known. They make connections. They suspend judgement until the search is ended, at which point they might reach tentative conclusions.

(6) Researchers do *backsearches*. They work backwards from the most recent publication dates since these would tend to incorporate previous findings. In searching for material about the "free speech movement" of the early 1960s, it makes no sense to start with 1960 materials and move forward. Instead, begin with this year's tools and move backwards. Perhaps a definitive book was written last year, or perhaps through *Forthcoming Books* a researcher might find a book that is to be published in six months.

(7) Researchers make use of *serendipity*: a prepared mind can use organized browsing to find data that lie outside planned research. Using imagination and following intuition and hunches, the researcher can be inspired by the quality information she or he discovers. Watch for the relationships among ideas.

(8) Researchers *accurately document* all material in their files. They attribute all quotations, put page references to facts and figures, copy names exactly, add dates to resource materials. Bibliographic details are needed for completeness, and if researchers take accurate records the first time, then they don't need to re-check later.

(9) Researchers always study the *unique arrangement* of resources so that they understand how the source was put together and do not miss any information. They read the prefaces and the introductions: these tell what is in the tool (its scope) and how to use it. They check the contents page and the index to locate topic headings. They look for special features and appendices such as illustrations, maps, charts, bibliographies. They know the regular content of periodicals

and newspapers, the use of indexes, and quirky computer access protocols. They always skim through materials first to see if the source does contain what looks like needed answers.

(10) Researchers keep *focused on needs,* and have a written needs statement before them as they select and use resources through the research log. They constantly analyse need in terms of what they are doing – drifting away is sometimes incvitable, but researchers who drift must be prepared to change the scope of their research. This continual analysis helps to organize thoughts and search patterns.

(11) Researchers determine *what kinds of resources* they'll use. Not all sources will be appropriate, and relevance must be determined by an evaluation of answers or coverage (e.g., time or geographic limitations). Most researchers start with general works for background, then move to specific sources as the research focuses. These organized sources will lead to unorganized sources, such as unindexed magazines, government publications, and dissertations.

(12) Researchers need to know when to *terminate* a search. Part of any successful project is knowing when enough data have been accumulated, evaluated, and verified. At that point, it is time to stop collecting data. All of this is predicated on how much time is available for research: five minutes, five hours, five weeks. The shorter the time span, the more shortcuts researchers will take and the rougher the evaluative assessmcnt will be. Researchers need to decide which method of data collection will be most productive before they begin. Teamwork is effective here if the deadline is tight: one can use the telephone, another can do a literature search, someone else can check for relevant documents or visit a courthouse. Sometimes nothing special turns up, and then common sense should be applied to finish the project. There is no need to be tenacious. If, however, the researcher refuses to admit defeat, everything must be rethought, for the value of the project is going to dictate the amount of research time.

(13) Researchers scan the *bookshelves* for resources in the subject area of the books already retrieved by looking at neighbouring classification numbers. They record bibliographic notes of these sources (author, title, imprint, pagination) and check out the subject tracings found on the page after the title page. They add these new terms to the research log and use them to extend the search. Also, they check these additional books for indexes, footnotes, and bibliographies.

(14) Researchers consult with *reference librarians,* who can assist with computer searches and in keyword generation for controlled vocabulary, suggest highly specialized sources that researchers don't yet know about, and provide an entrée to other libraries. They have been trained to find information, while researchers have been trained to recognize whether that information is correct, up to date, or even relevant in terms of their current projects.

(15) Researchers who are *unhappy with the published sources* they have found go directly to identified experts, such as university faculty, government bureaucrats, lawyers, accountants, doctors, engineers, or business executives, who might be able to provide the needed information or suggest other avenues of approach or documentation. This is often a trial-and-error process, especially since the only expert available might be someone who would not have been worth consulting if printed sources had been better.

(16) Researchers can *locate supporting evidence* by constructing a search strategy based on biased questions and then consulting the appropriate sources for answers to these questions. Researchers need to identify the type of source (e.g., whether historical or current, fact or opinion, personal narrative or scientific study, statistics, experts), then identify the access point: database catalogues, indexes, telephone calls, and so forth. The answers, of course, need to be rigorously cross-checked.

(17) Invariably, researchers will find *conflicting answers.* These are to be expected. Resources are compiled by humans who are subject to error and prejudice. Researchers need to be cautious here and keep searching until there are a majority of verifications, either print or non-print. The simplest way to resolve conflict is to make sure that answers are current and up to date. This means checking with the latest possible current fact sources or comparing the bases from which the data were derived.

(18) Researchers are always on the lookout for *omissions.* Some research will lack a context or even credibility. Incomplete information leads to a thin product and will reflect badly on the researcher. Never accept a source without some kind of verification. The act of verifying may even supply needed data that were missing. Researchers need a gut reaction: What is missing here? Is more explanation needed? Should the research matrix be reworked? Researchers let their natural curiosity lead them to

themes and connections, perhaps even invoking the paper trail or the bibliographic trail. Creative problem-solving techniques such as brainstorming are also useful.

(19) When searching through databases (both print and online) with *keyword descriptors,* researchers can add the following, where relevant, to all terms: any subdivisions of the subject, names of prominent researchers and scholars, names of institutions, generic names such as the name of an industry. Search with these modifiers either independently or attached to the subject, or both.

(20) Researchers *take the time* to plan a search strategy. This will structure all possibilities (planned and accidental) and leave room for the interplay between critical evaluation and creative problem-solving. How much and what kind of information a researcher needs depends on the size and depth of the research project, and this size can be determined only by proper planning.

(21) Researchers are prepared to *modify the research.* As they unearth new and contradictory evidence, they may even reverse their original position. They may limit it to a certain time frame or limit it to certain characteristics, or even develop arguments that run counter to research statements. Throughout, researchers are in touch with their environment through investigation and observation.

(22) Every subject area has its jargon, and research is no exception. Researchers understand the *basic terminology* of research, which involves library usage, computer usage, bureaucratic jungles, and interviews with people: the types of publications (monographs, periodicals, government documents), the types of information controllers (abstracts, bibliographies, catalogues, indexes), the types of references (citation, annotation, abstract), the types of access (BT, NT, RT, UT, thesaurus, controlled vocabulary, call number).

(23) Researchers know that there are two kinds of *focus*: the logical focus for the solid background of the facts, and the contextual focus for the perspective, linkage, and relationship to both larger and smaller issues. Always be on the alert for side issues and for the need to follow up; accidental leads and tips are an important part of the process and should not be ignored.

(24) Researchers break down *complex problems* into simple queries that call for pinpoint data or yes-no answers. They use decision flow charts as thought processes and try to invoke the parameter

checklist of angles and handles early on to identify person/place/date. They zero in on the most significant point of each handle and brainstorm for sources that will provide information and that will verify information already obtained, remembering that questions are the creative act of intelligence.

(25) In researchers' *evaluations* of answers, they try to decide whether they are looking for proof beyond a reasonable doubt or proof based on the balance of probabilities. Whichever they choose will affect how much verification and cross-checking will be needed.

Some Shortcuts

The ability to find data in an efficient manner is a great asset. The more researchers know about materials and methods necessary for the efficient gathering of information, then the more productive and less time-consuming will be their research. There are a few measures that experienced researchers use in learning about a new subject area, but these also demand a certain level of competence and previous mastery of research techniques. No one system works for everyone, nor is there one source that will answer all questions on all subjects. Every research project is new and unique to the researcher who does it. There are no really deep secrets to research, but there are five major shortcuts that will produce a voluminous amount of data rather quickly.

(1) Do a *systems analysis*. Figure out how the system of the subject area works. This varies from subject to subject, but a systems analysis provides researchers with background and contacts. For example, to find out how a government agency spends its money:

(a) Get a government organization manual and phone directory to find the structure.

(b) Get a copy of the agency's annual budget, which will show where the money comes from and where it is going (along with an explanation of why a program is getting more or less money in the coming year, its relationship to other programs, and what specific bureaucracy administers the program). Often such budgets include salary figures and office expenses. The worth of the program is also clearly indicated by how important it is to the elected officials.

(c) Review applicable federal and provincial laws and regulations (plus relevant city by-laws and codes), which indicate how things are supposed to work. By paying attention to laws that can be bent, ignored, or broken, a researcher can see some of the exceptions, exemptions, loopholes, and emergency sections.

(d) Merge the system knowledge of legislated materials with the budget documents and review recent decisions. With contacts in the searchable records offices, a researcher could do a pretty thorough job in finding out what is supposed to happen, certainly learning enough to recognize any deviations or quirks in this particular system of spending money.

(2) Use the BRITE formula (background, relationships, issues, terminology, experts) for a *quick start*. Find the key issues, generate general and specific synonyms from an index or guidewords or cross-references of a printed resource, tighten the focus for completeness, and get experts to evaluate early on. "Look before you leap." This allows researchers to maximize their time and efforts by identifying the proper source of information (people, documents, files, articles), asking the right questions, and recording the answers in a usable form. This research matrix lets people know where they are on the information spectrum at all times.

(3) Look for *definitive articles*. Check out citation indexes for related subject areas and authorities, look for review articles or journals, search for business and industrial trade magazines through *Ulrich's International Periodical Directory*. Incorporate all these into the research log.

(4) *Cultivate contacts*, whether in subject fields or in research areas. Contacts such as other researchers, records custodians, librarians, association officers, government officials, and reporters must be in place before extensive research commences. Beginning researchers need to build up their networks before they can use them. Know about the major organizations, associations, and government agencies for contacts in the subject field, and know the specialized publishers and information centre personnel in that subject field.

(5) While it is useful to think that information is *available*, the reality is that information may not be readily accessible when it is wanted. The time of day may be wrong, the expert may not be

available, the data are no longer kept, the document has been classified: researchers need to be flexible in their approach. They use resources in another time zone when information centres are still open. They look for additional, back-up experts. They find alternative sources, since the data have to be verified anyway. They privately obtain documents, modify the scope of their research, change the form of their final product, or even delay the whole project (and maybe even cease to work on it).

Some Failures

Despite one's best intentions and methods, there are also failures in search strategies. There will be situations where the answers are elusive. Researchers will have tried, by this time, a given number of approaches, tested several hypothetical solutions, and yet still come up empty. If the search goes wrong or bad, then either the sources or the researcher are mistaken. For instance, if a researcher finds wrong data, then maybe the source is inaccurate or an older document was used. Or if the researcher finds no data, then maybe the source is (again) inaccurate or the wrong places were searched. Nobody or nothing is infallible, whether the researcher or the source. Neither can be better than the information that went into it.

One of the toughest problems with information work is the real-life situation where the information required exists (or did exist) but it is almost impossible to retrieve because it was never collected (e.g., Canadian voter lists with racial designations), it was never kept or disseminated (e.g., family records, church records), it has not yet been published in a usable way (e.g., unprocessed census data), or it is interdisciplinary and requires the exploration of many sources and systems with different angles.

Some of the more common search errors need particular attention. Experienced researchers watch out for and avoid these:

- copying incorrectly with misplaced (or missing) quotation marks or lack of attribution;
- obtaining information that is too current (just collected but unprocessed), too local (or too national), or too controversial (either in the past or in the present, for a full range of

opinion on a sensitive issue has always been impossible to gather);
- illegible handwriting, from themselves, from experts, from sources;
- time pressures: haste makes waste, incorrectness, not enough material gathered on which to base conclusions, too much material gathered but too little time to sort it all out;
- wrong spellings, variant versions, older spellings;
- not verifying; however, in some cases it may be impossible to document the data because the tools used to identify them do not yet exist;
- insufficient attention to detail, such as transposing numbers or letters;
- lack of a follow-through for the references;
- lack of a context and a perspective;
- problems with printed resources: not locally available, not up to date, inadequate index, no index, or information not listed in such a way that queries can be properly answered;
- not enough translations handy for foreign source materials.

Other search errors are more subjective and relate to attitude. Beginning researchers need to watch out for these signs.

(1) Improper use of skills of reading, thinking, and organizing, such as wasting time, sloppiness, or poor evaluation. Researchers must be able to express themselves in terms that can be translated into possible access points to a system. Failing to scan a source, i.e., simply checking the index and the table of contents, before beginning a detailed search is a waste of time. Researchers should never base an entire evaluation of the worthiness of material on length rather than contents, nor on an author's name or the fact that he publishes frequently. Depth means more than frequency of publication.

(2) Not checking assumptions and biases of information. Researchers should not waste time looking for what is expected rather than what is found.

(3) Lack of motivation on the part of the researcher, leading to a mind unprepared to recognize relevant information. Sometimes researchers do not understand an explanation but are still willing to accept it because of the name of the expert.

(4) Doubting, or searching with the feeling that what is needed is not there.

(5) Dislikes: of libraries and books; of institutions and agencies; of personal contact; of telephone use; of modern technologies such as the computer or the fax machine.

(6) Not enough time devoted to the research end of a project. Perhaps more relevant, more important information *does* exist, but the researcher does not venture beyond the immediate, close-at-hand resources. A potentially more important source could be missed because "any answer" is perceived as better than "no answer."

Some Successes

Research technique is a breeze, once beginning researchers have a good attitude and proper motivation to slog away at uncovering, checking and verifying, and reconciling conflicting data. I always advise beginners to proceed at their own pace for self-confidence. They should enjoy the adventure of searching in order simply to find out: it is very pleasurable to uncover knowledge. Personally, I make considerable use of two conditions: *serendipity* (prepared browsing) and *analogues* (routines). Much information searching is only a pattern, and this kind of activity lets researchers keep an eye out for recognizing the unusual and the deviations.

Indeed, many deviations are recognized only when researchers are denied access to information or to the available documents, for then they become suspicious and begin to question motives; they become hungrier for the real facts. Limiting researchers' ability to gather information has only an opposite effect. Denial fans the flames of interest, leading to the question "why?"

In addition to attitude, researchers need to remember where they are along the information spectrum. They need the research matrix, which varies from project to project and researcher to researcher. If the researcher is not really interested in a project – this occasionally happens – or if his or her mind is otherwise preoccupied, then the researcher will have a tough time of it unless organized for the information search. The more you know about research techniques, the better off you will be. A properly devised research matrix provides the structure while the research log provides the organization.

Professional researchers have few worries about motivation. They are continually employed at using their skills. Another name for such professionals is "information brokers." These work in an information environment, usually as full-time employees in a special library or in a for-profit company. They know the ins and outs of all the major computer databases (the protocols, the saved strategies, the thesauri), the major print resources (vocabulary control, bibliographic citations, article retrieval), and how to obtain names and addresses. But most of them deal with quite specific questions or topics, and while they can get answers, they are not as well placed to evaluate these answers in terms of need. They normally don't write reports or come to conclusions. They are indeed "brokers": they provide a bridge between the information source and the user. However, they are usually unable to obtain documents privately, since they have few contacts beyond other professional brokers. They do what is asked of them, suspending judgement. They do, for their fee, save a lot of time and energy in the gathering of information, leaving it up to their client to sift through it all. They deal mainly with the first category of information (the warehouse) and some of the second (the documents). Librarians usually don't write reports unless they are also hired as researchers for special libraries, but information brokers may write reports if asked. This is very expensive, at corporate rates.

Free-lance researchers, who are part researcher, part librarian, and part information broker, have developed. They evaluate and write, acting sometimes as magazine writers or feature writers. They work out of their homes (where they map out their activities by planning and costing out their research), or a library, with access to a computer and to a large network of contacts. Most free-lancers are experienced, trading on their ability to obtain information privately. Their organization depends on a quiet atmosphere: they outline all that they know about the subject, beginning with some kind of a research matrix and a research log (great for the taxman and for the fact checker). Then they look for parameters and generate ideas for everything that they do not know or would like to know more about. All of this becomes the search strategy, and preliminary forays are made in the personal home library, a collection of basic resource tools, files of local sources such as libraries and associations, phone numbers for contacts, and computer databases.

Time and costs are considerations here, since free-lancers are usually paid by the piece, with (or without) expenses. On the one hand, the publication or the company paying the bills wants to keep its expenditures low, but on the other hand researchers need to make a living. Some research is even tendered out, and usually the low bid wins. There is a difference between the conscientious researcher and the hack researcher, a difference based on time and cost. Before submitting a bid, then, the researcher must carefully examine the purpose, the time requirements, and the cost of the proposed research, and beginning free-lance researchers need to be aware of the pitfalls of bidding high or low.

Those researchers with the most experience are able to pitch their projects at the right level for costing. In addition to their own well-developed personal libraries and files, they also have favourite information centres for visits, where they have access to the stacks (access that may not be granted to other people), browsing facilities, creature comforts, technology (telephones, fax machines, photocopiers, online computer systems) that they can use, plus service from the staff. These researchers are known to the librarians, who can provide quick answers, point the way, or establish contact with other brokers in the information network. With proper cultivation of many different librarians, researchers gain immense benefits: librarians often look up material in response to a phone call so that no personal visits are involved, and librarians often alert researchers to a number of new or overlooked items in the subject field being researched.

But libraries, files, computers, and documents are not enough. Experienced researchers have networks of contacts to rely on, from impersonal experts through to the librarians, the records custodians, the public relations personnel, their own colleagues, and their inside contacts. It has been said that contacts count for more than ability. Researchers, then, must be good at what they do to gain the respect of their contacts and to be able to use these contacts to get a competitive edge. Beginning researchers vitally need to develop their own networks of sources: they cannot exist in isolation. They must be aware of their own personalities. Most – but not all – researchers fit into the "left" brain mode of analytical thought: logical, rational, predictable behaviour, "vertical" thinking of hierarchies, looking for unique answers. But some also are strong in the "right" brain mode of creative thought: imaginative, unpredictable, "lateral" thinking of relationships, with a capacity to locate an infinite range of answers. Certainly each side of the brain can learn from the other. Then at some point the researcher sifts the information collected, makes his judgements, and can be satisfied that his efforts have resulted in *finding answers*.

Summary

This chapter explores the researcher mode. With advice, tips, shortcuts, and explanations for successes and failures, the point is made that time saved means money saved. A researcher who is quick and efficient will be able to handle more income-generating projects or have more leisure time. Researcher attitudes, motivations, and thought processes are also discussed within the context of finding answers.

APPENDIX I

ADDITIONAL SOURCES FOR RESEARCH TECHNIQUES

Armstrong, C.J., and J.A. Large. *Manual on online search strategies.* Boston: G.K. Hall, 1988. 831 pp.

Barzun, Jacques, and Henry Graff. *The modern researcher,* 5th ed. New York: Harcourt, Brace, Jovanovich, 1992. 450 pp.

Berkman, Robert I. *Find it fast; how to uncover expert information on any subject.* New York: Harper & Row, 1987. 260 pp.

Black, Hawley. *The Canadian investor's resource book.* Toronto: Harper Collins, 1991. 195 pp.

Bruser, Robert S., and Brian MacLeod Rogers. *Journalists and the law; how to get the story without getting sued or put in jail.* Ottawa: Canadian Bar Foundation, 1985. 106 pp.

Buckwalter, Art. *Investigative methods.* Toronto: Butterworths, 1984. 240 pp.

Clarke, Bernadine. *Writer's resource guide,* 2nd ed. Cincinnati: Writer's Digest Books, 1983. 473 pp.

The Columbia Knight-Bagehot guide to economics and business journalism. New York: Columbia University Press, 1991. 400 pp.

Crawford, Michael G. *The journalist's legal guide,* 2nd ed. Toronto: Carswell, 1990. 320 pp.

De Stricker, Ulla, and Jane Dysart. *Business online; a Canadian guide.* Toronto: J. Wiley, 1989. 335 pp.

Demers, David. *Precision journalism; a practical guide.* Beverly Hills: Sage, 1987. 130 pp.

Gates, Jean. *Guide to the use of libraries and information sources,* 6th ed. New York: McGraw-Hill, 1988. 352 pp.

Hillard, James M. *Where to find what; a handbook to reference service.* Metuchen, N.J.: Scarecrow Press, 1991. 351 pp.

Horowitz, Lois. *Knowing where to look; the ultimate guide to research.* Cincinnati: Writer's Digest Books, 1984. 168 pp.

Katzer, J. *Evaluating information; a guide for users of social research,* 2nd ed. Reading, Mass.: Addison-Wesley, 1982. 236 pp.

Kessler, Lauren, and Duncan McDonald. *Uncovering the news; a journalist's search for information.* Belmont, Calif.: Wadsworth, 1987. 244 pp.

Levy, Harold J. *A reporter's guide to Canada's criminal justice system.* Ottawa: Canadian Bar Foundation, 1986. 230 pp.

Mann, Thomas, Jr. *Guide to library research methods.* New York: Oxford University Press, 1987. 199 pp.

McCormick, Mona. *The fiction writer's research handbook.* New York: NAL, 1988. 256 pp.

McCormick, Mona. *The New York Times guide to reference materials,* rev. ed. New York: NAL, 1986. 272 pp.

McLaughlin, Paul. *How to interview; the art of the media interview,* 2nd ed. Vancouver: International Self-Counsel Press, 1990. 233 pp.

Meyer, Philip. *The new precision journalism; a reporter's introduction to social science methods.* Bloomington: Indiana University Press, 1991. 320 pp.

Nilsen, Kirsti, and Claire England. *Guide to reference materials for Canadian libraries,* 8th ed. Toronto: University of Toronto Press, 1992. 596 pp.

Ouston, Rick. *Getting the Goods; information in B.C. – how to find it, how to use it.* Vancouver: New Star Books, 1990. 150 pp.

Overbury, Stephen. *Finding Canadian facts fast,* 2nd ed. Toronto: McGraw-Hill, 1989. 192 pp.

Printed reference material and related sources of information, 3rd ed. London: Library Association, 1990. 589 pp.

The reporter's handbook; an investigative guide to documents and techniques, 2nd ed. New York: St. Martin's Press, 1991. 576 pp.

Rubin, Rebecca. *Communication research; strategies and sources,* 2nd ed. Belmont, Calif.: Wadsworth, 1990. 273 pp.

Ryder, Dorothy. *Canadian reference sources,* 2nd ed. Ottawa: Canadian Library Association, 1981. 311 pp. (updated annually in the February issue of *Canadian Library Journal*)

Sheehy, Eugene. *Guide to reference books,* 10th ed. Chicago: American Library Association, 1986. 1560 pp.

Sproull, Natalie L. *Handbook of research methods; a guide for practitioners and students in the social sciences.* Metuchen, N.J.: Scarecrow, 1988. 425 pp.

Strobl, Walter M. *The investigator's handbook.* Toronto: Butterworths, 1984. 176 pp.

Ward, Jean, and Kathleen Hansen. *Search strategies in mass communication.* White Plains, N.Y.: Longman, 1987. 274 pp.

Wendland, Michael F. *The Arizona project; how a team of investigative reporters got revenge on deadlines.* Kansas City, Kansas: Sheed Andrews and McMeek, 1977. 276 pp.

Wilhoit, G.C. *Newsroom guide to polls and surveys,* 2nd ed. Bloomington: Indiana University Press, 1990. 82 pp.

INFORMATION
RESOURCE TITLES

Many of these titles are also available as CD-ROMs or as online databases.

1. Contacts, Documents

(Primary sources: first-hand accounts and original works such as letters, diaries, manuscripts, historical documents, laboratory and field reports, surveys, speeches, and interviews)

A. Human Resources
(also check Institute Resources, Biography, and Directories)

A1. *National Directory of Addresses and Telephone Numbers (U.S.)*
A2. *Consultants and Consulting Organizations Directory*
A3. *Sources*
A4. *Directory of Federally Supported Research in Universities*
A5. *Canadian Register of Research and Researchers in the Social Sciences,* 1982-
A6. *Metro Toronto Community Services Directory*
A7. *Connexions Directory of Canadian Organizations for Social Justice*
A8. *Canadian Peace Directory*
A9. *Directory of Experts, Authorities, and Spokespersons*

A10. City directories (most major cities)
A11. Electronic Yellow Pages

B. Quotation Books
(see also newspapers, Oxford Eng. Dict.)

B1. *Bartlett's Familiar Quotations*
B2. *Oxford Dictionary of Quotations*
B3. *Home Book of Quotations*
B4. *Colombo's Canadian Quotations/New Canadian Quotations/Dictionary of Canadian Quotations*
B5. *Dictionary of Canadian Quotations and Phrases*
B6. *Simpson's Contemporary Quotations*
B7. *Canadian Speeches*
B8. *Quotation Location; a quotation seeker's source guide*

C. Institute Resources
(agencies, associations, universities, research centres)

i. Foundations

C1. *International Foundation Directory*
C2. *Foundation Directory* (U.S.)
C3. *Canadian Directory to Foundations and Granting Agencies*

ii. Research Centres

C4. *International Research Centers Directory*
C5. *Research Centers Directory*
C6. *Government Research Centers Directory*
C7. *Research Services Directory* (for-profit facilities)
C8. *European Sources of Scientific and Technical Information*
C9. *World of Learning*
C10. *International Handbook of Universities*
C11. *American Universities and Colleges*
C12. *Directory of Canadian Universities*
C13. *Scientific and Technical Societies in Canada*
C14. *Scientific and Learned Societies of Great Britain*
C15. *Scientific, Technical and Related Societies of the U.S.*
C16. *World Guide to Scientific Associations and Learned Societies*

iii. Governments

C17. *Microlog, 1979-*
C18. *Guide to Federal Programs and Services*
C19. *Canadian Federal Government Handbook*
C20. *Corpus Administrative Index*
C21. *Directory of Services for the City of Toronto*
C22. Government telephone directories (prov., fed., U.S.)
C23. *Government Relations Handbook*

iv. Directories

C24. *Directory of Information Sources in Canada*
C25. *Directory of Directories, 1981-*
C26. *Current European Directories, 1981-*
C27. *Yearbook of International Organizations, 1948-*
C28. *Encyclopedia of Associations, 1956-*
C29. *Canadian Donor's Guide to Fundraising Organizations in Canada*
C30. *Directory of Labour Organizations in Canada*
C31. *Directory of European Associations*
C32. *Directory of British Associations*
C33. *Directory of Associations in Canada, 1973-*
C34. *Associations Canada, 1991-*
C35. *Canadian Almanac and Directory, 1848-*
C36. *Corpus Almanac and Canadian Sourcebook, 1966-*
C37. *Directory of Business and Financial Services*
C38. Financial Post Corporation Service, 1929-
C39. Financial Post Surveys, 1924-
C40. *Canadian Key Business Directory, 1974-*
C41. *Canadian Trade Index, 1900-*
C42. *Fraser's Canadian Trade Directory, 1913-*
C43. Scott's Industrial Directories, 1858- (provinces)
C44. *Standard & Poor's Register of Corporations, Directors and Executives, 1928-*
C45. *Thomas' Register of American Manufacturers, 1905-*
C46. *Moody's Investor Service, 1909-*
C47. *FINDEX; the directory of market research reports, studies*
C48. *D & B – Canadian Dun's Market Identifiers*

C49. *Directory of Trade and Professional Associations in Metro Toronto*

C50. *Directory of Public Companies in Canada*

C51. *WTCA World Business Directory*

D. "Fugitive" Material

(manuscripts, archives, papers, technical reports, conference proceedings, standards, patents, translations, theses, dissertations, etc.)

D1. *Union List of Manuscripts in Canadian Repositories*

D2. *Directory of Canadian Archives*

D3. *Scientific Meetings, 1957-*

D4. *World Meetings, 1963-*

D5. *Conference Papers Index, 1973-*

D6. *Index to Scientific and Technical Proceedings, 1978-* (ISI)

D7. *Proceedings in Print, 1964-*

D8. *World Patents Index, 1974-*

D9. *Standards Council of Canada's Directory and Index of Standards*

D10. *World Transindex, 1978-*

D11. *Scientific, Engineering and Medical Societies Publications in Print, 1976-*

D12. *Canadian Theses, 1921-*

D13. *Dissertation Abstracts International, 1938-*

D14. *Comprehensive Dissertations Index, 1861-1977*

D15. *Research Abstracts, 1976-*

D16. *Index to Current Legal Research in Canada, 1972-*

D17. *Government Reports Announcements and Index, 1946-* (U.S.)

D18. *Index to Social Sciences & Humanities Proceedings, 1985-*

2. Background and Quick Facts

(secondary sources: finding facts fast – books, textbooks, indexed periodicals)

E. Encyclopedias

E1. *Encyclopaedia Britannica, 30 vols.*

E2. *Encyclopedia Americana,* 30 vols.
E3. *Collier's Encyclopedia,* 24 vols.
E4. *Academic American Encyclopedia,* 21 vols.
E5. *World Book Encyclopedia,* 22 vols.
E6. *New Columbia Encyclopedia*
E7. *The Canadian Encyclopedia,* 4 vols.
E8. *Encyclopedia of Philosophy,* 8 vols.
E9. *Encyclopedia of the Social Sciences,* 8 vols.
E10. *International Encyclopedia of the Social Sciences,* 17 vols.
E11. *McGraw-Hill Encyclopedia of Science and Technology,* 15 vols.
E12. *McGraw-Hill Encyclopedia of World Art,* 15 vols.
E13. *Encyclopedia of Religion,* 16 vols.
E14. *New Grove Dictionary of Music and Musicians,* 20 vols.
E15. *Encyclopedia of Music in Canada*
E16. *McGraw-Hill Encyclopedia of World Drama,* 5 vols.
E17. *Complete Encyclopedia of Popular Music and Jazz,* 5 vols.
E18. *Worldmark Encyclopedia of the Nations,* 5 vols.
E19. *Van Nostrand's Scientific Encyclopedia,* 2 vols.
E20. *International Encyclopedia of Psychiatry, Psychology, Psycho-analysis, and Neurology,* 12 vols.
E21. *Encyclopedia of Bioethics,* 4 vols.
E22. *Encyclopedia of Education,* 10 vols.
E23. *Encyclopedia of Educational Research,* 4 vols.
E24. *Encyclopedia of Social Work,* 2 vols.

F. Handbooks
(miscellaneous facts: use its index first!)

F1. *Britain; an official handbook,* 1950-
F2. *Guinness Book of Records,* 1955-
F3. *People's Almanac,* Nos. 1, 2, 3 +, 1975-
F4. *Brewer's Dictionary of Phrase and Fable* (and ... *Twentieth Century Phrase and Fable*)
F5. *Benet's Reader's Encyclopedia*
F6. *Funk & Wagnall's Standard Dictionary of Folklore, Mythology, and Legend*
F7. *The New Golden Bough*
F8. *Everyman's Dictionary of Fictional Characters*

F9. *Oxford Companion* Series (… to Canadian Literature, Music, Art, etc.)

F10. *Literary History of Canada*, 4 vols.

F11. *The International Cyclopedia of Music and Musicians*

F12. *Larousse Encyclopedia of Modern Art*

F13. *Focal Encyclopedia of Photography*

F14. *International Dictionary of Films and Filmmakers*, 5 vols.

F15. *Encyclopedia of Painting*

F16. *Canadian Business Handbook*

F17. *Anniversaries and Holidays; a calendar of days*

F18. *Holidays and Anniversaries of the World: everyday*

F19. William Langer, *An Encyclopedia of World History*

F20. *World Christian Encyclopedia*

F21. *Handbooks and Tables in Science and Technology*

F22. *CRC Handbook of Chemistry and Physics*, 1914-

F23. *The Science Almanac*, 1985-

F24. *Awards, Honors and Prizes*, 1969-

F25. *Handbook of Canadian Chronology*

F26. *Canadian Awards and Prizes*

F27. *Canadian Writer's Market*

G. Geography

i. Guides

G1. *The Maps of Canada; a guide to official Canadian maps*

G2. *The Travel Book; a guide to the travel guides*

G3. *The Travel and Tourism Index*, 1984-

ii. Atlases

G4. *National Geographic Atlas of the World*

G5. *Times' Comprehensive Atlas of the World*

G6. *National Atlas of Canada*

G7. *Canada Gazetteer Atlas*

iii. Gazetteers

G8. *Columbia Lippincott Gazetteer of the World* (& suppl.)

G9. *Webster's New Geographical Dictionary*

G10. *Geo-Data; the world almanac gazetteer*

G11. *Macmillan Book of Canadian Place Names*

iv. Current

G12. *Background Notes* [U.S. Dept. of State], 1960-
G13. *Area handbooks and country studies* [U.S. Army]
G14. *Deadline Data on World Affairs,* 1955-
G15. *Constitutions and Countries of the World,* 1971-

H. History
(see also Biography, Statistics, Geography)

H1. *Cambridge Ancient History,* 17 vols.
H2. *Cambridge Mediaeval History,* 8 vols.
H3. *Cambridge Modern History,* 13 vols.
H4. *New Cambridge Modern History,* 13 vols.
H5. *Cambridge History of the British Empire,* 9 vols.
H6. *English Historical Documents,* 15 vols.
H7. *A Sourcebook of Canadian History*
H8. *Shepherd's Historical Atlas*
H9. *Historical Atlas of Canada,* 3 vols.

I. Current Data Sources
(see also Statistics, newspapers)

i. Almanacs

I1. *Information Please Almanac,* 1947-
I2. *World Almanac and Book of Facts,* 1868-
I3. *Whitaker's Almanack,* 1869-
I4. *Canadian Global Almanac,* 1987-

ii. Yearbooks (can cover more than one year)

I5. *Europa Yearbook,* 1926-
I6. *Statesman's Yearbook,* 1864-
I7. *Political Handbook of the World; governments and inter-governmental organizations*
I8. *Quick Canadian Facts,* 1945-
I9. *Commonwealth Yearbook,* 1951-

iii. Annual Reviews (only cover the year listed)

I10. *Britannica Book of the Year,* 1938-
I11. *Britannica World Data Annual,* 1985-

112. *Americana Annual*, 1923-
113. *World Book Year Book*, 1962-
114. *McGraw-Hill Yearbook of Science and Technology*, 1962-
115. *Yearbook of the United Nations*, 1946-
116. *Annual Register; a record of world events*, 1758-
117. *Canadian Annual Review of Politics and Public Affairs*, 1960-
118. *International Motion Picture Almanac*, 1929-
119. *International Television Almanac*, 1956-

iv. News Summaries, News Indexes

120. *Keesings' Contemporary Archives*, July 1, 1931-
121. *Facts on File*, Oct. 30, 1940-
122. *Canadian News Facts*, 1967-
123. *Editorials on File*, 1970-
124. *Editorial Research Reports*, 1924-
125. Online newspapers: *InfoGlobe* (1977-), *Dow-Jones* (1979-), *CP Newstex* (1974-), *New York Times*
126. Online broadcast: *Burrelle's Broadcast Database* (U.S.+NPR)

J. Statistics
(see also all Current Data Sources)

i. Indexes

J1. *Statistics Sources*
J2. *Source Book of Global Statistics*
J3. *American Statistical Index*, 1973-
J4. *Statistical Reference Index*, 1980-
J5. *Index to International Statistics*, 1982-
J6. *DATAMAP; index of published tables of statistical data*
J7. *Canadian Statistics Index*, 1985-

ii. International

J8. *European Historical Statistics*, 1750-1975
J9. *International Historical Statistics, Africa and Asia*
J10. *Statistical Yearbook of the United Nations*, 1948-
J11. *Monthly Bulletin of Statistics*, 1948- (UN)
J12. *Demographic Yearbook of the United Nations*, 1948-

J13. *Yearbook of International Trade Statistics, 1951-*
J14. *Unesco Statistical Yearbook, 1963-*

iii. Canada

J15. *Historical Statistics of Canada, 1867-1980*
J16. *Canada Yearbook, 1885-*
J17. *Canadian Statistical Review, 1926-*
J18. *Statistics Canada: Census, 1851-*
J19. *Ontario Statistics, 1975-*
J20. *Annuaire du Québec, 1914-*

iv. Great Britain

J21. *British Historical Statistics*
J22. *Annual Abstract of Statistics, 1863-*
J23. *Monthly Digest of Statistics, 1946-*

v. United States

J24. *Historical Statistics of the United States, Colonial Times to 1970*
J25. *Statistical Abstract of the United States, 1878-*
J26. *Economic Indicators, 1948-*
J27. *Survey of Current Business, 1921-*
J28. *Business Statistics, 1922-*

K. Biography
i. Indexes

K1. *Biography Index, 1946-*
K2. *New York Times Obituaries Index, 1859-1978*
K3. *Obituaries from the* [London] *Times, 1785-*
K4. *Biography and Genealogy Master Index*
K5. *Pseudonyms and Nicknames Dictionary*

ii. Universal

K6. *Webster's New Biographical Dictionary*
K7. *Chambers' Biographical Dictionary*
K8. *Current Biography, 1940-*
K9. *McGraw-Hill Encyclopedia of World Biography, 12 vols.*
K10. *New Century Cyclopedia of Names*
K11. *International Who's Who, 1935-*

iii. Canada

K12. *Dictionary of Canadian Biography*
K13. *The Canadian Who's Who*, 1910, 1936-
K14. *Macmillan Dictionary of Canadian Biography*
K15. *Canadian Obituary Record*, 1988-

iv. Great Britain

K16. *Dictionary of National Biography + Concise DNB*
K17. *Who's Who*, 1849-
K18. *Who Was Who*, 1897-
K19. *Burke's Genealogical and Heraldic History*, 1826-
K20. *Debrett's Peerage*, 1713-

v. United States

K21. *Dictionary of American Biography + Concise DAB*
K22. *Who's Who in America*, 1899-
K23. *Who Was Who in America*, 1607-
K24. *Biography News*, 1974-
K25. *New York Times Biographical Edition*, 1970-

vi. Subject Areas

LITERATURE
K26. *Author Biographies Master Index*
K27. H.W. Wilson "Author" Series
K28. *Contemporary Authors*, 1962-

PERFORMING ARTS
K29. *Performing Arts Biographies. Master Index*
K30. *Who's Who in the Theatre*, 1912-
K31. *Baker's Biographical Dictionary of Musicians*
K32. *Who's Who in Music*, 1935-
K33. *Biographical Dictionary of Dance*

ART
K34. *Who's Who in Art*, 1927-
K35. *Who's Who in American Art*, 1935-
K36. *Artists in Canada; a union list of files*

SPORTS
K37. *Who's Who in Canadian Sport*

BUSINESS

K38. *Who's Who in Finance and Industry,* 1936–
K39. *Financial Post Directory of Directors,* 1931–
K40. *Standard and Poor's Register of Corporations, Directors and Executives,* 1928–

POLITICS

K41. *Canadian Parliamentary Guide,* 1862–

LAW

K42. *Canadian Legal Directory,* 1911–
K43. *Canadian Law List,* 1883–

RELIGION

K44. *Butler's Lives of the Saints,* 4 vols.

EDUCATION

K45. *National Faculty Directory,* 1970–
K46. *Directory of American Scholars*

SCIENCE

K47. *American Men and Women of Science,* 1906–
K48. *Who's Who in Technology,* 1981–
K49. *Dictionary of Scientific Biography + Concise DSB*

L. Language (English)
(updates: *OWLS* [Oxford]/*Language Research Service* [Merriam-Webster]/*Barnhart Dictionary Companion* [quarterly])

i. Dictionaries: Great Britain

L1. *A New English Dictionary on Historical Principles* (OED)
L2. *Concise Oxford Dictionary of Current English*

ii. Dictionaries: United States

L3. *Dictionary of American English on Historical Principles*
L4. *Dictionary of Americanisms on Historical Principles*
L5. *Dictionary of American Regional English,* 1983–
L6. *Webster's Third New International Dictionary*
L7. *Webster's New Collegiate Dictionary*
L8. *Random House Dictionary of the English Language*
L9. *Barnhart Dictionary of New English*

iii. Dictionaries: Canada

LIO.   *Dictionary of Canadianisms on Historical Principles*
LII.   *Gage Canadian Dictionary*

iv. Usage, Style

LI2.   *Oxford Dictionary of English Etymology*
LI3.   *Comprehensive Etymological Dictionary of the English Language*
LI4.   *Dictionary of Word and Phrase Origins*
LI5.   *Dictionary of Slang and Unconventional English*
LI6.   *Dictionary of American Slang*
LI7.   *Fowler's Dictionary of Modern English Usage*
LI8.   *Follett's Modern American Usage*
LI9.   *Webster's New Dictionary of Synonyms*
L20.   *Roget's Thesaurus of English Words and Phrases*
L2I.   *Acronyms, Initialisms and Abbreviations Dictionary*

v. Special-Term Dictionaries: some examples

L22.   *Webster's Sports Dictionary*
L23.   *McGraw-Hill Dictionary of Modern Economics*
L24.   *Dictionary of Canadian Economics*
L25.   *McGraw-Hill Dictionary of Scientific and Technical Terms*

3. Information Controllers

(tertiary sources: sources about sources, continuously updated and almost all "online")

M. Lists of Bibliographies
i. Books

MI.   *A World Bibliography of Bibliographies*
M2.   *Bibliographic Index*, 1937-
M3.   *American Reference Books Annual*, 1970-
M4.   *Canadiana* [National Library of Canada]
M5.   *British National Bibliography*
M6.   *National Union Catalog* [United States]

M7. *A London Bibliography of the Social Sciences* [LSE]
M8. *Subject Collections; a guide to special book collections*
M9. *Subject Collections in European Libraries*
M10. *Directory of Special Collections of Research Value in Canadian Libraries*
M11. *Cumulative Book Index,* 1898-
M12. *Books In Print* + Subject Guide
M13. *British Books in Print*
M14. *Canadian Books in Print* + Subject Guide

ii. Libraries

M15. *Directory of Libraries in Canada*
M16. *American Library Directory*
M17. *Directory of Special Libraries and Information Centers*
M18. *Encyclopedia of Information Systems and Services*
M19. *World Guide to Special Libraries*
M20. *Newspaper Libraries in the United States and Canada*

iii. Newspapers, Magazines

M21. *Canadian Advertising Rates and Data,* 1928-
M22. *Gale Directory of Publications and Broadcast Media,* 1869-
M23. *Standard Periodical Directory,* 1964-
M24. *Ulrich's International Periodicals Directory,* 1932-
M25. *Newspaper Press Directory,* 1846-
M26. *Willing's Press Guide,* 1874- [Great Britain]
M27. *Editor and Publisher International Yearbook,* 1921-
M28. *Newsletter Directory*
M29. *Literary Market Place,* 1940-
M30. *Union List of Serials in Libraries of the United States and Canada*
M31. *New Serial Titles,* 1950-
M32. *Guide to Periodicals and Newspapers in the Public Libraries of Metro Toronto*
M33. *Union List of Canadian Newspapers*
M34. *British Union Catalogue of Periodicals*
M35. *Union List of Scientific Serials in Canadian Libraries*
M36. *Checklist of Indexes to Canadian Newspapers*
M37. *Matthews Media Directory*

N. Indexes

i. Newspaper Indexes

N1. *Canadian News Index,* 1977-

N2. *InfoGlobe,* Nov. 14, 1977-

N3. *New York Times Index,* 1851-

N4. *London Times Official Index,* 1790-

N5. *National Newspaper Index,* 1979- [U.S.]

N6. *CBS News Index,* 1975-

N7. *NEXIS,* 1977-

N8. *Infomart* [Southam, TorStar]

N9. Maclean Hunter: *Financial Post, Maclean's*

ii. Consumer and Trade Magazine Indexes

N10. *Reader's Guide to Periodical Literature,* 1900-

N11. *The Magazine Index,* 1959-

N12. *Canadian Periodical Index,* 1924-

N13. *Canadian Magazine Index,* 1985-

N14. *Applied Science and Technology Index,* 1913-

N15. *Business Periodicals Index,* 1958-

N16. *Canadian Business Index,* 1975-

iii. Journal Indexes

N17. *Humanities Index,* 1907-

N18. *Social Sciences Index,* 1907-

N19. *British Humanities Index,* 1951-

N20. *British Technology Index,* 1951-

N21. *General Science Index,* 1978-

iv. Specialized Indexes: important examples

N22. *Public Affairs Information Service Bulletin,* 1915-

N23. *Essay and General Literature Index,* 1900-

N24. *MLA International Bibliography of Books and Articles on the Modern Languages and Literatures,* 1921-

N25. *Short Story Index,* 1900-

N26. *Speech Index,* 1935-

N27. *Granger's Index to Poetry*

N28. *New Cambridge Bibliography of English Literature*

N29. *Canadian Literature Index,* 1974-

N30. *Play Index*, 1900–
N31. *Film Literature Index*, 1973–
N32. *Film Canadiana*, 1913– [Can. Feature Film Index]
N33. *Music Index*, 1949–
N34. *Art Index*, 1929–
N35. *Sculpture Index / Costume Index / Illustration Index / World Painting Index*
N36. *Photography Books Index*
N37. *Sport and Recreation Index*, 1974–
N38. *Encyclopedia of Business Information Sources*
N39. *Funk & Scott Index of Corporations and Industries*, 1960–
N40. *Accountants Index*, 1912–
N41. *Consumers Index*, 1973–
N42. *Index to Legal Periodicals*, 1908–
N43. *Index to Canadian Legal Periodical Literature*, 1961–
N44. *Index to Canadian Legal Literature*, 1987–
N45. *Religion Index One and Two*, 1949–
N46. *Philosopher's Index*, 1940–
N47. *Education Index*, 1965–
N48. *Canadian Education Index*, 1965–
N49. *Composite Index for CRC Handbooks* [science]
N50. *Merck Index*, 1960–
N51. *Science Citation Index*, 1961–
N52. *Biological and Agricultural Index*, 1916–
N53. *Index Medicus*, 1879–
N54. *Gallup Opinion Index Reports*, 1965– [U.S.]
N55. *Current Contents on Diskette*
N56. *Computer-Readable Databases*

O. Abstracts: some important examples

O1. *Psychological Abstracts*, 1927–
O2. *Sociological Abstracts*, 1952–
O3. *International Bibliography of the Social Sciences*, 1952–
O4. *Economic Titles and Abstracts*, 1953–
O5. *Historical Abstracts*, 1955–
O6. *International Political Science Abstracts*, 1951–
O7. *Biology Abstracts*, 1926–
O8. *Chemical Abstracts*, 1907–
O9. *Engineering Index*, 1885–

O10. *Pollution Abstracts,* 1970-
O11. *Energy Abstracts,* 1974-
O12. *Geo Abstracts,* 1972-
O13. *Nutrition Abstracts and Reviews,* 1931-

P. Reviews
(see also periodical indexes and abstracts)

P1. *Book Review Digest,* 1905-
P2. *Book Review Index,* 1960-
P3. *Canadian Book Review Annual,* 1975-
P4. *Masterplots*
P5. *New York Times Theater Reviews,* 1870-1976
P6. *New York Theater Critics' Reviews,* 1940-
P7. *New York Times Film Reviews,* 1913-
P8. *Magill's Survey of the Cinema*
P9. *Film Review Annual,* 1980-
P10. *Film Review Index,* 1882-1985
P11. *Index to Record Reviews,* 1949- [classical music]
P12. *Annual Index to Popular Music Record Reviews,* 1972-

Q. Guides
(these outline, survey, and suggest strategies)

Q1. *Native Canadian Anthropology and History; a bibliography*
Q2. A. Robert Rogers, *The Humanities; a selective guide to sources*
Q3. *Handbook of American Popular Culture,* 3 vols.
Q4. Richard Altick, *The Art of Literary Research*
Q5. Frederick Bateson, *A Guide to English and American Literature*
Q6. Donald Ehresmann, *Applied and Decorative Arts; a bibliography*
Q7. Lois Swan Jones, *Art Information: Research Methods and Resources*
Q8. Marshall Nunn, *Sports*
Q9. *Picture Researcher Handbook*
Q10. Vincent Duckles, *Music Research and Reference Materials*
Q11. David Cheshire, *Theatre: history, criticism, reference*
Q12. Peter Bukalski, *Film Research*

QI3. William Webb, *Sources of Information in the Social Sciences*

QI4. Barbara Brown, *Canadian Business and Economics; a guide to sources*

QI5. Lorna Daniells, *Business Information Sources*

QI6. *AHA Guide to Historical Literature*

QI7. Mary Dykstra, *A Bibliography of Canadian Legal Materials*

QI8. Pauline Bart, *The Student Sociologist's Handbook*

QI9. Esther Stineman, *Women's Studies*

Q20. Ching-Chih Chen, *Science and Technical Information Sources*

Q2I. Harold Levy, *A Reporter's Guide to Canada's Criminal Justice System*

Q22. *Interdisciplinary Approaches to Canadian Society; a guide*

Q23. *Columbia Knight-Bagehot Guide to Economics and Business Journalism*

Q24. Barbara Pruett, *Popular Entertainment Research*

INDEX

This index lists important names, concepts, and resources mentioned in the text. Titles of information resources are only noted wherever there is a substantive discussion of the tool and not a mere list.